From
New Towns to
Green Politics

STUDIES IN HISTORY, PLANNING AND THE ENVIRONMENT

Series editors	*Professor Gordon E. Cherry,*
	University of Birmingham
	Professor Anthony Sutcliffe,
	University of Leicester

Forthcoming titles

The Garden City
Past, present and future
Edited by Stephen Ward

Planning Europe's Capital Cities
Thomas Hall

To Bronwen, Rowan, Gemma and Alexis

From New Towns to Green Politics

Campaigning for town and country planning, 1946 - 1990

E & FN SPON
An Imprint of Chapman & Hall

London · New York · Tokyo · Melbourne · Madras

UK	Chapman & Hall, 2–6 Boundary Row, London SE1 8HN
USA	Chapman & Hall, 29 West 35th Street, New York NY10001
JAPAN	Chapman & Hall Japan, Thomson Publishing Japan, Hirakawacho Nemoto Building, 7F, 1-7-11 Hirakawa-cho, Chiyoda-ku, Tokyo 102
AUSTRALIA	Chapman & Hall Australia, Thomas Nelson Australia, 102 Dodds Street, South Melbourne, Victoria 3205
INDIA	Chapman & Hall India, R. Seshadri, 32 Second Main Road, CIT East, Madras 600 035

First edition 1991

© 1991   Dennis Hardy

Typeset in 11/12pt Times by Rowland Phototypesetting Ltd
Bury St Edmunds, Suffolk
Printed in Great Britain by St Edmundsbury Press Ltd
Bury St Edmunds, Suffolk

This book was commissioned and edited by
Alexandrine Press, Oxford

ISBN 0 419 15580 5

British Library Cataloguing in Publication Data
Hardy, D.
From new towns to Green politics.
I. Title
307.10941
ISBN 0-419-15580-5

Library of Congress Cataloging-in-Publication Data
available

CONTENTS

PREFACE

Writing a history of an ongoing organization is rather like trying to paint a landscape from a moving train. It is not just that the view from the window rapidly recedes, but also that one's perception and interpretation of earlier views is shaped by where one is now. Whoever it was who suggested that the past stays the same has clearly never engaged in contemporary history!

But if this project has been a labour, it has also been a labour of love. Having already researched the first phase of the Town and Country Planning Association's life, from its inception at the end of the last century through to the 1946 New Towns Act (Hardy 1991), there was a story to be completed. To this extent it was an obligation, but it has proved to be more than that. For the story since 1946 has been no less eventful than that of the earlier period, and no less illustrative of wider trends in the emergence of modern town planning.

As for the earlier phase, this volume is written with three objectives in mind. The first is to offer a record of a sustained campaign by an organization that has its origins in the garden city movement, but which has long since held a wider brief for town and country planning. Secondly, such a record, can, in turn, demonstrate the workings of a pressure group, an insight of added value at a time when such groups have achieved an important place in environmental politics. Finally, the campaign can be located within a broader context of postwar planning, using the records of a 'non-official, non-professional' body to cast fresh light on events.

A continuing theme throughout the postwar period is that of the idea of a political consensus, and this theme is explained in the opening chapter. The subsequent chapter offers a summary review of 'the story so far', drawing out the main points from the history of the campaign between 1899 and 1946, particularly as they bear on what is to follow. In the next five chapters, events are traced chronologically, from the time when a State programme of new towns was introduced, through to 1990 and the notable shift into the arena of green politics. Each of these chapters sets the political and social scene before considering the policy objectives of the Town and Country Planning Association in that period and the way in which it conducted the campaign. Pointing to a constant interaction between society-wide trends and the specifics of the campaign in question is another theme of the book.

After these chronological chapters comes a thematic treatment of four particular campaigns that date from the start of the 1970s, relating to environmental education, planning aid, public inquiries and new communities. The final chapter returns to the overall objectives – reviewing the general campaign of the Association, and locating it within a wider context of pressure group theory and modern planning history – before concluding with a tentative glance into the future.

The fact that it is concluded that a 'non-professional' town planning pressure group still has a role to play is a conclusion derived not from blind loyalty and misguided hope but from the evidence of political processes over a long period. Consistent campaigning for policies advocating the decentralization of power to regions and communities, an inherent concern for a decent environment for all, a respect for the judgement and wishes of ordinary folk, and the importance of communicating in plain, non-technical language, are all refreshing qualities in a period when planning has too often been ill-served by over-zealous bureaucrats and professionals.

Such qualities, it is believed, remain as worthy to champion in the 1990s as they have been in the past.

Dennis Hardy
London, 1990

Acknowledgements

The research would not have been possible without the generous support of the Economic and Social Research Council. Through the award of a grant I was able to call on the expert and much valued assistance of the following, who have contributed to key sections of the ensuing work: Jennifer Armstrong on public inquiries; Mehmet Ali Dikerdem on planning aid; Paul Smith on pressure groups; Colin Ward on environmental education and on parts of the conclusion; and Andy Wood on new communities.

As this (with its companion volume, *From Garden Cities to New Towns*) represents the official history of the Town and Country Planning Association we have relied upon and received the willing and enthusiastic support of staff at Carlton House Terrace. Our thanks are due, especially, to the Director, David Hall, who was always generous with his time and whose memory of past events has proved to be an archival source in itself; to the Deputy Director, Chris Gossop; to David Boyle and Nick Matthews, Editors past and present; and to Fred Attard, Jennifer Hindle, Shirley Peterson and Jan Woodworth. In addition to the TCPA's own records we have made good use of the Frederic Osborn papers at Welwyn Garden City, and wish to record our thanks to Michael Hughes and Angela Eserin.

Apart from the above, the research team has interviewed and enjoyed conversations with various 'key actors' in the Association's history – including Brian Anson, Maurice Ash, John Blake, Rob Cowan, Derek Diamond, Tony Fyson, Tony Gibson, Stephen Joseph, David Lock, Kelvin Macdonald, Mary Riley, Peter Self, Carol Tyrell and Wyndham Thomas.

Middlesex Polytechnic has once again provided me with a support-ive setting in which to undertake the project. Edmund Penning-Rowsell, Dennis Parker and Dave North have all helped me to free time, while, on the technical side I am indebted to Steve Chilton, Mike Torrington, Nick Beesley and Ian Slavin. Special thanks, though, must go to Sandy Weeks, who has now word processed her way through some ninety years of planning history, making adept use of changing technologies along the way.

Last but not least, in preparing the manuscript for publication, I have again been very fortunate to gain from the editorial advice and understanding of Ann Rudkin. Her contribution is greatly appreciated.

In the end, of course, for all the support I have enjoyed, errors, omissions and quirks of interpretation remain my own responsibility.

Abbreviations

BEE   *Bulletin of Environmental Education*
CEGB   Central Electricity Generating Board
CUSC   Council for Urban Studies Centres
DOE   Department of the Environment
GLC   Greater London Council
JRTPI   *Journal of the Royal Town Planning Institute*
LPAS   London Planning Aid Service
MKDC   Milton Keynes Development Corporation
RIBA   Royal Institute of British Architects
RTPI   Royal Town Planning Institute
TCP   *Town and Country Planning*
TCPA   Town and Country Planning Association

1

INTRODUCTION:
THE LURE OF CONSENSUS

There are various threads woven into the ensuing narrative. The story of a sustained campaign – a story composed of its own multi-coloured strands, depicting the efforts of individuals, and of corporate strategies and tactics – is but one such thread. Another has to do with the way in which this campaign can be seen as illustrating the work of a pressure group, pursuing various ends – sometimes on its own, sometimes with others – on that unclaimed territory beyond the formal realm of government. Yet other threads are interwoven within the wider tapestries of developments in modern planning and the whole story of postwar social and political change. Each of these threads is picked out to distinguish rather than to disentangle it from the basic fabric and to show how it inter-relates with the rest.

Yet there is, in addition to the above, an overriding theme, a *motif*, to hold it all together. This *motif* is the idea of consensus, an idea that is beguilingly simple to define and attractive to behold, but remarkably difficult to achieve in practice. Like the mythical mermaid of Lorelei its enchanting call has lured many a traveller into deep and treacherous waters, yet, undeterred and unsuspecting, fresh travellers make the same hopeful quest.

In the context of postwar politics consensus has played a central role, and the history of an individual campaign in this period cannot fail to address the implications. The work of the Town and Country Planning Association has been inextricably caught up in wider developments in politics and planning, and it has itself championed the cause of consensus as a vital source of enduring change. While the details of the TCPA's own claims on consensus will be considered in the following chapters, this introduction can help to set the scene by tracing some of the main landmarks in the debate.

THE IDEA OF CONSENSUS

> Consensus . . . while retaining a favourable sense of general
> agreement, acquired the unfavourable senses of bland or shabby
> evasion of necessary issues or arguments. Given this actual
> range it is now a very difficult word to use . . . (Raymond
> Williams, 1976, p. 68)

In essence, the idea of consensus means little more than agreement.
Used in a political setting it carries with it the idea of general support
(whether tacit or open) for a policy or more universal political
approach. But a definition as simple as that is a quicksand that
obscures hidden depths and dangers.

For one thing, the concept is simply too important, as a mainstay of
modern democracy, to rely on a glib definition. Political theorists
have for centuries wrestled with the notion of consent and the
argument that power and authority in society can only reasonably be
exerted with the willing support of the governed. Here is a fundamental issue that has featured in debate from Ancient Greece through to
the present day. The English Revolution of the seventeenth century,
the framing of the American constitution in the following era, and the
evolution of systems of liberal democracy in modern industrial
societies have all provided a setting for vigorous discourse about
political rights and acceptance. The likes of John Locke, Jean
Jacques Rousseau, Auguste Comte, J. S. Mill and Emile Durkheim
have all contributed to a continuing debate.[1]

That there should be a general acceptance of the prevailing system
of government in a democratic society is axiomatic. Governments
should govern, but not without the support of the people – hence the
importance of free elections to register preferences, of rights of
speech, and of education and material well-being to enable participation. None of these sources of consensus has been won lightly and
the path has been marked with successive campaigns to secure and
then to maintain progress.

The allure of consensus is hard to miss. It offers a means of
peaceful and effective government, with the governed not passive
recipients of policy but active citizens, aware and involved in the
political process. And if these general principles are applied to an
area of policy like town and country planning the parallels are
obvious. For planning is an interventionist process, requiring the full
force of government to make changes on the ground. A critical line is
crossed, marking, on the one hand, the opposing interests of a free
market and rights of private property and, on the other, a world of
regulations and bureaucratic interference. It is a line that is fraught

with contention, a Berlin Wall of old between West and East, the crossing of which has to be carefully manoeuvred.

Such is the vulnerability of planning. It is not a natural right of government to regulate the use of land (any more than government itself is a natural right), but, instead, it is something to be negotiated – and constantly renegotiated in the light of changing circumstances – with the people of the country. Short of imposing a system of planning on an unwilling population, the idea of intervention in this field must be agreed (in principle, at least) between all parties. If it is to be effective, a consensus for planning has to exist.

Yet, even if a broad measure of agreement can be reached, critics will point to shortcomings in the very idea of a consensus. A pragmatic response is that consensus is little more than a code-word for weak government. As exemplified by the record of politics in Britain in the 1980s, there is the view that consensus has been used in the past to avoid confronting difficult issues.[2] A consensus may well have surrounded certain issues but a tacit conspiracy exists to avoid others – it has served as 'a policy of avoiding or evading differences or divisions of opinion in an attempt to "secure the centre" or "occupy the middle ground".'[3]

A more fundamental source of criticism is that which takes issue with the way that consensus is applied by some advocates as a kind of glue to hold society together. The object of criticism is the functionalist school, which views society as a set of inter-related functions where the various parts somehow fit together like the pieces in a giant jig-saw. As a number of writers have shown, planning has derived much of its modern inheritance from the functionalist tradition, ranging from a superficial use of concepts of community and neighbourhood to a continuing application of systems theory.[4] In a nutshell, what the critics are saying is that consensus (if used in a functionalist sense) is in danger of being used as a gloss to maintain the *status quo*, appearing to reflect the agreement of society but, in reality, promoting most of all the interests of those in power. What is portrayed as 'the public interest' (a concept widely used in planning) is, argue the critics, seldom that.

Of these critics, those most opposed to a liberal democratic brand of consensus come from the Marxist camp.[5] The whole idea of consensus is seen as a nonsense because, at root, society is irretrievably divided along class lines. So long as a capitalist system persists, interests will remain sharply opposed and the very idea of a consensus must necessarily be a fallacy. It is conflict rather than consensus which is the order of the day. Of course, there are times when a consensus may appear to exist, but that will be a hoax, explicable in terms of 'false consciousness' (where the real interests of the working class are obscured) or the powerful idea of 'hegemony' (where ideological dominance creates an appearance of agreement). Consensus is an illusion – appearing to meet the needs of a plurality of interests but in effect meeting only some – the real purpose of which is to secure the legitimacy of the government of the day, if not that of the political system itself.

For planning, this argument about fundamentals is central to an assessment of its recent history. Flying under the banner of consensus, has it (as various critics continue to argue) really been a great confidence trick? Has an elaborate system of land-use and environmental controls been introduced, not to serve the interests of the people, but – to the extent that these two sets of interest are not compatible – simply to safeguard the interests of capital? Has the so-called consensus that has figured so prominently in the record of postwar planning been a mere sham?

The evidence in the chapters to follow may provide a basis for a more reasoned assessment but by no means a conclusive answer. For the presentation of the evidence itself is shaped by one's own values, and the issue at stake is not, in any case, one that lends itself to a hard-and-fast resolution. Thus, the subject is approached openly, recognizing both the sincerity and vigour of the quest for consensus in postwar Britain, but also the frailties of deals that were made and a constant tendency to pull apart into opposing factions rather than to pull together. Consensus remains an alluring concept, but like the mythology of Lorelei, this is not a story with a guaranteed happy ending; in some respects, the happiest episode comes at the start.

CONSENSUS PLANNING

> The history of British town and country planning is the story of the rise and fall of a loosely-knit alliance – the creation of several generations of a reforming coalition of diverse groups with common interests in the orderly management of land, and the recent disintegration of that coalition. (Donnison and Soto, 1980, p. 3).

Whether or not (as the previous section concludes) the happiest episode in the story of postwar planning comes at the start, there can be little doubt that the ending of the Second World War released an overwhelming sense of commitment amongst the British people to pull together and jointly to build the good city. Underpinning the efforts of planners was a wider set of political aspirations, based on still vivid memories of prewar unemployment and poverty. As a last-minute swing to Labour in the 1945 General Election showed, there could be no turning back; the Conservatives might have appeared to be no less committed to change, but chances could not be taken.

Whatever else was to be done, the bottom line for postwar governments was a cast-iron commitment to economic management to
secure growth and employment for all, and the construction and
maintenance of a Welfare State to guarantee basic material rights and
to enable social equity. These two objectives, economic and social,
were the load-bearing joints of a postwar consensus that was to enjoy
a broad measure of support across the political spectrum.

Planning fitted neatly into this. In many ways it could serve as
the physical arm of both policy initiatives, economic and social. It
could provide the new infrastructure that was required if Britain was
to modernize and to compete effectively with other economies, and,
filled with social promise, a means to secure environmental improvements for a population long condemned to substandard living and
working conditions. Modern egalitarian Britain needed planning.

This is the promising setting in which the TCPA began its postwar
campaign. Whereas in its earlier campaigns it had put at the top of the
agenda the importance of planned overspill to bring relief to the
conurbations and to provide an attractive alternative, now its brief
was widened to encompass the entire cause of town and country
planning. It became, in effect, *the* planning pressure group. And,
eschewing alignments with any one political party or faction, the
Association was at the very centre of the business of consensus-
building. It contributed to and thrived on the immediate postwar
planning consensus, just as in later years it worked to prevent it
falling apart. Its own campaign and the record of the postwar
consensus are inseparable.

Bringing the two strands together (the TCPA's campaign and
developments in planning), Chapters 3 to 7 provide an account of
changing fortunes in each of the decades between the mid-1940s and
the end of the 1980s, with Chapter 8 offering some case studies from
the 1970s and 1980s. The evidence from this period will show that, in
certain respects, Donnison and Soto (in the quote at the beginning of
this section) are correct in their assertion that it has been a story of
'decline and fall'. The high-water mark of 1945 was soon passed, and
planning was seriously challenged along the way. But the story is
more complex than that.

For one thing, the immediate postwar consensus was not necessarily as strong as it is sometimes claimed to be. It was (as Donnison
and Soto rightly say) 'loosely-knit' and it was not to take much to pull
apart the weave. Nostalgia for this period has done much to exagger-
ate the strength and durability of this consensus. Some years on, and
speaking more generally of the political scene at this time, Edward
Heath (as Prime Minister) rejected the idea that the parties ever
came together in their policies;[6] while, more recently, Peter Jenkins
concludes that 'the post-war consensus had never been much of a

consensus.'[7] Certainly, if there was a consensus in planning, it proved to be more fragile and less enduring than it is sometimes assumed to be.

So, in a simple depiction of 'decline and fall' one has to be wary about overstating the opening case. At the same time, while planning has been eroded over time, it would also be wrong to overstate the extent of its demise. As the following chapters will show, the case for planning has been weakened but by no means demolished.

As evidence of how soon it was weakened, the immediate postwar consensus did not even survive the 1940s. New legislation was passed and a planning system very quickly became a landmark on the new administrative map of Britain, but it will be seen that critics were already at work in questioning not only the details but the very basis of this form of intervention.

In the 1950s this process continued. A key feature of the immediate postwar legislation (to do with compensation and betterment) was effectively removed, and (particularly in respect of housebuilding) the private sector was encouraged to take a more assertive role in the development process. Conservatives were in power for most of this period, and while they were reluctant to take any major new initiatives on the planning front, their record shows that they were prepared to retain the system largely intact and to accept a role for planning as part of their wider strategy. To that extent, the consensus survived the decade.

Similarly, for most of the 1960s both Conservative and Labour Administrations continued to subscribe to the value of planning. Indeed – in response to rapid socio-economic changes and demands for new housing, modern buildings and an improved infrastructure – this was to be a particularly active period, with a range of new initiatives from both parties. The two leading politicians of this period, Harold Macmillan and Harold Wilson, found common ground in a commitment to economic management and to a process of modernization, and planning was called upon to play a key role, just as it had in the 1940s. Conflating the names of Butler and Gaitskell into 'Butskellism' has offered a ready characterization of the postwar consensus, derived from ideas spanning the political divide, yet the record of the 1960s shows that Macmillan and Wilson might have offered no less of a symbol of commonality.

Towards the end of the 1960s, though, danger signs were in the offing. Economic management had failed to secure an adequate rate of growth, while the Welfare State had not removed poverty. Planning itself was acquiring an unenviable record, one that was marked by unpopularity for insensitive plans and a disregard for the real needs of communities. Such trends were to be reinforced in the 1970s, accelerated by an international recession in the wake of higher oil prices. Not only were the basic tenets of Keynsianism questioned (to the extent that under the Callaghan Administration of 1976–79 the first cautious steps were taken towards monetarist policies), but the various institutions of the Welfare State were to experience the first of a wave of cuts in public expenditure. Edward Heath's claim that 'there never was a consensus'[8] sounded less outlandish at the end of the decade than when it was made at the beginning.

It was not a particularly distinguished period for planning, and the election in 1979 of a Conservative government led by Margaret Thatcher seemed to many to sound the death-knell not only for planning but for the whole postwar consensus. Keynsianism was quickly discredited, and the ideology of the new régime was distinctly anti-planning. Observing the demoralization that set in amongst planners, Peter Self (a stalwart of the TCPA, with a campaigning record that dates back to the 1940s) offers the recent view that 'by 1982 planners had lost interest or faith in the possibility of building a coherent planning strategy.'[9] Not simply the direction of planning, but, indeed, its very rationale had been called into question.

But was it all over? Had the so-called postwar consensus now completely disintegrated? Analysing the politics of the Thatcher years, Andrew Gamble is one analyst who reserves judgement.[10] Certainly, he (along with other commentators on this period) concedes the fact of a significant shift in the composition of the policy agenda. Thatcher's single-minded commitment to the goals of a free economy and a strong State did, with the benefit of three election victories, inevitably bring changes in their train. The political debate could never be the same again. Yet Gamble (even before the resignation of Margaret Thatcher in November 1990) is not convinced that these changes run as deep as might at first appear. Old assumptions have been challenged but more needs to be done before they are effectively replaced: 'Thatcherism should be seen as an attempt to clear the way for a new hegemony, not as that new hegemony itself.'[11]

Gamble's caution is vindicated by the state of town and country planning at the start of the 1990s. It has been challenged and changes have been forced upon it, but the system remains recognizable and largely intact. More than that, there are grounds (spelt out in the final chapter) for considering the case for a new coalition of interests. Planning, in spite of earlier premonitions of doom, is here to stay. But its role and purpose needs to be reformulated. The world of the 1990s is very different to that of the 1940s, and, as the following chapters will demonstrate, in moving towards a new consensus there is no shortage of historical experience to draw upon to show where planning can succeed as well as where it can fail.

NOTES

1. A comparative summary of the place of consensus in the history of political theory is provided in Partridge (1971).
2. This view, closely identified with Margaret Thatcher, is pursued in the next section of this introduction and in Chapter 7.
3. Raymond Williams (1976), p. 67.
4. See, for instance, Simmie (1974) and Bailey (1975).
5. Over the past twenty years, planning (and with it, the underlying notion of consensus) has been the object of a sustained Marxist critique. See, for instance, Paris (1982, part Three) and Ambrose (1986).
6. Evidence cited in Jenkins (1989), p. 4.
7. Jenkins, *op. cit.*, p. 4.
8. Quoted in Jenkins, *op. cit.*, p. 4.
9. Self, P. (1989) 'Planning's search for a political consensus', *The Planner*, Vol. 75, No. 24, pp. 20–21.
10. Gamble (1988).
11. *Ibid.*, p. 236.

2

FROM GARDEN CITIES
TO NEW TOWNS

The New Towns Act was passed in 1946. For nearly a half century before that campaigners had been working to spread the idea of new settlements in the form of what were originally conceived as garden cities.[1] The nature of this preliminary campaign sets the scene for what follows in the postwar period. Established patterns and goals of campaigning as well as the continuing involvement of leading figures in the movement provide threads of continuity in the new setting of Britain after the Second World War.

What happened before 1946 may be seen in terms of three phases of activity. The first largely belongs to the Edwardian era, starting with the formation of the Garden City Association towards the end of Queen Victoria's reign and witnessing early progress in this country and overseas in the years before the outbreak of the First World War. In turn, the war years and the ensuing period through to the eve of fresh hostilities in 1939 offer a record of mixed fortune, with hopes raised amidst the euphoria of a 'homes for heroes' campaign, only to be dashed during the 1920s and the first half of the 1930s, prior to a fresh impetus for planning at the end of this period. This impetus is carried forward into the Second World War and its immediate aftermath, culminating *inter alia* in legislation for a national programme for new towns.

The record shows that this unbroken campaign was conducted by a small organization with limited resources and a total membership numbered, for most of this period, in hundreds rather than thousands. Yet the record also shows that it was remarkably influential, the ideas it promoted being central to the practical and intellectual development of modern town planning. The question remains, however, as to whether or not the campaign led directly to the New Towns Act or whether comparable State action would have been taken in any case, in the face of an impelling need for more planning to guide land-use change and settlement development. Was the work of the pressure group the key factor or was the change that came about a product of wider, structural forces? It is a question that will be shown to be applicable no less to the period after 1946 than to that before it.

HOWARD'S WAY

> Howard's synthesis has stood the test of experiment and the cross-examination of public controversy. It is I believe the key to the planning of the coming period. All its essential elements stand: moderate-sized industrial and trading towns in close contact with a surrounding agricultural countryside, each a healthy, well-equipped and coherent community; zoning of areas within each town for ready access between homes, workplaces, shops and cultural centres; limitation of density to safeguard light, gardens and recreation space, but not exaggerated to the pitch of urban diffusion; civic design aiming at harmony rather than standardization; planned internal and external communications; and unified site-ownership coupled with leaseholds, reconciling public interests with freedom of choice and enterprise. (F. J. Osborn, in Preface to Howard, 1946 edition, September 1945)

At the end of the Second World War, F. J. Osborn (hitherto active in the development of the only two garden cities of the day, Letchworth and Welwyn, and instrumental towards the end of the 1930s in redirecting the efforts of the then Garden Cities and Town Planning Association towards broader planning goals) reviewed the situation. He was the first to admit that a campaign that had started at the end of the last century had secured only minimal gains; yet he was also foremost in asserting that the basic principles that had underpinned the very formation of the Association had successfully stood the test of time. Indeed, it was these principles that were now brought forward for use in the brave new world that dawned.

Osborn's above quote elucidates the essence of these principles and its source indicates that the fount of inspiration was to be found in a book by Ebenezer Howard that was first published in 1898. In that book, *To-morrow: A Peaceful Path to Real Reform*, Howard presented to the world his ideas for what he eventually termed garden cities. More than a new settlement scheme, Howard was thinking of nothing less than the reconstruction of society, 'a new commonwealth' less wedded to the dictates of capitalist competition and more to cooperative socialism. Within three years, however, (as evidenced in the title of his revised book, *Garden Cities of To-morrow*) he had been forced to moderate his aims and to settle for the creation of garden cities as an end in itself.[2]

Moderation was a price to pay for practical progress. Within a year of the publication of the original manifesto, the Garden City Association was formed with the dual objectives of spreading the ideas contained in Howard's book, and setting in motion the building of the world's first garden city. High in idealism but with little else to sustain it, the new organization achieved little in its first year, until the arrival of a respected lawyer of Liberal Party persuasions, Ralph Neville, who assumed the Chairmanship of the Association. It proved to be a turning-point in more ways than one.

On the one hand, Neville's arrival heralded a more secure future. His very presence added a degree of respectability to the infant organization, as well as an *entreé* to a world of influential politicians, fellow lawyers and industrialists. As an early list of nearly 100 Vice Presidents testifies, the Association found little difficulty in enlisting at least nominal support from the 'great and the good'; in the context of a wider public concern for 'the housing problem' the garden city was accepted as a worthy cause. Neville also had an eye for sound organization, and one of his first acts was to appoint a full-time Secretary, Thomas Adams, who arrived knowing little about the garden city and went on to become one of the world's leading town planners in the first half of the twentieth century.[3]

Yet, on the other hand, Neville's intervention drew Howard and the Association away from its origins amongst those fervent groups of radicals that characterized the fringes of late-Victorian and Edwardian political life, gathering in meeting rooms and institutes to read each other's tracts and newsletters, and to discuss ways of changing the world. The Garden City Association (through Howard's personal contacts) had itself been sponsored by the Land Nationalisation Society, and in the early years of the new body a number of key members held dual membership.[4] Howard was at home in this milieu, a shorthand clerk of limited means, sharing a radical belief in the power of rational persuasion (he was himself a compelling speaker and writer), and without apparent self-interest in pursuance of his cause. He was an idealist, but also a realist, and, believing that the garden city would best be promoted by moderate means, was not to resist the ascendancy of more hard-headed characters within the organization.

In pragmatic terms, Howard's acquiescence was justified, at least to the extent that capital was raised to enable the purchase in 1903 of land for the first garden city at Letchworth in Hertfordshire. Building began in the following year, and the Association (although it hived off the management of Letchworth to a separate company, keeping for itself a general propagandist role) had secured a place on the international map. Visitors came from around the world to see for themselves this embryo utopia, a foretaste, so it was promised, of a new era of settlement planning. Along with the aeroplane, claimed Lewis Mumford some forty years later, the garden city was one of the great inventions of the twentieth century and a harbinger of a new age.[5] Although early visitors (who discovered work in progress but certainly not on a scale that lived up to expectations) may have placed more reliance on the aeroplane than on the garden city, the influence of Letchworth as a demonstration project was considerable, particularly in the context of a growing lobby for a national system of planning legislation.

The term 'town planning' only came into common usage in about 1904, but a campaign rapidly gathered pace to press for something that went beyond the improvement of housing in isolation. A majority of housing reformers (including the National Housing Reform Council, formed in the year after the GCA, and especially influential in the municipalities) sought to guide new development towards the suburbs, while the Garden City Association looked for sites further afield. Both factions, however, were agreed on the need for planning legislation, and, although it fell short of what was called for, the 1909 Housing, Town Planning, etc. Act marked the formal start of twentieth-century planning. It provided for the more orderly development of new suburbs, leaving greenfield settlements of the sort advocated by the Association for a later agenda. Undeterred, the GCA claimed much of the credit for this enactment, and promptly changed its name to that of the Garden Cities and Town Planning Association to reflect a wider brief as the foremost body to represent the interests of planning.[6]

This adoption of a wider brief showed progress in one sense, but it also led to a dispute within the organization as to whether or not it was abandoning its true garden city principles. The fundamentalists argued that the garden city was the only true doctrine, as opposed to those (led by the influential Secretary, Ewart Culpin) who were willing to embrace well-planned garden suburbs within the list of objectives for the Association. A strong card in the hand of the new guard was that Letchworth remained the only garden city (still well short of completion), and that it was important to keep abreast of and to encourage related forms of development.

Thus defined, the 'garden city movement' proved to be the main source of town planning ideas in the period before 1914, in which year the professional body, the Town Planning Institute, was established. Leading figures in the garden city movement – such as Raymond Unwin (along with Barry Parker, the architect of Letchworth) and Thomas Adams – were to play key roles in the new organization. Moreover, the influence of the garden city movement was not confined to this country. Elsewhere, Germany, France and Belgium were amongst those with their own garden city organizations; and it was the officers of the Association who were instrumental in convening an international gathering in 1913 that, in turn, led to the formation of the International Garden Cities and Town Planning Association.

By 1914 the campaign had led to one garden city and to numerous hybrid forms of development which bore at least some of the hallmarks that Howard had imprinted. Town planning had entered the statute books, and its early development was closely linked to garden city principles. If not exuberant, the campaigners were at least optimistic about the future.[7]

Then came the war, and it seemed that hopes would be dashed and early progress lost. In fact, wars may have a contradictory impact, inflicting great losses on a nation yet also unlocking latent impulses for domestic reform. This was the case with the First World War, an event of immeasurable human suffering which, at the same time, witnessed limited social and political progress on the home front. Of particular significance was the growing involvement of the State, in contrast with a long tradition of minimizing intervention where at all possible, with housing reform singled out for special attention. It was widely accepted during the war years that greater public intervention would be essential to tackle a severe housing shortage that was beyond the reach of the private sector alone to resolve. The lurking threat of political instability if this and related social problems were to be ignored added to the need for concerted action.[8]

The main response, under the banner of 'homes for heroes', remains one of the better-known political initiatives of this period. It became a point of focus of the GCTPA, which sought to secure that the greater part of the promised postwar housing should be directed to garden city locations. It was not enough, argued the Association, to build more houses without paying equal attention to the planning implications. Involvement in this episode, particularly between 1918 and 1920, proved to be one of the more high-profile phases in the Association's long campaign, though with Lloyd George's coalition government soon to lower targets, the euphoria and prospect of a radical breakthrough in planning as well as housing proved to be short-lived.

With little faith in the State as an agent of fundamental change, and sensing the likely outcome well before the postwar housing drive was curtailed, the old campaigner, Ebenezer Howard, parted company with the Association's wider brief. Almost single-handed, he set about establishing the second garden city, not many miles away from Letchworth, at Welwyn in Hertfordshire. It was a remarkable achievement, and others within the organization, notably C. B

Purdom and F. J. Osborn (the latter of whom had in 1918 written a short volume, *New Towns after the War*) soon followed Howard to the new settlement, to practise in an undiluted form what the main organization no longer preached.[9]

In one sense, at least, Welwyn's gain was the Association's loss, for (although those who went to live and work there remained members) the main energies of Purdom, Osborn and others were now directed towards the strenuous task of community-building. Meanwhile, for the London-based organization, compared with the pioneering days of the Garden City Association and the excitement of the 'homes for heroes' phase, most of the 1920s, and the first half of the 1930s is an unexceptionable period in the movement's history. The lobbying continued, and influential figures on both sides of the House – not least of all Neville Chamberlain, a future Prime Minister – were won over to the idea of the garden city. Labour's brief spell of government, between 1929 and 1931, offered some hope of a broader acceptance of planning, one outcome being the establishment of a government committee to report on the feasibility of satellite towns.[10] But any immediate hopes of a breakthrough were dashed by the severity of the economic depression of those years, and by the depth of entrenched resistance to further government intervention.

Paradoxically, it was that same economic depression (which had forced Labour from power and which was used by opponents of planning to argue for freer rather than more restrictive policies) which, in time, led inexorably towards a more interventionist approach. The underlying structural problems that were revealed and the manifestation of uneven development, in terms of great regional disparities, forced upon unwilling politicians a commitment to act. With a growing lobby in favour of planning (in the broadest sense, to include the crucial area of economic management, as well as town and country planning), the trend was unmistakable.[11]

The tide was turning, and for the Association the return of Osborn in 1936 to an active role as Honorary Secretary marked a revival of its fortunes and influence. Osborn, himself, for all his direct experience at Welwyn, was now the first to admit that garden cities should no longer be on the front line of the Association's claims; nor should there any longer be ambivalence about the role of the State (as opposed to voluntary effort, favoured by the pioneers) to secure lasting change. First, argued Osborn, there had to be a comprehensive system of land-use planning on a national basis, and only when that was secured could one hope to achieve the effective building and rational distribution of garden cities.

Over the next ten years, Osborn led the Association in a sustained and remarkably influential campaign for just these objectives: for a national system of planning and for a programme of new towns located in line with regional priorities. An early opportunity for him to publicize these views to maximum effect came in 1937 with the establishment of what was generally known as the Barlow Committee, formed, in the face of continuing regional problems, to consider trends in the distribution of population and industry and to make policy recommendations. Although Barlow did not report until 1940, it proved to be an important milestone along the road to postwar planning legislation. Osborn had doubts as to whether it really went far enough, but was adept in using the recommendations to pursue his case in the war years.[12]

The 'stepping stones' along the way to a comprehensive planning system are well-recorded, following a course from Barlow to Scott and Uthwatt, through the labyrinth of wartime reconstruction politics, and into the brave new world of 1945 with its promise that all would change.[13] In all of this, Osborn was tireless, cajoling politicians in all parties, broadcasting on the radio, organizing conferences, and writing endless letters and policy documents. In turn, the esteem of the Association (which changed its name to Town and Country Planning Association in 1941) was high, with an accepted role as the main source of ideas for the planning system that seemed increasingly likely as a feature of postwar Britain.

Sure enough, (apart from wartime legislation designed to meet immediate building needs) fresh laws were promptly passed to plan for the future of town and country, of industry and recreation. The 1945 Distribution of Industry Act, the 1947 Town and Country Planning Act, and the 1949 National Parks and Access to the Countryside Act were all broadly consistent with the Association's objectives (though, inevitably, none of these statutes contained all that the Association hoped for, and a division of responsibilities between different Ministries was a major stumbling block). Of all the postwar legislation, however, that which came closest to the heart of the Association was the 1946 New Towns Act.

In this, with its provision for a State programme of new towns around the country, it might have seemed that nearly half a century of campaigning had met with success. Instead of the piecemeal and hitherto very limited process of forming new communities through voluntary initiative, the way was now open for a national system of planned overspill. As if to endorse its commitment, in the same year that the Act was passed, the government designated Stevenage (symbolically, located between Letchworth and Welwyn) as the first of the postwar new towns.

In fact, the Association was satisfied rather than euphoric. The Act was lacking in certain important respects, and there were serious doubts as to whether the State was the right agency to create organic and innovative communities of the sort experienced in the first garden cities. But this was not a time to carp (in public, at least) and with a sense of pragmatism that had characterized its earlier campaigning, the Association set about carving a new niche for itself as a monitor of progress rather than as the inventor of an idea. Planning and new towns had now been accepted, and the task ahead was to ensure that standards were upheld and visionary goals not lost. Something of a political consensus surrounded the new initiatives, but the consensus was delicate and would need careful tending. That was all a part of the Association's brief.

INFLUENCING EVENTS

> I think (after the most critical examination and continual re-examination of the facts) that I personally have been a decisive factor in the evolution of the new towns policy and that this evolution is extremely important historically. I mean no less than that without my fanatical conviction and persistent work in writing, lecturing and especially lobbying the New Towns Act of 1946 would not have come about, at any rate in that period.
> (F. J. Osborn, in correspondence with Lewis Mumford, 16th October 1962, in Hughes, 1971, p. 327)

Osborn's considered claim that he was personally responsible for the 1946 Act is, by any standards, extravagant. Even allowing for the fact that he might have been implicitly acknowledging the work and persistence of others in the Association, it remains a claim the meaning of which needs to be teased out. For what it is really saying is that government policy can be shaped by agencies (whether individuals or groups) working from an extra-Parliamentary base. And this, in turn, is a thesis that is fundamental to an appraisal of the campaign conducted by the Association, not only before 1946 but also since.

Clearly, a pressure group such as that which campaigned for garden cities and town planning would not have stayed in business had it not been for an underlying belief in its own capacity to influence events. There is little if any evidence of self-doubt on that front; instead, the energies of its leaders from the date of its very inception have been directed towards ways of organizing the most effective campaign within its means to pursue its declared aims. The record before 1946 bears out the unquestioning persistence of this objective.

To the extent that the Association follows an evolutionary path into the postwar period, certain features of its early history are worth noting. For a start, although the idea of the garden city and the case for town planning was clearly and loudly articulated, it has never been a mass movement. Typically, total membership has been numbered in hundreds rather than thousands, the exceptions being those times – coinciding with the formation of Letchworth, the 'homes for heroes' phase, and the end of the Second World War – when public interest was especially aroused by the idea of planning. On two of these three occasions, numbers exceeded two thousand; but these peaks were matched by periods of relative quietude, as in the mid-1920s, when less than 500 members were attracted.[14]

The fact that it has never been a large organization has had a consequent effect on the way that the campaign has been conducted. A low annual income has left the Association in a constant state of financial insecurity, and this has inevitably limited what it might do. Equally, it has been unable to employ a large office establishment, managing with no more than a handful of permanent staff supplemented with a small but ready band of volunteers. The influence it has exerted has been in spite of rather than because of its resource base.

Instead, what it has relied on has been the leadership qualities of a number of outstanding individuals, a network of influential contacts, and the cumulative effects of sheer persistence. Ebenezer Howard, Thomas Adams, Raymond Unwin, Barry Parker, Ewart Culpin, C. B. Purdom, Seebohm Rowntree, R. L. Reiss, Frederic Osborn and Patrick Abercrombie are all key figures in the early history of modern town planning, and each (in different ways) played an important role in the garden city movement. This was by no means a monopoly of town planning talent, for there were those who were not a part of the garden city movement, like Thomas Sharp and Trystan Edwards, who were not opposed to small settlements but who preferred higher density development; and subscribers to the Modern Movement, who had a totally different concept of urban form, and who were cast by the likes of Osborn in the role of twentieth-century barbarians. These competing schools notwithstanding, the garden city movement enjoyed considerable influence throughout this period.[15]

Indeed, a cluster of what is popularly but erroneously termed 'anti-urban' ideas, including but also going beyond Howard's original garden city, was to have a signal influence in shaping modern town planning thought and practice, in Britain and overseas. Largely through the work of Raymond Unwin, architect of Letchworth and later Chief Architect in the Ministry of Health (the department with responsibility for public housing), many of the elements of the garden city were transferred into a garden suburb setting. Relatively low density housing set in individual gardens, a romantic style of cottage architecture and street layout, and landscaping in sympathy with natural form were amongst the features that came to characterize not only interwar municipal estates but also the output of private builders.

In furthering its cause, as well as drawing on the work of key professionals, the Association was also effective in nurturing an extensive network of contacts, who were able to help financially and in terms of political leverage. Stemming from the arrival of Ralph Neville as Chairman in 1901, the approach has been consistently pursued ever since, through to the present day. A figurehead post of President was established in 1907, with Neville assuming the first title, to be followed, in succession, by a landowner and aristocrat with an interest in housing reform, the Marquess of Salisbury (from 1914), the politician and member of the newspaper family Cecil Harmsworth (from 1919), and (from 1929) the Earl of Lytton, a former Governor of Bengal, landowner and Chairman of the Hampstead Garden City Trust. To these were added lengthy lists of Vice Presidents, spanning an impressive range of British public life, and politicians of various persuasions. Particularly, towards the end of the 1930s and during the subsequent war years, the Association was also locked into a powerful body of intellectual opinion that had coalesced from various standpoints to argue the case for planning.

Yet all of this, the work of key individuals and the support of the 'great and the good', cannot be seen in isolation from the cumulative effect of campaigning year in and year out, repeating and refining the same basic message to all who would listen. If Osborn's above claim to omniscience is overstated, there can be little doubting the sense of another observation: 'I think it was the persistency with which our group stuck to one objective, and even over-simplified it, that lodged the idea in the political mind.[16] For nearly fifty years, from the date of Howard's seminal publication, the case for new settlements to relieve 'the urban condition' was advanced with unfailing vigour. To that extent, at least, evidence of the pressure group's influence was beyond question.

A mark of how far it had come is the extent to which the Association (and Osborn, in particular) was seen by government as a key consultative body in the drafting stages of new town planning policy and legislation. The campaign may have achieved few of its objectives on the ground in the preceding period, but it had certainly, as Osborn claims, 'lodged the idea in the political mind'.

This notion of an autonomous pressure group ostensibly influencing policy accords with a pluralist explanation of power and politics. It is posited on liberal democratic assumptions of access to decision-making and on an underlying belief in the capacity of rational argument and persuasion to win the day. Opinion forming (sometimes over a long period) is an important part of the process, effectively preparing politicians and others for the time when the proposed initiative can be introduced. Pluralists speak of 'policy windows' that open at particular times, and of 'policy entrepreneurs' who are ready to take advantage of a more conducive situation.[17]

All of these stages are evident in the case of the garden city movement. The idea had no particular standing at the time of its inception, and it was purely as a result of sustained advocacy that it came to occupy a central position in early housing and town planning debates. 'Policy windows' seemed within reach at various times, but it was not until the 1940s that a real opportunity emerged. At that point, Osborn played the classic role of a policy entrepreneur, bringing to bear the full weight of accumulated arguments and experience to press home the Association's case. The postwar enactments might be seen as testimony of the effectiveness of pressure group politics.

And, in one sense, of course, the whole episode had been remarkably effective. Howard's vision, so it would seem, had been brought to fruition. The problem is that the pluralist explanation tells only part of the story. It locates the campaign and key agents within it, but it fails to explain why the policy window opened at that time in the 1940s and in the way that it did. To answer those questions one must look beyond the specifics of the campaign and to the structural context within which all this occurred.

At root, the real issue was that of a basic confrontation between a role for governments which is non-interventionist (or, at least, which favours minimal intervention), and that which favours planning in the broadest sense. In the face of a succession of reforms and interference with 'natural' economic processes, the classic doctrine of *laisser faire* had long been adapted out of recognition (as compared with its theoretical origins in the eighteenth century). Yet, at least until the 1940s, an ideological resistance to planning remained the prevailing order of the day. And it was less the force of rational argument, valuable though that was in preparing the ground, which caused the change than the force of new circumstances.

The failure of traditional economic policies to resolve the problems of the 1930s and fear of the political consequences of allowing large-scale unemployment to reappear; the success of the State in marshalling resources to lead the nation to victory in the war; popular enthusiasm and electoral support for the prospect of radical social reform; and an urgent need for policies to deal with the investment and rebuilding process when the war ended – all were circumstances that favoured a far more interventionist approach than hitherto. Within a new context of social reconstruction, town planning had a key role to play.

But it was also a circumscribed role. The new towns that were to be built, for instance, were not to be managed directly by the communities themselves, nor were the financial benefits of rising land values to be guaranteed for local use. Howard the pragmatist might have taken some comfort from the acceptance of the idea of planned overspill, but Howard the idealist would have lamented the heavy hand of the State and the loss of those elements that he considered crucial to the social success of the scheme.

Seen on a wider front, the post-1945 measures, far-reaching though they were, failed to achieve the irreversible shift of power and wealth that seemed to be in the offing. It was, in the nature of liberal democracy, a period of reforms but certainly not of revolution. Howard's 'new commonwealth' was not to be created through the ballot box.

To return to Osborn's claim that it was he (and implicitly the sustained advocacy of the Association) who was responsible for the 1946 Act, the pluralist might agree with the general thesis, but it has to be said that it is only a partial explanation. The 1946 Act was passed, not simply because a particular group wanted it, but because the State felt impelled at that time to respond to an urgent shortage of housing and to provide greenfield sites for new industries. It was this structural context which provided the opportunity, though the way that the opportunity was seized and the nature of the solution has much to do with the effectiveness of the Association's campaign.

In the chapters that follow, dealing with the period since 1946, this question of a balance and interaction between agency and structural factors will be pursued as a recurring theme. It is contended that the Association's policy can only satisfactorily be explained in relation to the changing social and political context of postwar Britain.

NOTES

Howard's Way

1. The history of the early campaign, from 1899 to 1946, is recorded in Hardy (1991).
2. A valuable interpretation of Howard's successive compromises is provided by Beevers (1988).
3. See Simpson (1985).
4. Two accounts of the linkages between the various radical organizations are those of Buder, S. (1969) 'Ebenezer Howard: the genesis of a town planning movement'. *Journal of the American Institute of Planners*, Vol. 35, pp. 390–398 and Fishman (1977).
5. Lewis Mumford, in his introduction, 'The garden city idea and modern planning', in Howard (1946).
6. Information on this episode is derived from contemporary reports in the Association's journal, *Garden City* (dating from 1904).
7. See, for instance, Culpin (1913).
8. This episode is well documented and basic references are included in

Hardy, D. (1990) 'War, social change and planning: the example of the Garden City Movement'. *Planning Perspectives*, Vol. 4, No. 2.

9. See, for instance, Osborn (1970).
10. This was known as the Marley Committee, reporting in 1933.
11. In the context of a widely-based lobby, Osborn organized a town planning alliance of interests known as the Planning Front.
12. See, for instance, the account of Osborn's wartime activities, in Hebbert (1981).
13. The official histories of these aspects of wartime planning can be found in Cullingworth (1975 and 1979) and Cherry (1975).

Influencing Events

14. The highest recorded membership figure was, in fact, in 1903, when the total reached 2500. At that time the annual subscription rate was 2s 6d (equivalent to about 12p).
15. The influence of the garden city movement is widely acknowledged amongst planning historians. See, for instance, Hall (1988).
16. Osborn, in correspondence with Lewis Mumford, 7th January 1947, in Hughes (1971), p. 145.
17. Kingdon (1984).

3

POST-1946:
A WATCHING BRIEF

The latter half of the 1940s proved to be a testing time not only for the Association but for the whole apparatus of modern planning. For the Association here was a new role, no longer campaigning for the advent of new legislation but now, instead, holding a watching brief over the young offspring. Everything was in place but would it grow to its full potential? Indeed, events in the early years suggested that the future of planning was far from secure, and public hopes turned very quickly to doubts. Inevitably, the two histories are intertwined – the record of the Association seeking to influence but, in turn, strongly constrained by developments at large.

In the three sections which follow, the first sets the scene in terms of the political climate of the late 1940s, the second focuses on the particular role of the Association in seeking to influence policies, and the third looks at the internal organization of a pressure group at work in the new political context of postwar Britain.

THE FRAGILE CONSENSUS

> The coalition in favour of planning was no more than a temporary alliance of unequal forces; it had forged no lasting consensus. (Donnison and Soto, 1980, p. 6)

It is part of the folklore of planning history that the postwar planning system was forged in a mould of social and political consensus. And, indeed, this interpretation of events is well enough founded. It fell to a Labour government to bring forward an array of new legislation, but each of the main planning Acts of the immediate postwar period had its roots in proposals already agreed within the wartime coalition. The shape of the postwar planning system had been outlined by politicians from all parties before the landslide victory of Labour in 1945.

There were, in fact, four new entries to the statute book, each of which was to map out the ground of postwar planning and each of which had been foreshadowed in the coalition debates over the previous five years. Both the Distribution of Industry Act of 1945 (passed before the end of the war) and the New Towns Act in the following year drew on some of the recommendations of the Barlow

Before we build—

—a plan

We all know that in Britain today there are towns that suffer from overcrowding and lack of planning. The twofold purpose of the Ministry of Town and Country Planning is to improve existing conditions wherever possible and to ensure that order and beauty shall come to our towns and cities of the future. These pictures show what intelligent planning can do and what it tries to avoid.

Poster to publicize the work of the newly-formed Ministry of Town and Country Planning.

Report of 1940; the most decisive sections of the Town and Country Planning Act of 1947, relating to the value attributed to development rights, had already been explored in the Uthwatt Report of 1942; while the ethos and priorities underlying the 1949 National Parks and Access to the Countryside Act can be traced back at least to the 1942 Scott Report.

With such a strong element of continuity and underlying agreement, spanning successive governments, Cullingworth's view that the content of postwar planning legislation would have been much the same regardless of which political party gained power in 1945 seems eminently reasonable.[1] Indeed, the pledges of the major parties in their respective manifestoes lend support to this view.[2] Predictably enough (in view of what subsequently transpired) the 1945 Labour Manifesto contained a firm commitment to building more houses 'in relation to good town planning – pleasant surroundings, attractive lay-out, efficient utility services, including the necessary transport facilities.' More than that, the electorate was reminded that 'Labour believes in land nationalisation and will work towards it', with proposals for compensation and betterment.

Less predictably perhaps (given the ideological challenge posed by planning), the Conservative Manifesto also contained a commitment to 'plans for the use of land which will take into account the needs of each locality and the opportunities offered by national resources.' Significantly, following Uthwatt, new legislation was promised with regard to compensation and betterment, 'so as to secure for the future the best use of land in the public interest, including proper reservation of open spaces and the best location of industry and planning.'

And to complete the triad of consensus, the Liberal Manifesto also reconciled the idea of planning and State intervention with its more traditional, individualist values. In a bold statement, comprehensive measures were called for, including the immediate acquisition of development rights outside built-up areas and the recoupment of betterment values for the community.

A legacy of bad housing (worsened by the embargo on new building during the war), the destruction of whole neighbourhoods through enemy bombing, and the urgent need to reconstruct British industry, together served as a powerful spur to set about the task in a planned way. The evidence before the nation cut ruthlessly across ideological lines, and it would have been a brave or foolish politician who would have used the election platform to deny the case for planning. Historically, 1945 was a high-water mark for a cause that had been decades in the making, yet which never before had enjoyed such popular and bipartisan support.

Subsequent commentators have endorsed this view. In their his-

Lewis Silkin, Minister of Town and Country Planning, one of the prime architects of the postwar consensus.

tory of postwar planning, for instance, McKay and Cox have pointed to an acceptance of new planning measures as 'absolutely necessary'.[3] In turn, Donnison and Soto have shown how it was possible for the Minister of Town and Country Planning, Lewis Silkin, to weave a consensus from different threads – appealing, as he did, to diverse interests who could each find something of benefit in the new planning legislation. He 'temporarily united one of the most contentious parliaments in British history with a vision of the liberal dream shared by the coalition of interests supporting the idea of town planning.'[4] Reade agrees that this was indeed the secret of the consensus, a package of measures that offered something for everyone – 'politician and professional, broad mass and socially-concerned elite, Left and Right, urban and rural, preservationist and modernist, layman and expert.'[5] There were different emphases here and there, argues Cherry, but such was the degree of consensus about planning that 'essentially the same pack of cards was being shuffled.'[6] A vision of a rebuilt land achieved through careful planning had now become 'a general expectation'.[7]

But if the immediate aftermath of the war was to be a golden period for planning it was also to be shortlived; the fragility of the consensus was soon revealed. It had never, in fact, been more than a 'loosely knit alliance',[8] and before too long the seams were beginning to come apart. The promise of a New Jerusalem very quickly gave way to the harsh everyday reality of shortages of food and building materials, of a severe winter in 1946–47 which reduced energy stockpiles to dangerously low levels, of a foreign exchange crisis and a subsequent devaluation of sterling, and of growing public impatience and intolerance with the very idea and practice of planning. It was not what planning could achieve which increasingly shaped its public image, so much as a harmful association with technical complexity and bureaucratic interference. As the 1940s progressed, the public perception of this association fuelled the fire of a populist critique.

Thus, instead of utopia, these were to be recalled as years of austerity; and the reputation of town planning as an arm of government suffered irrevocably in the process. Within a few years the bubble had burst – 'the attempt to forge an economic recovery based on central control, austerity and the careful deployment of resources had wearied the electorate.'[9] Controls, rationing and regimentation had seemed a fair enough price to pay to win a war, and, as the electorate showed, to build the peace that followed. But the public had not written a blank cheque, and, in the absence of an adequate return, the mood very quickly changed. Right across the board – doctors who were less than enamoured by the terms of Bevan's new National Health Service, miners frustrated by the realities of nationalization, returning soldiers and their families who found themselves on lengthening housing lists and sometimes forced to squat, and consumers who had more money to spend than before the war yet less to spend it on – amongst all these groups patience was wearing thin.[10]

Such was the context in which town planning came to terms with the world – a context of great expectations followed very quickly by fading hopes. And the question to be asked in relation to the campaign of the TCPA is where, in these first critical years after the war, was the organization that had worked so hard to bring about the new planning system? What part did it play in trying to hold together the fragile consensus, and how did it counter the loss of faith in planning that was so rapidly setting in? In the following section these issues are explored, revealing a sharp awareness of history in the making, of a turning tide threatening to sweep away gains that had been so painstakingly and recently won.

DISPERSAL ON THE RIGHT TERMS

That the policy of the Association has been formally accepted, and powers enacted to implement it, does not mean that our work is finished. Indeed, it may be said to be only just beginning.' (TCPA Annual Report for 1947, p. 4)

As the above statement shows, there was a recognition that the enactments of 1945, 1946 and 1947 – affecting, in turn, industrial location policy, new towns, and land values and development – marked a watershed in the emergence of modern planning. The long slope of campaigning had been ascended, but that was not the end of it. Stretching into the distance was uncharted territory, and that was where the efforts of the Association now had to be directed: 'the opportunity before us and the responsibility which rests upon the Association have never been greater.'[11]

Looking ahead to what was possible, the vision was clear enough – 'a long-term programme that can give most people the sort of dwellings they want, that serves the technical needs of industry, that safeguards 99 per cent of agricultural land, that provides for the revival of local communities, that relieves the congested cities and gives hope to the declining market towns, and that offers in new towns opportunities for the enterprising and scope for modern architecture and technique.'[12] A key concept for the Association (as it had always been) was that of dispersal; securing for people the opportunity to live and work in balanced communities.

If such a vision seemed utopian, it was, in fact, based on sound enough principles, long nurtured by the Association and carefully considered by the various wartime national planning committees. Moreover, the likes of Frederic Osborn, who had witnessed the sea change in public support, were only too aware that this support had been won on sufferance, and that, should the State become too heavy-handed, the public would very quickly become disillusioned. 'It is vital to keep in mind that there is no "community" interest apart from the interests of persons within the community',[13] a gentle warning that, as subsequent events proved, was to fall on deaf ears.

For the first two or three years after the ending of the war, there was little public indication that the Association had doubts about the course of events. Each new enactment was welcomed as a further step along the road to a better environment. Thus, the fiftieth annual report of the Association was a time to celebrate on the coming into

From soot–

The pall of smoke and dirt which hangs over our industrial cities, shutting out sunlight and filling the air with impurities, is another evil which must be done away with as soon as possible.

effect of the 1947 Act – seen as a sign of having 'succeeded in one of [our] aims: that of machinery for applying wise policy to the guidance of urban and rural development.'[14] But even at that early stage, while acknowledging the machinery, doubts were expressed as to whether it was being effectively used to develop planning policy in the right direction.

Thoughts turned back to the period after the First World War,

–into sunlight

Here is a modern smokeless factory. Very often nowadays permission to build a factory is given only if it conforms to certain conditions which affect design, screening and access to roads.

The promise of planning: government posters portray the contrast between the present and future.

when housing stole the show at the expense of overall planning, and once again (as the Association had done then) it was urged that only the 'genuine pursuit of a dispersal policy would reverse this housing emphasis.'[15] A more worrying parallel between the two periods was to recall that the 'homes for heroes' programme, ushered in by a relieved and rejoicing government under Lloyd George, had eventually foundered in the face of a downturn in the economy. Now, two years after the ending of the Second World War, the country was again in the grip of an economic crisis, and the question was raised as to whether the new planning system might too be disbanded. Probably not, was the opinion of the Association, but the prospects were far from good; at best, 'it may stand in danger of a setback in the fierce competition for man-power.'[16]

Thus, the first years of comprehensive planning were to be hard-fought, warding off growing fears of 'over-planning' and surmounting the difficulties of a Treasury under siege. Even the new towns programme, at the very heart of the Association's campaign, and enacted with so little political dissent, could hardly have got off to a worse start. In the same year as the Act, Osborn confessed to 'real anxiety as to what the new towns will be like', fearing that they might turn out to be little better than the mass housing estates of the interwar years.[17] Indeed, he might well have feared whether the programme would materialize at all. In spite of the rapid passing of the 1946 Act, and the early start in designating and acquiring land at Stevenage for the first of the new towns, the best-laid plans seemed to founder. Opposing interests at Stevenage offered a timely reminder that central planning in a democratic society would by no means be an easy process, and for a number of years there was little to see in this prominent 'shop window' of planning; the sorry record was that by the end of 1950 only twenty-eight houses had been completed.[18] Moreover, the same story was writ large across the entire programme (except for three of the newly-designated 'Mark One' new towns, exempted because of their potential industrial importance), to the extent that in November 1947 public expenditure restrictions halted further building for a year. Reflecting more general trends in planning, it has been concluded that 'the first four years of the new towns programme saw the replacement of idealism with disillusion about its feasibility and some ill-will about the mechanism for carrying it out.'[19]

In the event, the initial obstacles were overcome; a full-scale new towns programme was to become a distinctive feature of postwar Britain, and in the 1950s at least the doubts as to whether it would happen at all were to be dispelled. Additionally, the immediate effects of the 1947 Act could also be seen, as local planning authorities throughout the country set about preparing their first development plans.

But the doubts remained amongst the Association's campaigners. It was one thing to pass new Acts, to designate sites for new towns, and to make plans, but unless 'a larger share of the building effort is diverted to the new towns and to factories and housing in small country towns, the state of the big cities will continue to worsen, to the grave injury of the nation and of themselves.'[20] The fact is that, by

"MAGNIFICENT VIEW, ISN'T IT — ON A CLEAR DAY ONE CAN SEE EIGHT SATELLITE TOWN SITES AND TWENTY SIX REGIONAL BOARD HEADQUARTERS "

Controversy surrounded the designation of new town sites, and civil servants were soon to become a ready butt for public concern.

the end of the 1940s, there was still too little evidence on the ground to demonstrate what planning could achieve. And without that, quite apart from lost opportunities, how could the public be expected to lend support to the new system? This was a theme frequently returned to by Osborn and others; a critique based on the view that if planning was only to display its restrictive functions then it would hardly be surprising if public support dwindled. 'To regain prestige it must begin to show results that make a deep appeal to the ordinary man and woman, in the city as well as in the village and the country house.'[21]

Such exhortations went unheard, and the prognosis became steadily more dismal. The central concept of dispersal was simply not being adopted with the singlemindedness sought by the Association, and by 1949 it had to be admitted that 'our central campaign to stop the big cities expanding and increasing their density has so far failed';[22] reaffirmed in the following year in the conclusion that 'for the time being the dispersalist movement is losing out.'[23] In the face of defeat, the time had come to expose and to challenge competing interests within the so-called consensus.

For a start, the Association was concerned that countryside preservationists were beginning to oppose dispersal policies, in the face of alarmist reports of the loss of food-producing land that would result from new and expanded settlements.[24] The dispute was ill-founded, claimed the Association, and both should be working together to secure a balance between town and country. But, in fact, the alliance between preservationists and dispersalists had never been soundly-based, and, under pressure, was destined to weaken.

At least, however, concern about the preservationists breaking rank was expressed with a degree of restraint, unlike the broadside that was delivered to the high-density architects for embarking on policies that cut across some of the most sacred principles of the Association. War had been declared as long ago as the early 1930s, when Osborn (for whom density was to become something of an obsession in the years ahead) sought to demolish the case of the Modern school of architecture and the influence of the Continental architects who brought such ideas to Britain. Now, again, in the 1940s controversy flared, with Osborn correct in his belief that the initiative for postwar redevelopment was shifting away from the low-density, garden city approach and towards an altogether different model based on high densities and often high-rise development. 'Reactionary architects' were accused of destroying what was good and producing 'nothing in the least pleasant in its place.'[25] From across the Atlantic, Lewis Mumford (well primed on the subject by his correspondent, Osborn) joined battle with an attack on the 'barbarous Le Corbusier/London County Council type of overcrowding' exemplified by the LCC's scheme to accommodate 21,000 people at a density of 28 dwellings (as many as 100 persons) per acre.[26]

For Osborn (and because of his influence at that time, for the Association) density was all important for the success of the whole dispersal strategy. What is more, assessing the optimum density came to assume something of a mystique, with precise figures offered as the hard-and-fast dividing line between good and bad planning. In an article on what he called 'town cramming', Osborn asserted his belief that a density of twelve houses per acre was the most that should be considered and that anything above that could only result in a sacrifice of some aspect or other of amenity.[27]

The rigidity with which this was argued cut sharply through any lingering notion of a planning consensus, dividing the camp into 'believers' and 'non-believers'. Even the loyal and supportive Mumford was cast aside at one point, for daring to assert that the magical figure of twelve should be treated as a guideline rather than dogma.[28]

Thus, for the Association, the 1940s ended on a sour note, the hopes of the earlier years of the decade not exactly dashed but certainly not achieved. An impressive complex of planning machinery was in place but what was it all for?

The general public (as Osborn had warned) had been irritated rather than inspired, seeing the restrictions in the same light as ration books and queues, and losing sight of the vision that had been promised in 1945. It was already questionable whether the ground could be recovered; the fragile consensus was no longer intact.

'THE SHEEP AND THE LION'

> I am constantly amazed at its [the TCPA's] prestige all over the world, as in this country. Inside its mantle my sheep's bleat becomes a lion's roar. (F. J. Osborn, in a letter dated 6th March 1949, in Hughes, 1971, p. 173)

The quote above from one of Osborn's letters reveals the mutual dependence of person and organization as a feature not only of the 1940s but of the following decade too. One implication is that without the organization Osborn's voice would not have been as audible as it was in his capacity as Chairman of the Association's Executive. This may or may not have been true (with Osborn's committed views he quite likely would have found another platform), but what is less questionable is the inverse implication that, without Osborn, the Association would not have been the source of influence it was in this period.

In the quote, surprise is expressed at the prestige enjoyed by the

Association, but this is to ignore the fact that it had been campaigning consistently for half a century and its stance was by then widely known. It also plays down the fact that, for all its vulnerability, British planning in the 1940s was a source of world interest, and if only through its identification with the new system the Association inevitably gained from this wider esteem.

Personalities have always been important in the Association's history – accounting for by no means the whole story, but important nevertheless. Ebenezer Howard, Ralph Neville, Thomas Adams, Ewart Culpin, C. B. Purdom and R. L. Reiss were amongst those who had played significant roles in the earlier stages of the campaign. Immediately before and during the war years, it was Osborn who took the leading role, and this was to continue in the postwar period. 'I am always in the hope that new leaders will emerge,[29] declared Osborn, with a mixture of optimism and resignation, and, in explaining why he carried on regardless he was probably right in his belief that 'if I dropped the Association at present it would cease to have any effect.'[30]

The fact is that in this period Osborn stage-managed the campaign, determining the Association's policy and orchestrating the work of the organization from within. It remained a small organization with a handful of staff in its King Street office, and with a continuing reliance on voluntary support. A full-time Director was a key post, but the 1940s saw several changes. The appointment in 1946 of a recently-demobilized RAF officer, John Mumford, lasted only a year (before he left to become the Public Relations Officer of the Ministry of Town and Country Planning), and this was followed by the upgrading of Desmond Donnelly (who also came to the Association from the RAF in 1946) from the post of Organising Secretary to that of Director.

Donnelly was an aspiring politician, and Osborn, hopeful that he could play a valuable role in the years ahead, took time out to give advice on the art of campaigning. The TCPA would always have its enemies, noted Osborn, but, quite simply, 'forget these outside critics.'[31] There would also be doubters inside the Association, some of whom would think that with the new legislation the campaign had been concluded, but 'it is not at all difficult to show them that we have a great deal to do yet, and that our success to this stage is an additional reason for continued support.'[32] Osborn then tempered his advice with an acknowledgement of Donnelly's questioning approach: 'I approve your restlessness, because unless we are always dissatisfied with ourselves we shall get nowhere.'[33] But Donnelly, too, was shortly to leave, in his case to enter Parliament in 1949 as the Labour MP for Pembrokeshire.

Apart from the Director, the Association enjoyed the support, at least for part of this period, of dedicated officers, like Elizabeth

Baldwin (Business Secretary), Gladys Keable (Conference Secretary) and Elizabeth McAllister (Editor).[34] And, true to its tradition, it continued to attract as Vice Presidents some of the most influential figures of the day, 'heroes' of the planning breakthrough in the war years like Abercrombie, Beveridge, Barlow, Reith and Scott.

The central organization was important, but the Association (and especially Osborn) was constantly seeking ways to energize the cause at the local level. In the absence of 'enthusiasts who will give all their spare time to it [planning]', it was conceded that the most practical course might be to seek to promote planning through the work of local groups not wholly concerned with planning.[35] Elsewhere, an editorial in the journal (written by Donnelly, who for a time included the editorial role in his portfolio) called for 'members willing to help in the formation of local organisations of any kind in order to maintain that vigilant watch and to undertake education to promote informed public opinion.'[36] In the event, the creation of local networks seems to have been very erratic, with interest shown here and there by local groups but with nothing like a branch structure within the Association. A notable exception, however, was the vitality of the Scottish Section, which maintained a full programme of meetings and residential schools throughout this period.

Although the results were patchy, Osborn remained convinced that 'the urgent thing to provide' was 'a flow of supporting material and some organisational stimulus from our centre.'[37] One way to achieve this was to follow the well-tried path of lectures on demand, and key speakers continued the exhausting practice of touring the country to spread the message of planning. In 1946, for instance, nearly one hundred meetings, film shows or exhibitions were arranged, the majority of these being on various aspects of the first wave of proposed new towns. It was also the practice to cover as wide a spectrum of interests as possible, and this particular programme of meetings included audiences drawn from local authorities, joint planning committees and informal planning groups; political organizations like the Junior Conservatives and United Nations Rendezvous; business groups such as Rotary Clubs and the Progressive Business Men's Forum; women's groups such as Women for Westminster, Women Citizens, Soroptomists and Co-operative Women's Guilds; and a wide variety of other associations including a Co-operative Summer School, Eighteen-Plus Groups, Training and Technical Colleges, Ratepayers, Public Libraries, National Farmers' Union and Countryside Preservation Groups.

That same year also saw a number of conferences on topics as varied as 'Needs and problems of the family' (held in conjunction with the British Social Hygiene Council), 'Art for everyday in your own town' and 'The Greater London Plan'. Additionally, fortnightly lunchtime meetings were held at the Association's offices, at which various experts presented lectures on the new planning.[38]

Yet, for all the influence it claimed, and the intensity of its activities, the Association was consistently in need of more members and, even more so, a stronger financial footing. Even in 1946, when public interest and support for planning was at a peak, the Association could only attract 200 new members (in relation to an existing membership total of about 2,500) and at the end of the year recorded a net loss due to resignations and deaths. In the following years the total increased again (including new corporate members from the local authorities), though there were repeated calls for more financial support. Individual subscription rates stood at the 1921 level of a guinea, and the Association relied on donations to balance the books. At the end of the decade, members were asked for 'a voluntary increase of their annual support', with the warning that 'we enter a very difficult period in 1950'.[39]

One occasion which offered an opportunity for publicity (always with the prospect of bringing in new members and attracting influential support) and a time to reaffirm its purpose was the celebration in 1949 of the Association's fiftieth anniversary. It had come a long way since June 1899, when Ebenezer Howard rallied a small following with the idea of the garden city, and now, in the wake of new legislation covering all aspects of land-use planning, the Association advertised itself as the body which sought 'to promote planning education and propaganda' in the widest sense. In its proclamation was the clear message that it had long shaken off its preoccupation with garden cities (or even new towns) to the exclusion of all else. A Jubilee Dinner was held at the Waldorf Hotel, London, attended by the leaders of the new planning elite, and messages were received from Lewis Silkin, Herbert Morrison, Arthur Greenwood, the Archbishop of York, and the Lord Chancellor (Viscount Jowitt), the last of whom expressed the belief, repeated by others, that the achievements of planning in the 1940s would not have been possible 'without the constant and tireless work of the Association.'[40]

Such were the public utterances – a message of solid achievement and promise. In personal correspondence, though, it has already been indicated that, behind a prestigious facade, the organization was rarely at ease with itself. The financial situation was tenuous, and Osborn was the first to admit that too much of the work of the Association rested on his own tiring shoulders. Just months after the Jubilee Dinner he confessed that he was 'a bit worried at the moment about the Association' and anxious about its 'enthusiasm and solidarity'.[41] More tellingly, this was when he was also admitting that planning was losing the initiative that it had gained in 1945, and that public support was already waning. When the decade closed the

Association was still very much in business, but it was by no means in as strong a position as seemed possible at the time of the passing of the New Towns Act.

NOTES

The Fragile Consensus

1. Cullingworth (1975), pp. 241–249.
2. For each of the manifestoes cited in the text, see Craig (1975), pp. 113–137.
3. McKay and Cox (1979), p. 31.
4. Donnison and Soto (1980), p. 6.
5. Reade (1987), p. 50.
6. Cherry (1982), p. 64.
7. *Ibid.*
8. Donnison and Soto (1980), p. 3.
9. Ambrose (1986), p. 59.
10. Peter Jenkins analyses the broader reaction to planning in 'Bevan's fight with the BMA', in Sissons and French (1964), pp. 240–265.

Dispersal on the Right Terms

11. TCPA Annual Report for 1947, p. 6.
12. F. J. Osborn, 'Planning comes of age', *TCP*, Vol. XV, No. 57, 1947, p. 8.
13. *Ibid.*, p. 7.
14. TCPA Annual Report for 1948, p. 3.
15. *Ibid.*
16. 'Planning and the crisis', *TCP*, Vol. XV, No. 59, 1947.
17. Letter from Osborn to Mumford, 20th August 1946, in Hughes (1971), p. 129.
18. The early history of Stevenage is analysed in Orlans (1952).
19. Aldridge (1979), p. 43.
20. TCPA Annual Report for 1949, p. 3.
21. TCPA Annual Report for 1949, p. 4.
22. Letter from Osborn to Mumford, 6th March 1949, in Hughes (1971), p. 171.
23. Letter from Osborn to Mumford, 28th April 1950, in Hughes (1971), p. 185.
24. The issue was reported, for instance, in the TCPA Annual Report for 1949, pp. 3–4.
25. Letter from Osborn to Mumford, 8th July 1949, in Hughes (1971), pp. 178–179.
26. Letter from Mumford to Osborn, 12th September 1949, in Hughes (1971), p. 180.
27. F. J. Osborn, 'Town cramming: the art of maximising density', *TCP*, Vol. XVII, No. 66, 1949, pp. 90–96.

28. Mumford is less rigid than Osborn on the question of density. One instance where this difference surfaces is in a critique of an address by Mumford in 1946 to the Town Planning Institute, as contained in a letter from Osborn to Mumford, 20th August 1946, in Hughes (1971), pp. 130–131.

'The Sheep and the Lion'

29. Letter from Osborn to Mumford, 6th March 1949, in Hughes (1971), p. 173.
30. *Ibid.*
31. Letter from Osborn to Donnelly, 31st March 1947 (Osborn Papers).
32. *Ibid.*
33. *Ibid.*
34. Regular reports on staffing appear in the annual reports for this period. Elizabeth McAllister resigned her editorial post in 1947, and this was taken on by Desmond Donnelly, prior to his own resignation in 1949, at which point Osborn took over.
35. Letter from Osborn to Donnelly, 31st March 1947 (Osborn Papers).
36. 'The task and the opportunity', *TCP*, Vol. XVI, No. 62, 1948, p. 71.
37. Letter from Osborn to Donnelly, 31st March 1947 (Osborn Papers).
38. In addition to the TCPA Annual Report for 1946, a list of Osborn's public lectures is to be found in the Osborn Papers.
39. TCPA Annual Report for 1949, p. 5.
40. 'The Jubilee Dinner', *TCP*, Vol. XVII, No. 66, 1949, pp. 88–89.
41. Letter from Osborn to Donnelly, 22nd November 1949 (Osborn Papers).

4

1950s: HOLDING THE GROUND

The 1950s were something of a watershed for postwar planning. At issue was the question as to whether the new apparatus would be dismantled in the wake of a general public backlash against governmental restrictions and controls, or whether the foundations (laid in the 1940s) in the form of new town designations and development plan preparations could be built upon. In fact, the politics of this decade determined something between these extremes, neither the sweeping away of the new planning machinery nor the creation of a model environment. For the TCPA it was a frustrating period, full of activity but in many ways adding up to a defensive role, seeking to hold the ground and to make the best of what was politically possible. Dispersal policies remained at the heart of the campaign, but by the end of the decade the verdict was mixed; the campaigners could record progress on some fronts (notably, the building of new towns and the designation of green belts) but successive governments had still to grasp the nettle of regional planning.

The first of the following three sections provides a general profile of the decade, including an overview of town planning in the 1950s. This is followed by an analysis of the Association's campaign – its persistence in flying the flag of dispersal, and in arousing public opinion about planning generally – and, in the final section, by a review of the methods employed to pursue these goals.

FROM AUSTERITY TO AFFLUENCE

> Indeed, let us be frank about it: most of our people have never had it so good. Go around the country, go to the industrial towns, go to the farms, and you will see a state of prosperity such as we have never had in my life-time – nor indeed ever in the history of this country. (Harold Macmillan, in a speech in Bedford, July 1957, quoted in Barker, 1978, pp. 290–291)

British society travelled a long way in the 1950s. The decade started when its citizens still carried ration books and a weariness born of enduring the hardships of war followed by fresh difficulties in the immediate years of peace. Within a remarkably short period, however, towards the end of the decade the newly-appointed Prime Minister, Harold Macmillan, could inspire a collective belief in the unprecedented wealth and prosperity of the nation, encapsulated in the above slogan, 'our people have never had it so good'. Austerity was a thing of the past; now, so it was claimed, was the age of affluence.

Reality, is, of course, always more complex than political slogans would have us believe, but there is truth enough in the claim that, materially, the country was faring better towards the end of the decade than at the beginning. As a measure of how far Britain travelled, it is worth recalling that 1950 belonged to the immediate postwar austerity years. Labour had run its term of office, and a General Election in February offered an opportunity for the public to register its verdict on what had been achieved so far.

Anticipating that one of the issues on which the government would be judged was that of the electorate's willingness to endure what critics regarded as a growing interference in people's everyday lives – the sharp end of a philosophy of public intervention – an attempt was made before the election to simplify procedures and regulations across a wide range of activities. Harold Wilson, the young President of the Board of Trade, for instance, announced what amounted to a 'bonfire of controls' as literally thousands of licences were abandoned.[1] But the issue of existing controls was by no means the only item on the electoral agenda (nationalization proposals and foreign policy commanded more interest) and remedial action on that front was not enough to prevent a massive reduction in Labour's parliamentary majority to a mere five seats. The steam seemed to have run out of the promised socialist revolution, and, as Hugh Gaitskell later confessed, 'Most of us who were in the 1945–50 Parliament knew that we just about had as much as we could conceivably digest in those five years.'[2]

The new Labour Administration in 1950, exhausted and demoralized, still beset by daunting problems at home and abroad, clung to office for another twenty months, before succumbing to the Conservatives in the General Election of October 1951. On the town planning front (indeed, on any front) this short period of office was not particularly noteworthy; though, in symbolic terms, two events have a particular bearing on planning. The first event was little-publicized but a sign of things to come. Hugh Dalton, on succeeding Lewis Silkin as the new town planning Minister, lost little time (through the 1950 General Development Order) in relaxing controls over new development. 'An experiment in freedom', he called it,[3] seeking to steal a march on his critics, and, in effect, heralding the

Two captions from *Town and Country Planning* in the 1950s – the one stating that 'men predominate in the field of planning', the other that 'women take an eager interest in the Ideal Home Exhibition'.

start of a long process of 'simplification' which his successors were to continue in the years ahead. The high water mark of planning, as a comprehensive system of controls, had already been passed.

A second event that took place during this short-lived Administration was even more symbolic. In 1951, centred on London's South Bank, the public flocked to visit the Festival of Britain, widely interpreted as a colourful message to the nation and to the world that the war and the austerity that followed was over, and that a new age was beginning. For the Labour government it came too late – public disaffection was already too deeply entrenched, and the fanfare for the future turned out to be more of an overture for the incoming Conservatives. But it was a popular event in itself, and for town planning an ideal opportunity to show a sceptical public that the new Acts could be about much more than restrictions.

Fittingly, part of the Festival was located in East London, at Lansbury, where work was already underway to redevelop a blitzed and obsolescent district of the capital. Here, at last, was tangible evidence of what planning could do, and visitors were invited to follow a route through a 'town planning pavilion' (where the principles of planning were laid out in the form of sections dealing, in turn, with 'The Battle for the Land', 'The Needs of the People' and 'How these Needs can be Met') prior to walking through the new neighbourhood, to see the new buildings at first hand and to sample a pedestrianized shopping precinct. 'Lansbury', the public was reminded, 'is but one of the first steps in a national scheme of reconstruction.'[4]

The future of Britain was on show, and the main exhibition on the South Bank was marked by a sense of scientific discovery and progress. But it was by no means all science fiction, and in the colours and designs of everyday objects the public was given a glimpse of the immediate future – a preview of the 1950s. It all had a distinctive style, not one that was yet familiar, but one that soon would be: 'The Festival Style belongs firmly and squarely to the world of the New Towns, to the piazzas and pedestrian precincts, the espresso bars and community centres, to the blocks of council flats and rows of little houses, and, above all, to the office buildings of the idea that it expressed most, that of the post-war Welfare State.'[5] This, as political events unfolded, was to be the world that belonged, not to the collective philosophy of the government that had hosted the Festival, but to successive Conservative governments throughout the 1950s. Electoral victory in 1951 marked the start of it all.

For town planning it is generally regarded as a dismal decade. Politically, planning was not to feature in any of the manifestoes in the 1950s (and, indeed, the term was immediately dropped from the title of the government department with planning responsibilities, which was renamed the Ministry of Housing and Local Government) but at least, conceded its advocates, the system remained more or less intact. The most notable exception was the abandonment in 1953 of restrictions on development values (so that planning permission could result in development at its full land value, rather than that of existing use), a measure that aroused little public discussion yet which struck a body blow at the whole system of compensation and betterment that had been introduced in 1947. At a stroke, the potential cutting edge of the planning system had been blunted.

There was also a sense in which the system was eroded by default, not through the positive dismantlement of parts of the machinery but through a reluctance to push forward the frontiers of implementation. The most obvious example (and an issue of central importance to the Association) was the designation of only one new town, Cumbernauld, throughout the decade. Additionally (largely, though not entirely, the fault of central government) the approval of the first development plans very quickly fell behind schedule, leaving something of a vacuum in the face of a quickening rate of development in the country at large. And, in spite of the weight of a growing lobby and a carefully-argued case for regional planning, this remained, for some years to come, an area of neglect.

For the planning world, the 1950s were 'stormy and, on the whole, depressing',[6] but the decade was not without its gains. Some new features were added, like the 1952 Town Development Act (welcomed and indeed championed by the TCPA), enabling local authorities to arrange their own dispersal schemes as a complement to the new towns programme. And in 1955 Duncan Sandys, the then Minister of Housing and Local Government, introduced a national policy for the designation and protection of green belts (another measure that was warmly welcomed by the Association). There was also evidence of progress on the ground, in the form of developments in the new towns, in urban rebuilding schemes, and through a tighter control of development in the countryside.

But it is not for the gains so much as for the lost opportunities that the decade is recalled. Planning was becoming increasingly marginalized, and the changing face of Britain owed more to the priorities of housing and to investors in the new consumer society than to the elusive 'public good'. Harold Macmillan, as the newly appointed Minister of Housing and Local Government, set the agenda as early as 1951 with his personal commitment to transforming the house-building process. While Labour went into the 1951 Election with a pledge to maintain a rate of 200,000 new houses a year, Macmillan carried the banner of 300,000.[7] In his first full year of office, 1952, he could record a total of 240,000 (well in excess of Labour's best of 195,000), and in the following year passed his promised target, before going on to an even higher total of 347,000 in 1954. The political importance of this programme, after years of restraint and under-achievement, cannot be overrated, but for the planning lobby it seemed as if the cart was once again being put before the horse. For the Association (which had encountered a similar housing-led process in the interwar years) this was to be one of the crucial battlegrounds of the 1950s.

Moreover it was not just the character and extent of residential areas that was transformed in this period. Town centres, too, began to shake off their Victorian mantle, responding to the demands of a society discovering the attractions of consumer power. Old buildings and street patterns were cleared to make way for pedestrianized shopping centres, with new ring roads to cater for a growing number of private cars. Shops filled with modern furniture and electrical gadgets, fashionable clothing and records gave grounds for Macmillan's claim that the people had never had it so good, though a distribution map would have shown that this affluence was by no means evenly spread across the country. Once again, it was the South East and the Midlands which were forging ahead, and once again a regional policy was lacking to limit the disparities.

Such was the context of the campaign mounted by the Association in the 1950s, a constant effort to keep the show on the road to prevent the gains of previous years from being eroded and to keep pace with a quickening rate of development on the ground. It was a difficult campaign – more difficult in a way than if the planning system had been under explicit attack – and the outcome by the end of the decade was far from conclusive.

A SINGLE DESIGN

> It has to be remembered that the bolder aims of planning – the decongestion of cities, the creation of green belts, the establishment of new towns – essentially hang together as parts of a single design. In other words, none of the objectives will really succeed if it is pursued in isolation. (Peter Self, 1957, p. 166)

In 1957, in *Cities in Flood*, Peter Self wrote what was probably the most lucid and searching analysis of what he later termed the 'urban region' since Osborn's published evidence for the Barlow Commission in 1938.[8]

Significantly, in this connection, Self described his approach as partisan, supporting the Barlow policy for controlling the growth of the largest conurbations, particularly London. Of no less significance for the TCPA, the author was by then a member of the Association's

Executive and an Assistant Editor of the journal. The arguments developed in *Cities in Flood* therefore closely reflected and furthered the Association's position at that time, a mixture of satisfaction that some of the most important elements of dispersal were in the course of implementation, coupled with disappointment about lost opportunities and uncertainty about the future. Self's concern that with more than a decade of comprehensive planning it was 'still uncertain whether these efforts will prove to be the start of greater achievements or whether they will be written off as yet another piece of post-war idealism which failed to live up to its promises' was echoed in the writings of the Association.[9]

So too was Self's analysis of dispersal policy as 'a single design'. Under Osborn's leadership, the Association had been progressively drawn away from its traditional single-issue campaign of promoting garden cities, and in the 1950s the full implications of this were there to be addressed. The Association could simply not afford to focus on one part of dispersal policy to the exclusion of the rest; the new towns programme remained closest to its ideological heart, but what went on in the redeveloped districts of the conurbation and how the cities were to be contained was equally important if the whole strategy was to work. And it was to be the policy outcomes of these issues – planned overspill, urban redevelopment and green belts, the various components of a dispersal strategy – which set the agenda for the Association's campaign in this period.[10]

On the question of planned overspill, the Association sought not only to nurture the new towns programme but also to extend it through the addition of town expansion schemes. In spite of the slow start in getting building underway after the war, the early 1950s saw the existence of fourteen designated new towns and – following a short period of doubt, and some discreet lobbying when the Conservatives gained power in 1951 – there was no serious threat to the programme during the rest of the decade.[11] On the contrary, for a government committed to increasing housebuilding, it soon became clear that the new towns could make their own effective contribution. Nevertheless, the Association was always wary, seeing it as its duty to ensure the maintenance of the programme, as well as monitoring the way the new towns were developed, and, additionally, campaigning for further sites to be added to the list.

Inevitably, the pace of change was never fast enough for an organization that had for more than half a century seen small, planned settlements as building blocks that could be used to transform the whole of society. At the start of the decade, the slow progress that had been made to date in implementing the new towns programme was enough to prompt the view that town planning as a whole was 'at the crossroads'.[12] It was contended that more rapid

Contrasting views of new towns – the TCPA's belief in social benefits to be enjoyed, as opposed to Gordon Cullen's architectural perspective – decrying the lack of urbanity produced by low densities.

progress would serve to inspire public confidence in the worth of planning as a positive activity. The following year, in contrast, was one of 'marked progress',[13] with each new town receiving its own housing allocation.

Thereafter the rate of building in these pioneer settlements was carefully monitored but not again seriously questioned by the

Association. Indeed, within a few years the problem was less one of continuing growth than a concern that the various population targets should not be exceeded.[14]

Other aspects of the programme were to be criticized by the Association (the meagre provision of community facilities in the early stages, for instance, being a source of frequent comment), but the central task was seen to be more one of defending the very idea of new towns and of warding off critics of the whole concept. Of these critics, the architectural lobby was especially persistent, and Osborn lost no opportunity to respond in kind. A series of articles in the *Architectural Review* in 1953, for instance, claiming that the new towns were a social, economic and architectural failure, was like a red rag to a bull.[15] The social and economic arguments were dismissed by Osborn as inaccurate and exaggerated, but these were as nothing compared with the specious grounds for the aesthetic critique. J. M. Richards and 'his agoraphobiac colleague Mr. Gordon Cullen' were accused of going to any lengths to promote their own concept of 'townscape', including the use of cameras held low 'to make sixteen-foot roads and five-foot paths look like concrete prairies.'[16] Such visual distortions, combined with a pretentious use of language, amounted to no more than 'pseudo-sociology prompted by muddled aesthetic longings.'[17] Later publications in the same genre as the 1953 articles, notably two well-publicized essays in 1957, 'Outrage' and 'Counter-Attack', arguing for more 'urbanity' (equated by the Association with higher densities), drew similar venom as 'lapses from sense'.[18]

Critics of new towns had to be taken seriously and the integrity of the concept of new towns defended, but the real challenge for the Association during the 1950s was to see the programme extended. All the new towns together when completed could only accommodate a total of half a million people, significant in itself but inadequate in relation to national demands. Writing in 1953, Osborn believed that 'everybody sees that they [the first fourteen] are not enough to deal with congestion or rebuilding. There is still a need for a few more new towns but the present Minister [Macmillan] is against them.'[19] In spite of persistent advocacy, the rest of the decade brought only one additional designation, that of Cumbernauld in 1955, to serve the needs of Glasgow. Few doubted, however, that an expanded programme could only come through the public sector.

Thus, for all the concern within the Association about the number of new towns, little support was given to the housing campaigner, Stanley Jevons, when he called for the Association to take a lead in launching a third garden city, in the tradition of Letchworth and Welwyn.[20] The Association's view was that the 'balance of competent opinion seems heavily against the present practicability of a private-enterprise new town.'[21] In making the point, the implication was that if the new towns programme were to be expanded it was the government of the day that had to be convinced. The time for free experiment was over, and planning would either succeed or fail within the framework of the State.

Throughout the 1950s the association recognized this fact, and, though it was frustrated in its attempts to secure further designations through the New Towns Act, it was instrumental in helping to negotiate a new source of governmental support for planned overspill. Since 1943 the Association had, against a background of appreciating the attractions and compatibility of small town environments to accommodate an overspill population, supported the work of a Country Towns Committee. In the latter half of that decade it was already becoming apparent that, for all the potential of the 1946 Act, it was unlikely that the new towns programme alone would grow fast enough to meet existing demands and that other routes should be explored. The expansion of existing small country towns was one obvious possibility, although for this to be effective on a large scale new legislation was needed to enable local authorities to enter into the type of arrangements required. The advocacy of this approach coincided with the election of a Conservative government in 1951, committed to more housebuilding but less than enthusiastic about extending the role of the State through the mainstream new towns programme.

Within a year of taking office, fresh legislation was brought forward in the form of the Town Development Act, a measure 'warmly welcomed'[22] by the Association for creating the machinery and a promise of financial aid for the expansion of selected country towns ('expanded towns') for the reception of people and industry from congested cities. Thereafter, the Association viewed the new towns and the expanded towns programmes as complementary arms of dispersal policy, and to this end later established its own Dispersal Policy Committee with a brief to embrace both forms of overspill. And, just as pressure was constantly exerted to maintain the momentum for new towns, so, too, was the Association persistent in cajoling central government and local authorities (the London County Council especially) to make the fullest use of the opportunities for expanded towns.[23] Successive statements were sent (in March 1955 and February 1956, for instance) to the Minister of Housing and Local Government, lamenting the slow progress in realizing the full potential of the Town Development Act and suggesting financial and legislative changes to improve the situation.

By the end of the 1950s, the Association could at least draw satisfaction from the fact that the two programmes, for new and expanded towns, were both operational. And, for all the reservations about not meeting their potential, there was enough on the ground and in the pipeline to attract the envy and admiration of planners from around the world. So the Association was divided between singing the praises of the two programmes, and badgering governments and local authorities to do more and to do it better. It was only in private that Osborn confessed at the end of 1958 that, for all the success of planned overspill, 'dispersal and decongestion policy . . . is so weak at present that Britain is once more drifting.'[24]

Undoubtedly, an aspect of Osborn's concern had to do with what he saw as a failure by successive governments successfully to address the density question. Unless low densities for new housing could be achieved (in overspill settlements as well as in the redeveloped areas of the older cities), the aim of the whole dispersal strategy was jeopardized. There seemed to be little point in encouraging the relocation of large numbers of people, only to recreate housing conditions that were less than optimal. And for Osborn (and, effectively, the Association) anything above twelve houses per acre would be to build problems for the future; it was 'town cramming' rather than 'town planning'. Thus, in pursuit of this goal the Association was lured into the whole web of planning activity in the 1950s, to include a monitoring of the first development plans under the 1947 Act and a close watch on the pattern of redevelopment schemes in the conurbations.

In spite of a sustained campaign, the Association was less effective in countering the trend towards higher densities than it was in other aspects of dispersal policy. From the early 1950s onwards, there was dismay about the growing number of blocks of flats and higher-density schemes appearing in the major cities, not least of all in London. 'The tacit conspiracy between the countryside preservationists, the city authorities and the architects . . . has now succeeded, and generations of town-dwellers will suffer for it.'[25] Osborn made the point repeatedly, sometimes falling out with friends and allies in the process. At the public inquiry in 1953 into the London County Plan, Osborn found himself questioning Patrick Abercrombie on the density issue, and concluded that it was 'appalling that a distinguished planner can be so confused . . . I wonder sometimes whether I am wise to be so restrained and gentlemanly in view of the terrible importance to humanity of the matters at issue.'[26] It was this attitude of being absolutely right that also brought Osborn into conflict with his confidant, Lewis Mumford, who warned that he found 'a certain inflexibility in your [Osborn's] definition of good housing and planning standards, which I think damages our common cause.'[27] This latter *contretemps* simmered during the rest of the decade, with Mumford repeatedly proclaiming 'a more catholic and comprehensive view of what constitutes a city.'[28] and rejecting Osborn's stereo-

Mumford and Osborn: in a common campaign, but differing on the question of densities.

typed approach as akin to Le Corbusier's, with the one making a fetish of low and the other of high densities.

Sustained by the belief that he was championing a popular cause, in that most people wanted a house and a garden, Osborn persisted with the low-density argument. In a sense, time has proved him right, yet the Association had little to show for its efforts. Indeed, looking back on this period, Peter Self (who agreed with Osborn on the need to restrain densities) has reflected that the inability to counter the high-rise boom of the 1950s and 1960s was the Association's 'great failure' and that the density issue had not been properly tackled.[29]

In contrast, a more obvious cause for celebration was the achievement of Ministerial support for a national green belt policy. This was another essential component of dispersal policy, with roots going back to Howard's concept of an agricultural belt to encircle and contain the garden city. The concept was recognized in Abercrombie's wartime plan for Greater London, but only extended to the country as a whole through the initiative of the Minister of Housing and Local Government, Duncan Sandys.

Thus, the Associaition was quick to welcome a circular issued in August 1955 to local authorities, inviting them to consider including green belts in their development plans, though it was also quick to remind the Minister that the designation of green belts only added to the need to ensure the provision of planned settlements in the countryside beyond. Any criticism, however, was entirely positive, and, reflecting a close relationship with Sandys, the Association was pleased to respond to a request to advise on certain aspects of implementing the new policy. A Green Belts Committee was established and promptly reported on the purpose of a green belt, its ideal size, the control of development, and legal and financial implications.[30]

Encouraged by the success surrounding the introduction of a green belt policy, the Association was understandably self-congratulatory, in a way that it had not been since the introduction of the postwar legislation. There was, for a brief moment, a glimpse of the various components of dispersal policy falling neatly into place; the fulfil-ment, perhaps, of Self's 'single design':

> Stated briefly, the position reached in the Association's campaign is this. The main principles of our policy – decongestion, green belts, and planned dispersal – are (in Great Britain) officially accepted. The necessary laws exist and require only minor additions. Fifteen new towns are being built. The Ministry, at least four of the great cities, and a number of small towns are trying, with uneven resolution, to disperse overcrowded persons and work-places by the use of the Town Development Act. Certain clauses in the new Housing Subsidies Bill are intended to favour these efforts. The present Minister (Mr Duncan Sandys) is positive in his support both of dispersal and of the preservation of green belts. The fact that the Association has been such a prime mover in the formulation of a sound and practicable policy, and is active in the efforts to operate it, has brought us much prestige with the authorities and instructive opinion. Our influence is growing . . .[31]

Midway through the decade, this positive note was something of a high-water mark, between the uncertainties and disillusionment that coloured the end of the austerity era at the start of the 1950s, and a comparable low-water mark at the end of the decade when the Association was again calling for fresh initiatives. For the Associ-ation, the closing of the decade 'cannot be regarded with much satisfaction . . . [with] little sign that the Government was disposed to revise its policy in such a way as to give adequate stimulus and assistance to urban dispersal, without which the basic problems cannot be relieved.'[32] Fresh struggles lay ahead.

WIDENING THE NET

> Note particularly the memoranda submitted to the Ministry on many planning subjects, including Caravans, Green Belts, Dispersal, the Town Development Act 1952, other Planning Bills, Local Government, Costs of Central and Dispersed Redevelopment. Note also Committees set up to deal with policy questions, on which members and officers of local

authorities as well as other professional and business persons serve. Note also other activities, such as Conferences and Lectures, Holiday-Study Tours abroad, Home Tours, advice to enquirers, Weekly Bulletin, and monthly Journal. (F. J. Osborn, Notes on TCPA history, 1959, Osborn Papers)

Osborn's brief guide to the varied activities of the Association in the 1950s offers a fair indication of how wide the net had been cast – wide enough to embrace the full extent of the planning system. Although (as explained in the previous section) dispersal remained at the heart of it all, there was little to do with planning that did not have some bearing on this central issue. As such, the Association, eternally

Arranging visits for overseas planners and foreign study tours for British planners was a feature of the 1950s. The first of these photos shows a Russian delegation to Harlow, the second a study visit to Gothenburg.

surviving on limited resources, was enormously hard-pressed to cope with the volume of work during this period; and the records reveal a story of tireless endeavour mixed at times with a sense of desperation in trying to keep pace with relentless demands.

The pace was frenetic, and none felt the burden more keenly than Osborn. Having fought a ten-year campaign from 1936 through to the introduction of planning legislation in the 1940s, and then steering the Association through the period of the postwar Labour Administrations to 1951, Osborn was ready to hand over the reins to a younger man. 'I have temporarily exhausted my almost inexhaustible capacity to repeat myself,' he confessed in 1950,[33] adding in the following year that 'the TCPA undoubtedly needs a new figurehead and spokesman; but not a candidate is in sight. So for me, at present, there ain't no escape.'[34]

There was not, in fact, to be an escape for another decade, and the problem was worsened by a failure to appoint permanent officers for some of this time, leaving Osborn to take on additional duties. As well as chairing the Executive Committee and editing the journal, for some of this time he also assumed the duties of Director.

Desmond Donnelly had left this post in 1949, and the new appointment, Russell Kerr, stayed for only eighteen months, leaving Osborn and a small staff (including the loyal Miss Baldwin, who performed the varied duties of Business Secretary until she retired in 1956 after thirty-nine years of service) to run the office on a day-to-day basis. With the Association's finances inadequate to support a new appointment at that time it was not until 1955 that the main post, redefined as General Secretary, could be filled. An advertisement called for 'a man of energy and enthusiasm who will concentrate on the work', with an 'understanding of the human and economic importance of the dispersal and new towns policy; knowledge of planning procedure; and organizing ability.' The successful applicant was Wyndham Thomas, someone who proved to be a devoted new towns enthusiast and a key figure in the Association for the rest of the 1950s and most of the 1960s.

The presence of 'a man of energy and enthusiasm' in the office was a personal relief for Osborn, who confessed that 'the moral strain of this long fight has I think told on me to some extent in a loss of energy,'[35] and a boost for the Association, 'which is the only body doing anything at all to resist the drift away from sound policies . . .'[36] Additional relief was also felt with the growing involvement of Peter Self (a lecturer in Social Administration at the London School of Economics, and former journalist with *The Economist*), who joined the Executive in 1954 and was carefully groomed by Osborn as his most likely successor. By 1959, with Thomas and Self, and others like Maurice Ash in the wings, Osborn could write that at last he could see a possibility of resigning daily executive work, 'since younger people of real capacity have at last turned up'[37] – although an earlier comment that 'the line will be a little weakened when I retire to base'[38] reveals the true ambivalence of his position.

The fact is that under Osborn's leadership the Association was undoubtedly effective in getting across its message, but it was run with an autocratic hand. Osborn was never one to suffer dissent within the ranks, and was to rue the day he 'eased up' on his practice of restricting membership of the Executive to 'only genuine enthusiasts for our policy.'[39]

As well as questions of leadership and control, an indication has already been given that the financial basis of the organization was less than satisfactory (in that for some years the funds would not allow the appointment of a new Director), and in 1954 a measure of the loss was a shortfall in income of nearly £3,000 over the year. One reason for this was a fall (starting in 1950) in the membership total, following the high levels achieved amidst wide public interest in planning during the 1940s, though the main reason was due to the costs of an increasing range of propagandist activities. Raising the subscription rate (which had been one guinea since 1922) to one and a half guineas failed to redress the situation, and at Annual Meetings repeated warnings were given that the Association would be unable to continue with so many involvements without a fresh influx of income. Membership drives were launched, as well as appeals to 'industrialists, building societies, and other important interests whose support for a balanced policy of planning is essential for continuance.'[40] But it was not until the end of the decade, as a result of profits from conferences, a special appeal to mark the Association's sixtieth anniversary, and a modest increase in membership, that the financial crisis receded.

It is paradoxical that the very success of the Association in this period, measured in terms of the sheer volume of its activities, should also bring into question its very existence. Earlier episodes had shown that new members were more likely to be recruited when planning issues attracted national attention, and the fact is that in the 1950s most of the excitement that had surrounded the wartime and immediate postwar debates had waned. The 1950s was a time of implementation, and it is a constant complaint of planners that a large proportion of their work is unseen and unappreciated by the general public. Osborn was constantly aware of the need to atttact public support to the cause of planning, 'the 95 per cent of people who are, without any question, on my side in the matter of housing and town development standards,'[41] but like his predecessors realized the enormity of the task. His organization during this period never had more than nine members of staff in the office (and some of these were part-time), and the business of communication was always costly and time-consuming. The way for the Association to influence decisions was not to chase the elusive goal of a mass membership, but, instead, as it had always done, to seek to influence those in high office. And at this the Association was, on balance, very successful.

Although, when the Conservatives assumed office in 1951, the Association regretted the loss of 'planning' in the title of the renamed Ministry of Housing and Local Government, good relations were enjoyed with successive Ministers. Peter Self recalls that Harold Macmillan, Duncan Sandys and Henry Brooke were all invited to speak at various functions organized by the Association, and that the views of the Association were well-known in Whitehall.[42] Comments on policy initiatives were not only expected, but at times were invited (for example, when green belt policy was being formulated). Speaking as Prime Minister, Harold Macmillan was not being entirely platitudinous when, in 1959, he voiced the opinion that 'every Minister responsible for the subject [town and country planning] has had cause to be grateful for their constant and constructive criticism.'[43]

Of the key planning politicians in the 1950s, the relationship with Duncan Sandys is especially interesting. Shortly after he had been appointed as the Housing Minister, Osborn discovered that Mrs Sandys had sometimes attended the TCPA's wartime lunchtime meetings. A letter was quickly despatched, recalling the connection and arranging for free copies of the journal to be sent on a regular basis. 'Though we have to be neutral as between parties,' Osborn informed her, 'we do hope very much that if the present Government continues in office, Mr. Sandys will continue to be Housing Minister.'[44] Cordial letters were then exchanged with the Minister, who, on one occasion, replied that 'the policies which I am endeavouring to pursue are, I think, broadly in line with the kind of thing that you and your colleagues have been advocating for many years. I therefore warmly welcome your public support and your private advice.'[45] In other correspondence, Osborn privately endorsed his appreciation of the good work being done by Sandys, 'in striking contrast (remembering the former Minister's preoccupation with housing) to Macmillan's attitude to us and our recommendations.'[46] Elsewhere he attributed the 'exceptionally high' status enjoyed in government circles in 1956 to his own 'personal conversion of the present Minister.'[47] And it is no coincidence that in that same year, 1956, Osborn was awarded a knighthood – an honour that he gratefully accepted in the belief that 'this recognition will give a fillip to the Association.'[48]

Personal contacts of this sort were important, but in the world of politics they were always ephemeral, and other avenues had to be explored as well. Concerned, as always, that planning was not getting the attention it deserved in Parliament and in the press, Osborn sought the advice of Desmond Donnelly (who had become an honorary officer of the Association after leaving his full-time post to enter Parliament).[49] With his political experience as an MP, Donnelly advised that the Association should foster the support of 'one or two top level speakers in each debate.' Unfortunately, he warned, the 'principal speakers on housing and town planning are nearly all pedestrian and boring.' But the sharp advice was to concentrate more on Question Time; this was where he believed that campaigns were fought and won, and more should be done in the way of using it, 'week after week'.

As for the press, with the predictable disrespect of a politician, Donnelly revealed that 'the real truth about the British newspaperman is that on the whole he is rather a low level creature seeking sensation rather than solidity.' Town planning was poorly covered because journalists seemed to think of it as 'some sort of finicky architectural subject or . . . pure preservation.' The only hope was to approach the editors themselves, particularly 'Haley at *The Times*, Tyerman, Hodson at *The Sunday Times*, and Astor at *The Observer* (who will be more difficult but I will suggest a line of approach when I see you).'[50]

All of this was sound advice, and the Association had always been effective behind the scenes in lobbying 'the great and the good', through lunches in the Pall Mall clubs and carefully developed networks. At the same time, in the 1950s it continued the other side of its tradition, seeking every possible outlet to convey its message and to win a wider public support. This process, as it had always been, was diffuse in scope. Meetings and discussion groups were held at its offices, known as the Planning Centre, in King Street, where there was also a Members' tea room and bookshop; there were lectures and films on a variety of British and international planning topics; and the Association sponsored a regular programme of national and regional conferences. It was also in the business of organizing 'planning holidays' for members and their friends, and study tours to European countries. In turn, especially with the growing reputation of the new towns, the Association hosted visiting parties from abroad as well as responding to numerous enquiries.

While the record of regional branches remained (as it had always been) sporadic, the Scottish Section was a notable exception in this period. Annual conferences attracted a good representation from the Scottish local authorities, and a Planning Forum in Glasgow offered a regular programme of meetings on topics varying from the Crofting Commission Report to housing problems in the Clyde Valley. The Scottish Section was also instrumental in lobbying the Secretary of State for the designation of a new town at Cumbernauld, and for the nation's own Town Development Act (secured in 1957). The other notable regional initiative was the formation in 1956 of the Midlands New Towns Society, under the leadership of David Eversley, an initiative which Osborn could later record 'had substantial effects in the highly conservative and possessive Birmingham conurbation.'[51]

The net was cast wide, and new committees were formed to assist the Association in its tasks. As well as the Council (with about sixty members) and the smaller Executive (numbering about twenty), the decade saw the formation of a Local Authorities Committee – to keep under review the implications of planning at the local level; a Dispersal Policy Committee (inheriting the mantle of the former New Towns Committee) – to monitor the workings of the Acts for new and expanded towns; a Country Towns Committee – dating from the 1940s, and declining in importance with the formation of a committee specifically to look at town expansion schemes; an Industrial and Business Committee – to promote close contacts with the business community and to spread the message of good planning; and a Local Groups Committee – to liaise with civic organizations around the country.

In addition to responding to on-going developments on the planning front, the Association also continued its tradition of using anniversaries and special events as a way of bringing politicians and others into the fold. Osborn regretted a missed opportunity when Letchworth chose to mark its fiftieth anniversary with events in its own town as opposed to at least one dinner with invited guests in London, concluding that he was 'tired of being the one person in England who knows the importance of the garden city movement.'[52] In contrast, the Diamond Jubilee of the Association was an event that was not allowed to pass without appropriate celebrations. An appeal was launched to raise £60,000 (a target that was not, in fact, reached), and a distinguished list of sponsors (not only names from the past, like Reith and Beveridge, but also a future Secretary of State for the Environment and, later, President of the Association, Geoffrey Rippon) appeared in a jubilee brochure.

A New Towns Exhibition was held at the Royal Academy in October 1959, with support from the government and the New Town Development Corporations, but the timing clashed with the General Election of that year and attendances were disappointing. To conclude the celebrations, a prestigious dinner at the Mansion House attracted some 300 guests, including the Lord Mayor of London and the then Minister of Housing and Local Government, Henry Brooke.

In spite of Osborn's gloomy forebodings about the neglect accorded to planning, the 1950s was a period of high esteem for the Association. A reputation had been established in the formative years of the 1940s, and the Association was treated very much as a

Lord Beveridge with Wyndham Thomas (left) and Sir Harold Bellman, Chairman of the TCPA Council (right), at the 1959 New Towns Exhibition.

part of the political Establishment. No other organization carried such a wide planning brief, and its views were sought and heard on a variety of issues. Osborn's personal influence was obviously considerable during this period, but, painstakingly, a new team was assembled and ready to take over when the pre-1914 pioneer finally stood down as Chairman of the Executive in 1961. A combination of new personnel and changing circumstances in the country at large was to lead to a redirection of effort in the decade that followed.

NOTES

From Austerity to Affluence

1. Quoted in Sked and Cook (1979), pp. 90–91.
2. *Ibid.*, p. 97.
3. Hugh Dalton, quoted in Keeble (1961), p. 45.
4. Dunnett (1951), p. 47.
5. Banham and Hillier (1976), p. 9.
6. Keeble (1961), p. 51.

7. The origin of the figure of 300,000 is explained in Bogdanor and Skidelsky (1970), pp. 59–61.

A Single Design

8. Self (1957). A second edition was published in 1961.
9. *Ibid.*, p. xvii.
10. The official aims of the Association in this period were as follows:

    The Association advocates a national policy of land-use planning that will improve living and working conditions, advance industrial and business efficiency, safeguard green belts and the best farm land, and enhance natural, architectural and cultural amenities; so administered as to leave the maximum freedom to private and local initiative consistent with those aims.

    It supports the opening out of congested areas as they were rebuilt, and providing for people and industry thereby necessarily displaced in new towns and expanded country towns. In rural areas it stands for such grouping of towns and villages as will extend wherever possible the advantages of good services and social life and promote agricultural prosperity.'

11. Peter Self, in 'Sworn foe of the high rise disaster', *TCP*, Vol. 54, No. 5, 1985, p. 149, recalls that one of his first tasks on joining the TCPA Executive was to work for the retention of the new towns. One of his own contributions was to write anonymously in *The Economist* to demonstrate the economic value of new towns.
12. Editorial, 'Progress in the new towns', *TCP*, Vol. XVIII, No. 79, 1950, p. 440.
13. Editorial, 'New Towns', *TCP*, Vol. XIX, No. 81, 1951, p. 8.
14. For instance, see the statement by the Executive Committee, 'The future of the new towns', in *TCP*, Vol. XXVI, No. 6, 1958, pp. 217–220.
15. J. M. Richards, 'Failure of the New Towns' and Gordon Cullen, 'Prairie planning in the New Towns', No. 679, pp. 29–32 and 33–36; Lionel Brett, 'Failure of the New Towns', No. 680, pp. 119–120, *Architectural Review*, 1953.
16. F. J. Osborn, 'Success of the new towns', *TCP*, Vol. XXII, No. 117, 1954, pp. 10–12.
17. *Ibid.*, p. 12.
18. Editorial, 'Sense and sensibility – and nonsense', *TCP*, Vol. XXV, No. 6, 1957, pp. 237–238.
19. Letter from Osborn to Mumford, 2nd March 1953, in Hughes (1971), p. 212.
20. H. Stanley Jevons, 'A Third Garden City?', *TCP*, Vol. XXI, No. 107, 1953, pp. 230–235.
21. 'A Third Garden City?', *TCP*, Vol. XXI, No. 109, 1953, pp. 230–235.
22. TCPA Annual Report for 1952, p. 4.
23. Peter Self speaks of 'goodness knows how many meetings . . . over that difficult Act', and of success in persuading the London County Council 'to embrace the Act wholeheartedly'. See his article, 'Sworn foe of the

high rise disaster', (see note 11). The importance of the expanded towns programme in the Association's campaign was also reinforced in a personal interview with Peter Self in December 1986.

24. Letter from Osborn to Mumford, 24th December 1958, in Hughes (1971), p. 287.
25. Letter from Osborn to Mumford, 29th January 1952, in Hughes (1971), p. 204.
26. Letter from Osborn to Mumford, 8th June 1953, in Hughes (1971), p. 218.
27. Letter from Mumford to Osborn, 2nd July 1953, in Hughes (1971), p. 219.
28. Letter from Mumford to Osborn, 10th January 1957, in Hughes (1971), p. 275.
29. Peter Self, 'Sworn foe of the high rise disaster' (see note 11).
30. 'TCPA advice on green belts', *TCP*, Vol. XXIII, No. 140, 1955, pp. 555–558.
31. TCPA Annual Report for 1955, p. 3.
32. TCPA Annual Report for 1959, p. 3.

Widening the Net

33. Letter from Osborn to Mumford, 6th March 1950, in Hughes (1971), p. 184.
34. Letter from Osborn to Mumford, 26th October 1951, in Hughes (1971), p. 200.
35. Letter from Osborn to Mumford, 9th June 1954, in Hughes (1971), p. 227.
36. Letter from Osborn to Mumford, 24th October 1954, in Hughes (1971), p. 230.
37. Letter from Osborn to Mumford, 27th April 1959, in Hughes (1971), p. 288.
38. Letter from Osborn to Mumford, 1st August 1958, in Hughes (1971), p. 282.
39. Letter from Osborn to Mumford, 30th March 1953, in Hughes (1971), p. 214.
40. TCPA Annual Report for 1952.
41. Letter from Osborn to Mumford, 25th February 1957, in Hughes (1971), p. 269.
42. Personal interview with Peter Self, 4th December 1986.
43. TCPA (1959), p. 7.
44. Letter from Osborn to Mrs Duncan Sandys, 23rd May 1955, Osborn Papers.
45. Letter from Duncan Sandys to Osborn, 5th August 1955, Osborn Papers.
46. Letter from Osborn to Lord Balfour of Burleigh, 6th May 1955, Osborn Papers.
47. Letter from Osborn to Mumford, 30th April 1956, in Hughes (1971), p. 250.

48. Letter from Osborn to Mumford, 2nd June 1956, in Hughes (1971), p. 254.
49. Letter from Desmond Donnelly to Osborn, 6th January 1959, Osborn Papers.
50. *Ibid.*
51. Letter from Osborn to Mumford, 18th April 1969, in Hughes (1971), p. 452.
52. Letter from Osborn to Mumford, 2nd March 1953, in Hughes (1971), p. 212.

5

THE SECOND PLANNING
REVOLUTION

After the disappointments of the 1950s, a decade given over to trying
to prevent the draining away of idealism or at best to maintain the
status quo, the 1960s presented fresh opportunities. A succession of
governments that crossed the political divide shared a renewed
commitment to planning as an essential means of modernizing the
country. Old planning practices were overhauled and new measures
introduced in a spate of activity that reminded some observers of the
innovative days of post-1945. It was in this respect that, twenty years
after the first programme, planning experienced something of a
second revolution.

For the TCPA this was an important period. New leaders had
emerged within the organization and these were to be effective in
shaping the policies of the Association for the new context. Regional
planning featured high on the agenda, and the likes of Peter Self,
Maurice Ash, Derek Senior and David Eversley were all to make a
significant contribution to a vigorous national debate.

'INTO THE WHITE HEAT'

> It is a choice between the blind imposition of technological
> advance, with all that means in terms of unemployment, and the
> conscious, planned purposive use of scientific progress to
> provide undreamed of living standards and the possibility of
> leisure ultimately on an unbelievable scale . . . [of a New
> Britain] forged in the white heat of a technological revolution.
> (Harold Wilson, Labour Party Conference, Scarborough,
> October 1963)

Nothing better epitomizes the political context of the 1960s than the
stirring call to harness technology to transform the nation – casting
away, once and for all, the shabby vestiges of the first industrial

Bert Hardy's photo of Tyneside in the 1950s was used as a *Town and Country Planning* cover illustration to focus attention on the need for renewal in industrial cities in the 1960s. (Photo by courtesy of the Hulton Picture Company)

revolution and building a new future of material abundance and social justice. At the time, Harold Wilson's vision of a technological utopia caught the popular imagination, and (all too briefly as events showed) the 'white heat' from the crucible of the revolution radiated a warming sense of hope and direction.

Like all good populism the message came at the right time. Macmillan's assorted package of affluence, enthusiastically received at the time of the 1959 Election, had by 1964 (the year of the next General Election) already acquired an aura of 'shoddy goods'. Not only had the economic basis for continuing material stability been found to be wanting (exposed in a repetitive cycle of 'stop-go' policies of restraint and stimulus), but the Conservative Administration was by then tainted with the smear of successive scandals (the most notorious of which led to the resignation of the Defence Minister,

John Profumo). Moreover, Macmillan's successor in 1963, the landed aristocrat Sir Alec Douglas Home, was too easily caricatured as a product of Britain's past rather than a leader for the future. The nation was therefore receptive to a new message.

In setting the context for the TCPA's campaign in this decade, it is important to stress the change of mood that accompanied a change of government in 1964; yet, at the same time, it would be misleading to ignore the influence of the closing years of Conservative rule. For all the disappointments surrounding this chapter of political history, it was by no means a time of total retreat. Indeed, in some areas important seeds of modernization were sown. Inquiries were initiated in fields as diverse as railways, transport needs, ports, traffic in towns, company law, consumer protection, secondary and higher education, civil research and broadcasting.[1] And, in a significant reversal as compared with the 1950s – in a desperate attempt to gain control over the economy – the pendulum of government swung back from a *laisser faire* approach and more towards trying to establish a clear framework of planning and management.[2]

"I think I've found an answer to the unemployment problem in the north, sir."

Reproduced by courtesy of Punch

One sign of this shift that was of particular interest to the TCPA was in the government's unexpected revival of the new towns programme. After a decade with only Cumbernauld added to the list, six fresh designations were made between 1961 and 1964, providing for a projected population of half a million. None of these new designations was in the South East, though the problems of continuing growth in the metropolitan region were readily acknowledged. A departmental study of the region led, later in the decade, to policies that were in many ways a vindication of the position the Association had held from the time of Barlow. Elsewhere, unemployment figures encouraged the government to initiate new regional measures to promote growth, extending grant aid over a larger area of the country and offering special initiatives for the North East and Central Scotland.

Thus, in these remaining years of Conservative rule, against the run of what might have been expected, town and country planning remained secure within a political consensus that planning in some form or another was necessary for the nation. Relations between the TCPA and Conservative Ministers remained generally good, and, although there was always a tension between governmental priorities for more housing and the Association's concerns about where and how this new housing should be built, it will be shown in the following sections of this chapter that there was, at least, a constructive dialogue between the two sets of interests.

Predictably, the election of the first Wilson Administration in 1964 reinforced a commitment to planning in the widest sense – 'the point at which the popular fashions of the early sixties (so many of them built around the concept of managerial efficiency), and most of all the commitment to planning, became at last enshrined at the heart of official thinking.'[3] The election manifesto itself was written around the message of 'Planning the New Britain', with the promise of intervention in order 'to modernise the economy, to change its structure and to develop with all possible speed the advanced technology and the new science-based industries with which our future lies.'[4] A Parliamentary majority of only four did little to help the new government achieve its aims (although it was probably economic rather than political factors which imposed the tighter constraints), but a clearer mandate was given two years later, with Labour returned this time with a majority of nearly 100.

Modernization was on the agenda and new structures (like a Ministry of Technology and the Industrial Reorganisation Corporation) were put in place to plan and manage the reorganization of Britain's industry and infrastructure.

There was even a brief flirtation with the idea of a National Plan. But, having aroused high hopes, in terms of performance what followed was disappointing. Until the end of its term, the government was dogged with a damaging economic record, and divided within its own ranks over a series of issues. Materially, Labour could point to greater prosperity, if measured simply in terms of rising numbers of television sets, private cars and refrigerators, but even these symbols of affluence did not match up to popular expectations. Moreover, one area where it might have hoped for some relief, namely, the Welfare State, threw up its own problems in the form of a disturbing pattern of 'poverty in the midst of affluence'. More than twenty years of social legislation had failed to achieve its central goal of eradicating poverty. Sadly, the high hopes of the mid-1960s gave way to growing bitterness and disappointment, and, as a measure of how far things deteriorated, this period is now referred to as 'the decade of disillusion'.[5]

Town and country planning was, of course, a part of this process – enhanced at the outset by a national commitment to planning and management; responding to the environmental challenge and demands of modernization and affluence; and then getting caught up in a sweeping tide of disillusion (though a tide that was not really to engulf planning until the 1970s). Thus, in the context of rapid change, the second half of the 1960s proved to be an exceptionally busy period, witnessing 'a veritable flood of planning studies, planning reports, planning research, and, especially, perhaps, talk about planning.'[6] Not only were existing policies continued and extended, but it was also a time of new legislation and administrative reorganization.

This was clearly enough signposted in the 1966 Labour manifesto, with prominent sections on the need for reform in housing, urban renewal, traffic and the countryside:

The Britain we want has yet to be built. Many cities and towns are bursting at the seams with growing populations. Those spawned by the industrial revolution grew without vision or plan. They are utterly inadequate to the needs of today. But whether planned or unplanned, all our towns are choked with traffic, and their population overspill threatens the unspoiled countryside around.[7]

In the context of Britain's modernization, there was a job to be done, and the Government was not slow to act. A host of new measures were introduced, with implications for all parts of the urban and rural environment, and attracting to planning an interest that had not been experienced since 1945. Regional assistance schemes were intensified and extended (covering an area with nearly 20 per cent of the population), a rash of additional new towns and town expansions occurred, country parks and conservation areas were introduced, housing refurbishment took place alongside clearance schemes and rebuilding, yet another attempt was made to get a hold on rising land values, and transport within and between cities was the object of various initiatives. Moreover, in 1968 the plan-making system itself was overhauled, with the replacement of the old-style land-use development plans by structure and local plans. Throughout the land, Britain resembled a giant construction site, as local authorities and private developers ripped apart ageing town centres, encircled the new with ring roads, reshaped residential tracts in the inner urban zone around, tagged new estates onto the periphery, and linked cities with motorways.

What had been promised, then, was delivered; the cobwebs of the past were being swept away. It was, for planners as well as for others, a decade of renewed hope, and expectations amongst the public as well as the professionals were high. Understandably, the Association found itself in the very centre of this activity, seeking, as always, to influence policy and not being slow to criticize when its own ideals were not matched. Its own special contribution was to urge a rational framework of regional planning, although, to the extent that everything was interconnected, it was forced to cast its net widely. Successive Ministers and civil servants listened to the arguments, with lobbying assisted by a prevailing acceptance of pressure groups as a part of the political process. The Association's ability to influence events was as unconstrained as at any time in its history.

REDISCOVERY OF THE REGION

> . . . the TCPA's aims must now be pursued within two rather
> different frameworks. The first of these is the great urban
> region, best typified by London and the West Midlands . . . The
> second framework is the wider one of the nation as a whole, and
> concerns the measures which should be taken to revitalize those
> large parts of the country which are suffering relative decline.
> (Annual Report of the Executive Committee, 3rd April 1962)

In the 1960s the Association returned to the region. Central though the concept was to Howard's original garden city proposal, it was not until the aftermath of the First World War – encouraged by governmental use of regional boundaries during the war and further recognition after 1918 of the importance of the region as a planning concept – that the Association called explicitly for regional planning. Amidst concern in the 1920s about the outward spread of London, the idea of the city region remained on the agenda, but all this was as nothing compared to the redefinition of the concept in the second half of the 1930s. By this time, with the Barlow Commission offering a forum for debate, and the Association playing a central role, the importance of planning between as well as within regions became an issue of national concern. The Barlow Report of 1940 and subsequent planning legislation embodied the thinking of this earlier period, seeking to curb the growth of Greater London and the West Midlands, and to redirect industry to the outer regions.[8]

For some fifteen years after the Second World War, regional planning was accepted implicitly in official policies, and the thrust of the Association's campaign was directed more towards the components of the region (such as new towns, green belts and urban redevelopment) rather than to reassert the concept. It was only from

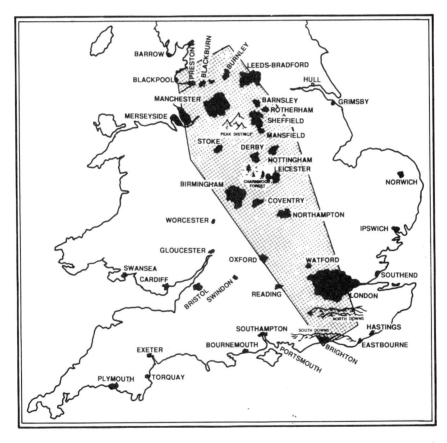

The concept of the 'coffin' was used to illustrate the concentration of development along an axis from the North West to the South East.

about 1960, by which time it was becoming clear that the 'newer' regions were growing too fast while the 'older' regions were still lagging behind, that attention is refocused on the region itself and on policies which by then seemed inadequate to the task. Thus, regional planning became the watchword of the 1960s, and at the very heart of the Association's activities.

The campaign that was mounted pursued various goals, but none so consistently as that of seeking to counter the rampant growth of Greater London and the South East. This remained at the top of the agenda throughout the decade, the key not only to the solution of problems within the capital itself but, no less, to the wellbeing of other parts of the country. It was a priority heralded by the new Chairman of the Executive, Peter Self, in the very title of his book, *Cities in Flood*, and in his persistent advocacy of new policies and governmental machinery to match the pace and intensity of metropolitan growth. His approach (closely reflected in the Association's policies) was very much an affirmation of the essential principles of the Barlow report, coupled with the need for a review and updating in the light of new circumstances.

From 1960 the Association started work on a series of statements on regional policy, the first of which was on the South East. A measure of interest in the issue is shown in the figure of more than 500 participants (many from local authorities) attending a conference at County Hall, London, in March 1961, called to discuss the nature of the problem and to consider the way forward. Following this event, the Executive produced a policy statement, 'The Growth of the London Region and the Future Development of South East England, 1961 to 1981'.[9] This pattern of consultation and policy memoranda characterized the Association's approach, seen as a way of stimulating 'public understanding of the scale and complexity of the problems to be resolved, and [enlisting] consequent support for bold and wide-ranging action by the public authorities mainly concerned.'[10]

The policy statement itself provided a framework for campaigning on this issue for most of the 1960s. It drew attention to the fact that the recommendations of the Barlow Report had never been fully implemented, and that some of the central assumptions underlying Abercrombie's 1944 plan for Greater London had been overtaken by events. In particular, the belief that the population level in the metropolitan region would remain static no longer held good; the average annual increase in the region was then about 100,000, and at that rate the total was expected to increase by nearly two million over a twenty-year period. Figures on employment rates were of no less concern. While the region accounted for 27 per cent of the national population, between 1952 and 1959 it attracted 45 per cent of the nation's new jobs. And this dual growth in population and employ-

Town and Country Planning Association Regional Conference

The London Region and the Future of South-East England

CONFERENCE HALL, COUNTY HALL, LONDON, SE1

10.45 a.m., Friday, 17 March 1961

MORNING SESSION Statements by three principal speakers, whose papers will be circulated beforehand.

1. MICHAEL WISE, Professor of Geography in the University of London.

2. WYNDHAM THOMAS, Director, TCPA, on "The Growth of the London Region".

3. PETER SELF, Vice-Chairman of Executive, TCPA, on "A Plan for the Development of the South-East"—the Association's policy proposals.

AFTERNOON SESSION To be devoted entirely to discussion of the Association's policy proposals which will suggest specific areas for development as new towns or town expansions; routes and priorities in major road building in the next twenty years; and the machinery and finance of new development.

Discussion will be opened with brief statements from representatives of five of the planning authorities primarily concerned with the regional problem. One hour will be left for discussion from the floor.

THE ASSOCIATION WILL RECONSIDER ITS POLICY RECOMMENDATIONS IN THE LIGHT OF THE CONFERENCE DISCUSSION BEFORE SUBMITTING THESE TO THE GOVERNMENT

Tickets: Members 15s. each. Non-Members 20s. each

The Minister of Housing and Local Government has sanctioned the payment by local authorities of certain expenses. Conference programme available from

TCPA, 28 KING STREET, LONDON, WC2 (TEMple Bar 5006)

ment led, in turn, to growing pressures on housing, land and transport. As a measure of demand, it was estimated that provision should be made to meet the needs of a million people in the countryside beyond the green belt. Central and local government authorities were urged by the Association to accept these facts and to revise planning strategies accordingly.

Arguments to promote the case were repeated and updated as new figures and research became available. In 1962, for instance, the Association produced a well-publicized booklet, 'The Paper Metropolis', which pointed to rapid office growth as a feature of the general problem.[11] In common with other studies, it drew from a thorough analysis of the problem various policy recommendations which were divided between what could be done to reallocate office uses within the region and what could be done to divert and prevent growth in that part of the country in the first place.

As well as initiating its own proposals the Association was no less active in responding to successive changes in official policy. Of these, the most important was the publication in 1964 of the *South-East Study*, marking official acknowledgement of excessive growth in the region and proposing a new dispersal policy to deal with it.[12] The policy included the designation of new cities and town expansions to accommodate about 1 million of the anticipated total population increase of 3.5 million over a twenty-year period in a region considerably larger in definition than earlier ones. True to form, the Association promptly convened a conference for over a thousand participants ('a new peak of activity – and we hope of influence')[13] addressed by the then Minister of Housing and Local Government, Sir Keith Joseph. This was followed in July 1964 with a memorandum, 'widely regarded as the most informed and authoritative comment on this subject.'[14]

Aspects of the *South-East Study* (considered as being 'revolutionary but not quite adequately revolutionary')[15] were welcomed, not least of all the underlying acceptance of the need for a regional strategy and the importance attached to planned overspill, but the tone of the memorandum was critical. The government was criticized for underestimating the rate of population growth, and for being too ready to accept existing employment trends within the region. In turn, alternative recommendations took the form of policies to restrain employment growth (including a plan to relocate offices in the North of England), new ways of accommodating dispersal beyond the green belt, and proposals relating to land ownership and betterment collection. It was concluded that the 'national as well as the regional issues involved in this concentration have to be faced, and a locational strategy adopted that is founded on fuller knowledge and a much greater willingness to explore far-reaching remedies.'[16]

The debate on London and the South East continued over the rest of the decade, embracing along the way contentious issues like the selection of a site for the Third London Airport (made, claimed the Association, in flagrant disregard for regional issues).[17] Increasingly, the shortcomings of the *South-East Study* as a framework for the rapid developments taking place within the region were exposed, and the Association was centrally involved in refining the critique and in formulating alternative proposals. An important step in this process was the publication in 1967 of another major policy statement. In this, the Association called for an integrated policy for the whole of the London city-region (extending along a diameter of some 100 miles).[18] This, in turn, was followed in August 1968 by what Peter Hall later referred to as 'a decisive intervention'.[19] It amounted to a proposal that plans for the region needed to concentrate future development not towards the periphery but in that area immediately beyond the green belt. 'By this statement, the Association was bringing out into the open a deliberate alternative to the policies which had first received expression in the *South-East Study* four years before.'[20] By all accounts the government took note, in that the essence of this approach was incorporated in a further revised plan for the region, published in 1970 as the *Strategic Plan for the South-East*.[21]

In pursuing its objectives, it was never an easy task, however, to get the balance right between what was an essentially intra-regional issue and the related business of matching growth between regions: 'Coordination of these two aims poses some tricky issues which have not been fully accepted', Self admitted, in his annual report in 1966.[22] For all these difficulties, the Association was careful in its regional campaign to address problems in the country at large, as well as those surrounding the capital. Thus, although its 1961 study of London and the South East was the first of its kind, it was closely followed by comparable studies for other parts of the country. In association with the Midlands New Towns Society, a conference in Birmingham in July 1961 led to a statement on the problems of that region, together with proposals for a new town to accommodate overspill. In turn, conferences were held and statements issued, in 1962 and 1963, for the North West and the North East.

In the same way as it did for the South East the Association was also quick to respond to the government's own regional initiatives, and White Papers in 1963 for the North East and for growth points in Central Scotland drew an appropriate response.[23] The former, in particular, was seen as containing many similarities to the Association's own earlier proposals, suggesting the degree of influence it was then exerting. While it constantly urged governments to do more, the very increase in regional activity was a source of satisfaction. It was seen as 'a true turning-point in national policy',[24] and it was claimed that 'the Association has certainly pointed the way in regional planning'.[25]

The mid-1960s represent a high-water mark in the Association's campaign, a busy and influential period with a seemingly close relationship between the Association's own dispersal policies and thinking in official circles. The regional reports had produced 'a real

revolution in thought,[26] and planning had (after twenty years) re-
turned to the political stage. At the time of the 1964 General
Election, 'now suddenly we see our Cinderella, transfigured as Miss
Britain, the glamorous centre of attraction at the Great Election Eve
Ball, with hopeful eligibles swarming from all angles to claim her as
partner . . .'[27]

The election of a Labour government in 1964 lent weight to the
mounting impetus for planning, although the Association drew satisfaction from the degree of political consensus that planning still
enjoyed. 'All the manifestoes gave prominence to it, and all promised, with differing accents, energetic central renewal, decentralization, green-belt protection, new towns, and guidance of the location
of industries and offices to check the drift to the South-East and
promote growth in the regions.'[28] This was duly interpreted by the
Association as a manifesto for the new government to pursue a
vigorous town and regional planning policy, and it continued to play
its own part to ensure that this happened. In December 1964, just
months after the General Election, a two-day conference, 'Planning
Britain's Regions', was mounted in Westminster to discuss the new
policies and to publicize the Association's own remedies. Government Ministers, Richard Crossman and William Rodgers, were
amongst the speakers.

A boost to the regional campaign came with the creation of a
Department of Economic Affairs (under the leadership of George
Brown), and the designation in 1965 of ten regional councils designed
to monitor the problems and potential of each of the nation's regions.
Although the lack of real powers for the new councils, and failure to
integrate their work with mainstream governmental policy-making
was a source of concern, the Association held back criticism until the
system had a chance to prove itself. Three years later, however, a
leading member of the Executive, Maurice Ash, resigned from the
South West Regional Planning Council, on the grounds that the
government had sacrificed the benefits of planning urban regions for
the wider goal of 'regional balance'. The policy of increasing aid for
outlying regions, as a substitute for a comprehensive regional policy,
was roundly condemned. 'I find it lamentable and unnecessary,'
concluded Ash, 'that a policy of indiscriminate aid to development
areas, not posited upon points of growth, should so soon have
brought about this conflict of regionalisms. We have seen a false
dawn.'[29]

The regional economic council experiment was to be a disappointment but not a disaster. Peter Self was later to recognize the shortcomings, but urged a note of realism. 'Let us face up to the fact that
there are no supermen in either Whitehall or Town Hall, and stop
kidding ourselves that our plans and procedures will ever be much

more comprehensive and objective than they are now . . . But even so it is a worthwhile endeavour to see how far each region can improve itself, despite external constraints and national limitations; and the vital step towards this is the coordination of local interests and actions in the work of the regional planning councils and boards.'[30] The Association could simply not afford to dismiss indiscriminately policies that were at least broadly on the right lines.

Nor could it afford to concentrate exclusively on the regional issue, central though this was to everything it did in this period. Related issues constituted an important secondary agenda at a time when planning was seldom out of the news. 'Things are moving fast here,' observed Osborn, with a turn of phrase that was reminiscent of the mid-1940s,[31] and his view is confirmed in the contents of successive annual reports. New towns, land values, housing, traffic and the planning process itself all attracted the Association's attention; with, as always, new towns holding a special place in the list of priorities.

After a lull in the previous decade, when only one new town was added to the list, the 1960s witnessed a fresh wave of designations. Skelmersdale was the first of the new wave, in 1961, and no less than fourteen more were to be added by 1973. It was also a time of major town expansion schemes, with some, like Swindon, more akin to a fully-fledged new town proposal. Taken together, this boost for planned overspill was warmly welcomed by the Association. Writing in 1966, Osborn captured the frenetic pace of it all:

> Every day now the papers and the radio report proposals for or protests against new towns or development projects all over the country. Tonight, for instance, comes news of the Greater London Council's schemes for two new towns of 40,000 as far away as Devonshire. And last week Crossman declared that in the S.E. there must be new towns to take another 1 million of London overspill. There are similar proposals for all the major conurbations; I can't keep pace with them in my aged and decrepit state of absorption.[32]

Osborn was writing nearly fifty years after the publication of his far-reaching book, *New Towns after the War*, and he could well look back with satisfaction at this latest spate of activity. A little over a year later, the Association joined in a retrospective glance at progress with a special new towns issue of *Town and Country Planning* to mark the coming of age of the new towns programme.[33] Twenty-one years had passed since the 1946 Act, and the record was celebrated not only for planning but as one of Britain's most notable postwar achievements. For all the progress, though, it was still a modest record in the face of the nation's continuing housing problems, and campaigners were urged not to rest on their laurels but to 'spearhead a movement which demonstrates the practicability of a renewal programme which by the turn of the century could make our great cities as fine to live in as the first new towns already are.'[34]

SHAPING POLICY

> What has the Association done in the last year? Statistically speaking, the tally includes seven policy statements, three major conferences, a number of discussion meetings, and some deputations to Ministries. Other activities were the giving of much information, the welcoming of overseas and other visitors, and the provision of speakers for various local meetings. Another feature of the year was the continued high quality of our monthly journal, *Town and Country Planning*, and the growing success of our weekly digest of news, *The Planning Bulletin*. (TCPA Annual Report for 1965, p. 3)

The events of 1965 (reported above) were typical of the pace and way of proceeding in the 1960s. Peter Self, as a dominant figure in this period, brought to the Association something of the London School of Economics (where he was a lecturer in Social Administration), encouraging lengthy and well-reasoned policy statements that would have done credit to any academic institution. Meetings, so it is recalled,[35] were frequently conducted like research seminars, and conferences attracted the leading planners, academics and politicians of the day. Throughout the decade, the Association operated at the very centre of the planning stage, respected for the consistency and quality of its contribution. There was much to be debated and the Association played a leading part.

Policy statements and memoranda to Ministers were part and parcel of the Association's history, resting on an unshakeable belief in the power of reason and persuasion to shape and reshape policy. For a pressure group with few other resources the effective communication of a good argument in circles of influence is really all it has. Yet, although the method was well-tried, in no previous period do the records reveal such a sustained output of policy documents. In 1967, for instance, six major statements were issued on a wide range of topics – on planning and housing policies for London and the South East, on leasehold reform, on a government scheme for a regional employment premium, on Stansted as the chosen site for London's third airport, on impending legislation for new town and country planning procedures, and on policy for regional growth points and assisted areas. It was a pattern of output that was repeated throughout the decade.

As well as a regular stream of policy documents, the various committees of the Association were organized to monitor and to seek to influence events. Within the organization, the Executive Committee continued as the driving motor, fuelled by a strong representation of professionals and planners. In 1963, for instance, the nineteen-member committee included the likes of Peter Self (who assumed the chairmanship following the resignation of Osborn in 1961), Maurice Ash, Lewis Keeble, Michael Dower, Derek Senior, Denis Howell and Michael Stewart. In turn, there were specialist committees and study groups dealing with particular topics, notably, a Local Authorities Committee, Dispersal Policy Committee (superseded by a Planning and Development Committee), CPRE/TCPA Joint Sub-Committee, and working parties on Regional Development, Urban Development, Employment Location Policy, Office Location, and Movable Dwellings. Rather than relying solely on the influence and reputation of a few, it had become very much a working organization.

Nor was it a closed affair. Public meetings were held at the Association's offices, including a regular programme (especially popular with students) organized by the Planning Forum. There was also a well-used information service, which included a monthly publication, *Planning Bulletin*, the Library, and the records and expertise of the staff. Visitors from abroad, schoolchildren and teachers, students, professionals and members of the public were amongst those who used the service.

The sustained pace experienced in the London office was matched by a comparable range of activities organized by the Scottish Section. Government decisions to add to the number of new towns and to offer assistance to encourage new factories in the central belt of Scotland were at the heart of much of the Section's activities. It was also closely involved in plans for the reorganization of local government, resisting encroachments onto Green Belt land, campaigning against further high-rise building schemes, and monitoring development plans in the region. And it continued to run a full programme of meetings and conferences to keep alive and develop the ideals of the Association north of the border. Appropriately, during such an active period, one of its founding members, Elizabeth Mitchell, wrote an autobiography, *The Plan that Pleased*, recording the long history of the Scottish campaign for dispersal.[36] Like her English counterparts, her assessment was that the Association had cause to rejoice in what it had achieved, but also regret that so few people were experiencing the real benefits of planning on a human scale. The high-density redevelopments in Glasgow heightened her anxiety that the essential message of Howard, transmitted over the years by the Association, had yet to be taken.

Taken together, south as well as north of the border, it all added up to a remarkably high-profile campaign in the 1960s. Planning was constantly in the news (in advance of a public backlash) and the visibility of the Association was high. Yet, as it had always been, the prolific output of the organization depended on a handful of skilled but voluntary campaigners and a small band of committed staff. This is the lot of a pressure group that cannot call on a large membership; its power rests on its ability to amplify a message. Such a pressure group is rather like the mythical Wizard of Oz, wondrous in his awesome power and booming voice, yet revealed as no more than a diminutive old man with a genius for showmanship. It is not (like the Wizard of Oz) that the message was a false one, but rather that it all rested on such a flimsy resource base.

Certainly, the Association's high profile was not enough to attract new members in large numbers. Totals edged up marginally during this period, but in no sense reflected the volume of work conducted on the public's behalf. For all the publicity it received, the number of individual members reached a peak of only 939 in 1969. Of greater satisfaction, however, was the solid base of local authority support, which, by 1969, added up to 574 members. And, in that same year, there were also 175 firms and other organizations with corporate membership. But a steady upward trend was not enough to check regular expressions of concern that an organization with a national reputation deserved better than that. Typically, the Chairman of the Executive Committee reported in 1966 that 'it remains only too true that if we are to function as effectively and energetically as we should do, then more support is necessary. The Association is coming to the point where it needs more money, more staff, and probably better offices as well, if it is to make an impact under modern conditions.'[37]

But more members on the scale required were not forthcoming, and two increases in the subscription rate (to a minimum of two guineas for individuals in 1962, and, again, to three guineas in 1967) had only a marginal effect. Indeed, by the end of the decade, the proportion of income derived from subscriptions had actually fallen. A financial surplus accruing from the Diamond Jubilee Appeal in 1959 helped the Association to withstand successive annual revenue deficits, but it was a source of constant concern that it could not rely on a steady flow of income to enable the campaigners to do all that was possible.

One obvious effect of the tenuous financial position was that of having to manage with a small staff team, on whom demands imposed were frequently acknowledged. 'The nature of our work requires frequent bursts of frenetic activity in organising conferences, preparing pamphlets, receiving visitors, and doing much else at short notice; while the Journal needs much careful and imaginative attention to sustain its high standards of interest and readability.'[38] Credit was given to the leadership of Wyndham Thomas, who remained as Director until 1967, before moving on to a post with the Land Commission. Recruited and groomed by Osborn, Thomas led the Association over a twelve-year period, contributing in a variety of ways to progress in respect of the new towns programme and the development of a clear regional planning stance. His successor, David Hall, (who brought with him local authority planning experience) was no stranger to the Association, through a spell as Chairman of the Planning Forum, and his arrival coincided with important changes in the structure of the planning system and with the first signs of a growing public disaffection with what planners were doing. This changing context was to provide a spur to reappraise the priorities of the Association and, in due course, for new issues to be addressed.

Another change occurred on the accommodation front, with a move from King Street (on the expiry of the lease) to elegant premises in Carlton House Terrace, shared with the Civic Trust. Symbolically, the new premises were to be within sight of Whitehall and the Houses of Parliament, the scene of much of the organization's lobbying. 'Across the park' came to refer to the short walk across St James's Park to talk to politicians and civil servants on the planning issues of the day.[39]

But was the journey 'across the park' worthwhile? Did anyone with power and influence actually listen to what the Association had to say? The evidence, in fact, is that a succession of Ministers and senior civil servants (though by no means all) were in agreement with the general arguments, and that there were at times clear indications of policy outcomes in line with the Association's thinking. Peter Self was in no doubt that the Association could 'take credit for a major part in stimulating these developments' (referring to initiatives on regional and traffic policy in the early 1960s);[40] a view shared by Osborn, who attributed the success in influencing policy to 'some excellent detailed work by the TCPA since I left.'[41]

Of those Ministers and other senior politicians who were receptive to the Association's arguments, a mutual respect developed with the Conservative Minister, Sir Keith Joseph. He readily attended conferences organized by the Association, and was at times warm in his praise: 'You should take the credit for pioneering the things that we take today as gospel – such as new towns, expanded towns, green belts, the idea of moving offices out of London.'[42] Although there were to be points of policy disagreement, the Association acknowledged that 'no previous Minister has shown a grasp of so wide a range of component factors.'[43] At the same time, keen as it always was to foster good relations on both sides of the House, the support of the leader of the Opposition, Hugh Gaitskell, was also courted; an effort rewarded with the promise that 'I shall try to get the Labour Party on the side of dispersal. I shall go farther than that – we are on the side of dispersal.'[44]

Gaitskell's untimely death was a particular loss to the Association, though Cabinet representation was assured through the rise to Ministerial status of Michael Stewart. While sitting as the Opposition frontbench spokesman on housing and planning, Stewart also served on the TCPA Executive Committee. The fact that he did not go on to become the Housing and Planning Minister was a disappointment, in that he was so well versed in the Association's ways (instead he first became the Minister for Education and Science, before moving to the Foreign Office), but consolation was taken from the fact that there were others in the new government who were also TCPA members.[45]

Richard Crossman, who took the job earmarked for Stewart, was not one of these, and the Association's first observation of him was that he was rather like a new boy in school – 'brave, but rather bewildered.'[46] He curried little favour by questioning the basis of the Association's policies, an attitude that provoked the response that 'we confess we would have expected a keen mind like Mr Crossman's to have got a bit further than this, even in a few weeks.'[47] Maurice Ash confirms that Crossman kept up this stance, and that meetings were sometimes acrimonious: 'How do you know?', he would ask, questioning the assumptions on which dispersal policy was based.[48] The frostiness was continued in a passage in Crossman's subsequent Diaries, where a private meeting with Peter Self was coloured by the unflattering view that 'the Town and Country Planning Association was a mere cypher.'[49] Crossman had, in fact, been briefed by Evelyn Sharp, the influential Permanent Secretary at the Ministry of Housing and Local Government from 1955 to 1966. Sharp was widely respected but difficult to persuade, and it was partly with her in mind that, in explaining the tactics of political lobbying, Maurice Ash concluded that usually it was 'the civil servants who are the real determinants of policy.'[50] In some cases this worked to the Association's advantage, a notable instance being the warm relationship that developed with the Chief Planner at the Ministry from 1961 to 1967, J. R. James. Osborn later revealed that in a private letter from James, the civil servant 'tells me he is 100 per cent for the new towns policy, and when he retires (a long way off yet) is going to replace me as cheerleader on the sidelines.'[51]

Looking back on the 1960s, in terms of the quantity and quality of material produced, and in terms of the sheer energy and skill of its lobbying, it is hard to deny that the Association communicated its basic strategies to a wider audience. It certainly made a mark on the planning debate of that period, which is not to assert that it was successful, so much as to note its involvement. Indeed, Maurice Ash reflects rather gloomily that the main thrust of the campaign (extending into the following decade too) actually failed:

> From the TCPA's point of view the story of the 1960s and 1970s is of the struggle to obtain comprehension and acceptance of the new form cities were taking; and of the failure of that struggle, which has resulted in the contempt into which planning has fallen through its divorce from reality . . . The struggle was lost through the ignorance of politicians, the obtuseness of the Civil Service, the power plays of local authorities, the professionalisation of planning and the romanticism of the media. In retrospect, we scarcely had a chance.[52]

This is a sad indictment, but probably not one that would have been levelled in such forthright terms at the end of the 1960s. In the decade that followed, planning in general entered a trough, and Ash was not alone in talking of failure.

NOTES

'Into the White Heat'

1. McKie and Cook (1972), pp. 13–14.
2. For instance, see, Bogdanor and Skidelsky (1970), McKie and Cook (1972), and Sked and Cook (1979).
3. McKie and Cook (1972), p. 2.
4. Included in Craig (1975), p. 259.
5. This is the title used by McKie and Cook for their book (1972) on the political history of this period. They also quote Roy Jenkins in a speech to the Labour Party Conference in 1971, declaring that 'We do not want the period in which we live to be remembered as the politics of disillusion. And there is some danger of that.' (p. 5).
6. Reade (1987), p. 59.
7. Included in Craig (1975), p. 298.

Rediscovery of the Region

8. The early campaign for regional planning is detailed in Dennis Hardy, 'Regionalism in Interwar Britain: The Role of the Town and Country Planning Association', in Garside and Hebbert (1989), pp. 77–97.
9. *TCP*, Vol. XXIX, No. 6, June 1961, pp. 225–233.
10. TCPA Annual Report for 1961, p. 7.
11. 'The Paper Metropolis', *TCP*, Vol. XXX, No. 5, 1962, pp. 191–197.
12. Ministry of Housing and Local Government (1964).
13. 'Planning Commentary', *TCP*, Vol. XXXII, No. 5, 1964, p. 213.
14. TCPA Annual Report for 1964, p. 3.

15. Letter from Osborn to Mumford, 1st April 1964, in Hughes (1971), p. 361.
16. 'TCPA on the South-East: A statement by the Executive Committee of the Town and Country Planning Association on the South-East Study and White Paper of March 1964', *TCP*, Vol. XXXII, Nos. 8 and 9, 1964, pp. 341–348.
17. 'Stansted Airport and Regional Development: A memorandum to the Government by the Executive Committee of the Town and Country Planning Association', *TCP*, Vol. XXXIV, No. 1, 1966, pp. 1–4.
18. 'Planning and Housing in London and South-East England: A policy statement by the Town and Country Planning Association', *TCP*, Vol. XXXV, No. 3, 1967, pp. 134–142.
19. Hall *et al.* (1973), Vol. 1, p. 475.
20. *Ibid.*
21. South-East Joint Planning Team (1970).
22. TCPA Annual Report for 1965, p. 3.
23. The TCPA's response was reported in 'Stay North, Young Man!', *TCP*, Vol. XXXI, No. 12, 1963, pp. 461–462.
24. *Ibid.*
25. Chairman of the Executive, in TCPA Annual Report for 1963, p. 3.
26. 'Cinderella at the Election Ball', *TCP*, Vol. XXXII, No. 4, 1964, p. 173.
27. *Ibid.*
28. 'Cinderella was there this time', *TCP*, Vol. XXXII, No. 11, 1964, p. 435.
29. Maurice Ash, 'Realism – and regionalism', *TCP*, Vol. 36, No. 4, 1968, pp. 206–208.
30. Peter Self, in 'Regional planning – a national view: Some notes and comments on the TCPA conference in London on 24–25 June 1968', *TCP*, Vol. 36, No. 9, September 1968, p. 407.
31. Letter from Osborn to Mumford, 28th March 1965, in Hughes (1971), p. 382.
32. Letter from Osborn to Mumford, 11th January 1966, in Hughes (1971), p. 393.
33. Special new towns issue, *TCP*, Vol. 36, Nos. 1–2, January–February 1968.
34. Wyndham Thomas, 'The achievement and the objectives', *TCP*, Vol. 36, Nos. 1–2, 1968, p. 9.

Shaping Policy

35. Recollections of Maurice Ash, in a personal interview, 10th March 1987.
36. Mitchell (1967), an autobiography that provides a fascinating insight into the dispersal campaign in Scotland from the pioneering days of the TCPA.
37. TCPA Annual Report for 1967, p. 4.
38. TCPA Annual Report for 1963, p. 11.
39. The phrase was used by David Hall in a personal interview, 22nd June 1987.

40. TCPA Annual Report for 1963, p. 3.
41. Letter from Osborn to Mumford, 24th December 1963, in Hughes (1971), p. 354.
42. Speech at TCPA Annual Conference Dinner, 18th October 1961.
43. *TCP*, Vol. XXXII, Nos. 8 and 9, 1964, p. 337.
44. Speech at TCPA Annual Conference Dinner, 18th October 1961.
45. Denis Howell and Arthur Blenkinsop were both Labour MPs who served on the Executive Committee in the 1960s.
46. Speech at Annual Conference, 1st–2nd December 1964.
47. 'Prospect', *TCP*, Vol. XXXIII, No. 1, 1965, p. 2. A passage in Crossman (1975), p. 114, adds an interesting insight from the Minister's side: 'One of my first engagements as Minister was to be the guest of the T.C.P.A. at their annual dinner and there I found myself sitting next to Molson [the Chairman]. Perhaps I had drunk too much, perhaps I was merely irritated by his stuffy manner . . .'
48. Personal interview with Maurice Ash, 10th March 1987.
49. Crossman (1975), p. 24.
50. Personal interview with Maurice Ash, 10th March 1987.
51. Letter from Osborn to Mumford, 11th January 1966, in Hughes (1971), p. 393.
52. Note written by Maurice Ash, following a personal interview, 10th March 1987.

6

1970s: THE END
OF THE BEGINNING

As the previous chapter has indicated, the much-heralded 'second planning revolution' came to little. By the end of the 1960s, the enormous promise of the postwar planning system still remained largely unfulfilled. Far from arousing popular support, an anti-planning blacklash was setting in, a product not simply of what planning had not done but, ominously, of what it had done wrong. By the 1970s, the tide that had carried planning along a broadly consensual path was turning. Determined to stay afloat, the TCPA sought not to jettison its heartland issues (like new towns and regional planning) but to bring aboard an additional cargo of participatory planning and community politics.

In the first section of this chapter, the eventful politics of the 1970s are traced as a backcloth to the history of the policies and organization of the Association. To the extent that the decade witnessed events that served to challenge the economic and political mainstays of the postwar consensus, not to mention the questions asked about planning, there is a sense in which this period marks 'the end of the beginning'. With hindsight, knowing what we do now about the 1980s, this interpretation is borne out by events to come.

THE AGE OF DISSENT

> If, in broad outline, the period of 'consensus' . . . could be seen as containing the story of the determination to escape for ever from the Depression conditions of the 1930s, the story of the middle and late seventies might well be seen as one of a return to the gloom of the 'devil's decade'. (Marwick, 1982, p. 188)

It would be wrong to portray the 1970s as marking a sudden fall from grace, yet it was, as Arthur Marwick suggests above, rather a gloomy period. Dramatic events played their part in fostering a new climate of opinion where hope was in short supply: the shock in 1972 of the first IRA bomb attack on the British mainland, the shared and bitter experience of a three-day week in 1973–74, with the nation seemingly held to ransom by a combination of militant miners and Middle Eastern oil potentates, and the 'winter of discontent' in 1978–79, when striking public service workers did little to increase public tolerance for trade union power.

More tellingly, it was the persistence of less dramatic indicators of British life that revealed the true superficiality of consensus and the extent of failure of postwar policies. Of these indicators, the economy was the most revealing, with neither a Conservative government from 1970 to 1974 (led by Edward Heath) nor its Labour successor from 1974 to 1979 (under, first, Harold Wilson and then James Callaghan) finding the key to economic growth. Rising unemployment figures and soaring inflation claimed the headlines, against a background of days lost through stoppages, low investment levels and industrial closures. An accompanying reduction in public expenditure (particularly from 1976, with Britain under pressure from the International Monetary Fund), with cuts in health, education and other services, merely added to the general spirit of malaise and sapping of confidence in the ability of either of the two major political parties to govern.

Indeed, the legitimacy of government became one of the central issues of the decade, emerging first amidst the turmoil of 1973–74, and again in the 'winter of discontent' in 1978–79 when rubbish was piled high in the streets and critics had an easy time portraying the unions as being the real power in the land. Thus, 'most commentators writing at the end of the decade were concerned with "crisis": crisis in the economy, crisis in law and order, crisis in racial and industrial relations.'[1]

None of this provided a particularly auspicious background for town and country planning. It was not just that the economic and political backcloth displayed a bleak picture, but the thin strands of consensus that had so far held it all together were now stretched to the limit in the face of growing public disaffection. There was even the memory of a dramatic event to symbolize the dilemma, in the form of the collapse of part of a tower block, Ronan Point, in East London in 1968, an event that lent itself all too easily to discrediting the whole postwar redevelopment strategy. And, a decade later, evidence of widespread corruption in local government affairs in the North East told the public what had already been suspected, namely, that a wide gulf had opened up between the goals of public improvement and the sordid reality of profits before people.

Academics lent weight to this critique, and the 1970s saw a number of critical texts, the most influential of which were informed by a close knowledge of local practice. What they shared was the damaging conclusion that it was not necessarily the absence of planning that created the worst problems, but sometimes its very presence; somewhere along the way, the needs of ordinary people had been nudged into the background. Norman Dennis, for instance, wrote a revealing analysis of housing policies in Sunderland, likening the intervention of planners to that of 'a clumsy giant crushing with heavy hoof things of whose value he has no conception.'[2] Another study from the North East likened planners to 'evangelistic bureaucrats', seeking to insulate themselves from the highly-charged, political nature of their work and effects of their actions.[3] For all the rhetoric of the postwar period, the author, Jon Gower Davies, contended that planning had served to benefit most of all those who were already well-off: 'in its effect on the socio-economic structure . . . [it had become] a highly regressive form of indirect taxation.'[4] From a different political perspective and a different part of the country (in this case, Greater London), David Eversley agreed that planners had become 'almost universally feared and disliked',[5] and choices within the profession

Award-winning tower blocks (like this one in Stepney) won little social acclaim, and in the 1970s urban renewal evoked a wave of community reaction.

had to be made if the process of planning was to regain public credibility.

Meanwhile, on the ground community groups were formed to protest at various manifestations of rapid change, opposing wholesale redevelopment schemes and transport plans which threatened landmarks and neighbourhoods.[6] *Goodbye, Britain?* was the title of just one book to argue that things had gone far enough, and that citizens must take an active stand to stem the tide of ruin.[7] But a thin line divided the positive opportunities for participation in plan-making, now enshrined in legislation, and the cynicism that leads to outright protest. Too often, the planner had become the enemy rather than a saviour of society, and in town and country battle-lines were drawn up as if each new development proposal heralded the coming of Armageddon.

This sharply-divided political context of planning in the 1970s is central to an understanding of the work of the TCPA, with its traditionally bipartisan approach and fervent belief in planning as a source of good. The Association's increasing involvement in community issues and participatory politics is a reflection of a wider sense of disaffection with representative democracy. But this is by no means the whole story, and no less important to an understanding of the priorities of the Association in this period is the evidence of continuing developments. Planning was under siege, but it was by no means dormant. On the contrary, it was an active period for the Association and for the country, with both the Conservatives from 1970 to 1974 and then Labour to 1979 introducing new legislation and asserting a commitment to different parts of the planning system.[8] There was certainly no shortage of ideas.

For the Conservatives, a particular priority was to make headway with rationalizing the machinery of government. At the national level, this thrust is illustrated with the formation in 1970 of the Department of the Environment to enable a corporate approach to transport and environmental issues; while at the local government level plans were progressed for the reform of the entire system. This latter issue had been widely debated by the previous Administration, but Labour preferences for a unitary system of regional authorities (understandably favoured by the Association) were now rejected in favour of a two-tier system of counties and districts. In other respects, too, Heath's government reversed earlier policies, notably, in respect to Labour's attempt through the Land Commission to recoup a proportion of rising land values for the community – an ideological gesture which won few friends outside the property market at a time when property prices were soaring to new heights.

One other policy change at this time, probably less a product of party dogma than of demographic trends, was that of curbing the rate of further new town designations. A slowing of the rate of population increase led to a lowering of anticipated totals over the next thirty years, and, with that, less call for comprehensive dispersal policies. This weakening of the political base for new towns, with attention switching later in the decade towards the inner city, proved to be a key issue for the Association.

When Labour was returned to power full of Socialist promise (with a small majority in February 1974, enhanced in a second election in October of that year), planning issues were high on the agenda. Much to the satisfaction of the Association, the political football of land values was back on the pitch as the highlight of a new, positive land-use planning approach. With a former Council member of the Association, Anthony Crosland, as Secretary of State for the Environment, and with John Silkin (the son of the planning pioneer of the 1940s, Lewis Silkin) as Minister for Planning and Local Government, the omens were good. The 1975 Community Land Act restored the practice of betterment recoupment and required local authorities to purchase land at existing land values. But the faltering economy immediately undermined the financial basis of the initiative, which, in any case, proved to be less than effective in legislative terms.

In 1976, Peter Shore assumed the mantle of Environment Secretary (a diminished mantle with the shedding of transport responsibilities to a separate Ministry), and in his period of office 'British urban policy underwent what could arguably be called the first major departure from the post-war 'decrowding' and dispersal policies.'[9] This was effected in a variety of ways – through a switch of rate support grant priorities towards inner cities, coupled with new policy initiatives for these areas while, at the same time, cutting back on plans for existing and previously proposed new towns. Inevitably, this, an assault on its very heartland, proved to be an especially testing issue for the Association – in a period that was testing enough in itself with the failure of successive governments to secure a positive role for planning, and with public esteem at an all time low.

BEYOND NEW TOWNS

> . . . one cannot but sense that new towns face a questionable future. Will the old programme now move on, to greater achievements, or will it be dampened and diverted into developments which barely justify the name of new towns? The old metaphor – 'planning at the crossways' – is a true description of the 1970 situation in Britain; and reflection shows that it is a complicated crossways indeed. (Peter Self, 'A new vision for new towns', *TCP*, Vol. 38, No. 1, January 1970, p. 4)

Peter Self lifted a finger to the oncoming wind of the 1970s and rightly sensed a change of direction. New towns, he warned, faced a questionable future, although just how questionable he was not to know at that stage. For the Association this was to be a key issue of the 1970s, not simply seeking to shelter its prodigy from the chill wind of change but, more positively, planting fresh seeds from the nursery of ideas that had sustained the movement over the years.

A number of factors had alerted Self to the danger that 'the unfinished new towns may be treated as simply the last instalment of a public overspill programme which is running out of steam'[10] – including the absence of workable regional plans to provide a framework for overspill. To some extent the situation was eased later in the year with the publication of the government's 'Strategic Plan for the South East', a plan with defined growth areas as the main way to accommodate an increase of up to five million people in the region by the end of the century.[11] But this, important though it was at the time, proved to be more a product of progress on the regional front in the 1960s than a mandate for planning in the new decade. The real threat to new towns was to come, not from the absence of a regional framework, but from a shift in political priorities towards the inner city. Wrongly, as the Association argued, the issue was polarized as a choice between the two – between investing in new towns or diverting resources to the decaying acres of the large cities.

It was a false dichotomy, in that the original garden city concept had been conceived as an integrated strategy, designed as much to deal with the overcrowded conurbations as the new settlements on greenfield sites. And, firmly believing that the strategy was relevant to the 1970s, the Association took every opportunity to argue the case again. 'The missing half' was the title of an article by Colin Ward on this theme, reminding planners that 'Ebenezer Howard urged dispersal as a means to aid the inner city, since when attention and action have focused on dispersal and almost ignored urban renewal – a classic case of only half a policy.'[12]

The real confrontation was still to come, though, with the battle lines drawn up in September 1976 by Peter Shore, the Secretary of State for the Environment in the Callaghan Administration, in what is generally recalled as his 'Manchester speech'. Thirty years after the passing of the New Towns Act, Shore's speech was widely interpreted as a reversal of policy, closing the door on further new town initiatives in favour of a concentration of resources for inner cities. The problem was, claimed Maurice Ash, that at a time when planning was at a low ebb the new towns were there as convenient scapegoats, blamed for their own success in drawing away jobs and people from the urban centres.[13] Elsewhere, in an open letter to the Secretary of State, Ash questioned the basis for the policy switch, and warned that opportunities would be lost if inner cities were to be redeveloped at high densities. A regional perspective was needed, from which it would be apparent that 'planned dispersal and the rehabilitation of the inner cities must proceed together.'[14]

But the Association, while maintaining a high profile defence of new towns – which had achieved all that had been asked of them – recognized that, as far as a future for a concerted overspill policy was concerned, the writing was now very clearly on the wall. This, it could see, was not just a product of political whim but an inevitable outcome of greatly reduced population projections, from a previous expectation for Britain of some 70 million by the year 2000 to a revised total of little more than 58 million. Without abandoning the case for new towns the time had come to devote more attention itself to 'the other half' of its longstanding strategy, the improvement of the cities. Ash had earlier admitted that this side of things had been neglected: 'We took it for granted that lower densities were enough; that cities could virtually re-order themselves.'[15]

Turning adversity to fortune, in March 1977 the Association responded to the new situation by itself launching an inner-city initiative. In a policy statement, 'Inner Cities of Tomorrow', it was pointed out that an interest in inner cities was by no means new. 'We feel bound to say at the outset that the problems of inner city areas have been central to the Association's basic purpose since its foundation in 1899.'[16] True enough, but a refocusing on these issues was timely and, apart from recommendations to the government (with thirty-five points for immediate action), the policy document marks an increasing preoccupation in the late 1970s with inner-city and local community issues. This is where the political spotlight was now directed, and the Association was keen to play an active role in policy formulation and implementation.

One means of contributing to the debate was to advise politicians as to how they might most effectively spend their limited inner-city budgets. Expressing exasperation, Peter Self wrote an article directed to the government, entitled 'This time, listen!', reminding the Secretary of State that the Association had repeatedly offered ideas on how to get a grip on the central issue of land values, as well as ways of achieving acceptable forms of housing. It was vital, he argued, to ensure that public investment was not misdirected. The Association, concluded Self, was answering 'the charge that we have not concerned ourselves enough with urban problems. We have a good track record of advice, but this advice may often have been too negative. Now we mean to build more positively upon our understanding of the processes of urban change. So this time, listen!'[17]

Not that this was by any means the only issue requiring attention. That the Association had assumed an unchallenged role as the major pressure group for town and country planning is evidenced in the remarkable number and range of policy documents produced every year. In 1976, for instance, 'the most active year on record',[18] no fewer than twenty policy statements were issued on a wide variety of topics (all of which were listed and commented on in the Association's annual report for that year). It is worth noting these as an illustration of the Association's scope of work in that decade.

First of these was a reaction to the then Secretary of State's recent statement on the Greater London Development Plan, marking the culmination of one of the long-running issues of that period. The Greater London Council had originally submitted its plan in 1969, and the Association monitored progress closely in the early half of the 1970s, including representation at a lengthy public inquiry. More than thirty years before, Osborn had been centrally involved in the whole debate about London planning, and it was entirely consistent that the Association continued to see this as a crucial planning issue. In its 1976 statement, with governmental decisions already taken, the Association simply lodged its objection to the fact that the Secretary of State had not responded to a call for six growth centres in outer London rather than four.

Another saga of this period was that of airports strategy, with the Association issuing two statements in 1976 – the one being a comment on plans for the London area and the other relating to the other regions. Accepting the need for a third major airport close to London, the Association had consistently favoured a site on Maplin Sands (in the Thames Estuary) rather than Stansted. This location, it was argued, would be of greatest benefit to the region, particularly neighbouring East London which might be expected to attract associated investment. In addition to Maplin, the case was also made for a network of regional airports. These, it was argued, would serve not only to divert traffic from the congested South East but would also provide a valuable source of jobs and development where these were most needed.

This was also a period when regional devolution was under discussion, another issue of particular interest to the Association. In a continuing debate, the question to the fore at this juncture was that of whether local government would have to be further reorganized or whether it could be improved through the integration of certain regional functions. As well as regional government, the Association also had views on local government finance, agreeing with the findings of the Layfield Report that the division between central and local responsibilities was a source of confusion, and recommending that clarity should be secured in favour of greater local powers.

On national parks and the management of the countryside the Association made its views known in the form of evidence to the

The Maplin proposal was linked to the possibility of reviving the East London economy in the face of industrial decline in the London Docklands.

appropriate Environment Sub-Committee of the House of Commons Expenditure Committee. The evidence was detailed, and the Association saw fit to justify its submission by explaining that 'it had always sought to recommend policies which would achieve the sound planning of town and country in balance, so that countryside policies would be seen in the context of city/regional planning and vice versa.'[19] In his garden city scheme, Howard had long ago constructed a jig-saw puzzle, the pieces of which were still being fitted together; each of the Association's actions could be seen as part of a grand design.

Inevitably, new towns featured in the year's output of policy statements, with one commenting on arrangements for the transfer of housing assets from development corporations to local authorities, and another objecting in forthright terms to the government decision to abandon plans for a new town at Stonehouse, near Glasgow. The later was rightly seen as the start of an inexorable shift away from overspill policy in favour of inner-city redevelopment.

Regional plans were an obvious source of attention, and statements were prepared on strategies for South Wales, the South East (a review of the 1971 strategy), and the draft development plan for the London Docklands. Planning procedures also evoked a response, on the subjects of delays in development control, the control of office development, and amendments to general development orders. Additionally, specific topics – transport policy, commercial property development, and residential densities – were each the focus of detailed statements.

Finally, it was the mid-1970s when the Association became involved in energy policy and related public inquiries, and the report on activities in 1976 includes reference to lobbying for an inquiry to be held into the application by British Nuclear Fuels to expand its waste processing facilities at Windscale, and the National Coal Board's proposals to work the coal reserves in the Vale of Belvoir. These issues are considered further in the separate section on the Association's role in public inquiries.

Together, the above amounts to a weighty portfolio, though even that was by no means the sum total of the Association's activities. Separate initiatives to promote environmental education and planning aid for ordinary citizens were started in the 1970s, and (like the public inquiries) these are considered separately as distinctive campaigns.

The Director, David Hall, also developed a new dimension to the international role of the Association, through his growing involvement in the United Nations Habitat forum for non-governmental organizations. At the 1976 conference in Vancouver he argued that 'independent, well-informed organizations such as the Town and

Country Planning Association'[20] should be active in all countries; that Ebenezer Howard's concept of the social city retained important lessons for modern nations; that to achieve such a concept local government boundaries should be drawn to relate to the areas to be planned; that a system of land management should enable the purchase of land at existing use values and the return of betterment to the community; and that a genuine system of public education and participation was essential for good planning.[21] From its inception, the Association assumed a role in spreading the ideas that evolve from the garden city concept, and, as the above illustrates, this international educative role was still very much on the policy agenda.

PATTERNS OF CHOICE

> The Association is at a crossroads; it must either expand its activities or radically contract them. The Executive has chosen the former course. (Maurice Ash, Executive Chairman, TCPA Annual Report, 1970)

In his first report as Chairman of the Executive, Maurice Ash announced a decision that was to open up new policy dimensions for the Association in the 1970s. The boundaries of these new areas of interest (including environmental education, planning aid and public inquiries) have been mapped out in the previous section, but no less than their impact in the outside world this expanding portfolio was to have important implications for the internal philosophy and organization of the Association.

At the heart of it all is the question of what the Association stands for. Throughout its history, there were times when members questioned what seemed like radical departures from the basic principles enshrined in Howard's garden city concept. At such times, the dilemma for the Association was that of seeking to balance the desires of evolutionists, who could see Howard's ideas as a set of adaptable principles, and fundamentalists who equated adaptation with a weakening of the basic ties. The Association's strategy for the 1970s ushered in a new round of debate.

In fact, it was not as immediate or dramatic as all that. One reason is that old campaigns were not abandoned. A continuing commitment to new towns and regional planning was undisputed and reassuring. Maurice Ash himself had worked closely with Peter Self in the 1960s and was a strong advocate of the city region concept, seeing it as a natural successor to Howard's idea of social cities.[22] In reviewing priorities in May 1971, for instance, Ash put the issue of the implementation of regional plans at the top of his list.[23] The other reason why the new strategy did not lead to immediate debate was that the various initiatives heralded in 1970 took some years to materialize. Some of the ideological implications of getting involved in community issues did not fully emerge until the following decade.

But by the mid-1970s voices of dissent about the spread of activities could be heard, and a debate that was to continue well into the 1980s was underway. A restrained note of criticism was offered at the Annual General Meeting in 1973, when Professor William Robson politely questioned whether the Association was perhaps trying to pull in too many different directions at once:

> More and more of the energies of the Association seem to be taken up in responding to demands of one kind and another which it receives from outside organisations . . . rather than producing policies or statements on its own initiative . . . My remarks are directed rather to the question whether we are not spreading ourselves too thinly among a great variety of diverse topics which, through lack of resources, prevents us from doing our own thing.[24]

This, of course, begged the question as to what 'our own thing' really was, and a rejoinder came from a traditionalist, Arnold Whittick (a close associate and co-author with Osborn of a definitive book on new towns), making the case that the Association's heartland was nothing more or less than the ground covered by the original garden city aims of 1899. Once the Association accepted a wider town planning brief (and he thought that the rot had set in by 1909) it weakened the thrust of its central argument, claimed Whittick, and that was precisely the problem confronting the Association in the 1970s – it was trying to cover the whole field of town and country planning. Instead, it should concentrate all its efforts on persuading the government of the day to build more new towns.[25]

At regular intervals, the debate surfaced in Council, with members aware of the problems of diffusion but generally supportive of the new approach. In May 1975 a wide-ranging discussion acknowledged that 'the success of the original campaign was to a considerable extent due to the single-minded pursuit of one objective', but concluded that 'it would be a retrograde step to concentrate solely on new town matters.' There might be times when a particular issue should command extra attention (the Community Land Bill at the time was cited as an example), but not at the expense of the new ventures into environmental education and planning aid. The meeting was unanimous that 'no choice should be made about whether in future the TCPA should assume *either* an educative *or* a pressure group role'; both were essential to the pursuit of the Association's aims and underlying philosophy, which remained 'currently as relevant as ever.'[26]

Discussions such as the above did not resolve the issue. Resources were limited and choices had to be made. In the summer of 1975, members of the Executive Committee and staff of the Association spent a weekend at Dartington to reconsider priorities and future direction.[27] Little was resolved as a result of it, in that support for environmental education and planning aid was endorsed, a new role was suggested for the TCPA in the EEC, and a more populist style for the journal was mooted. In only one area was there a proposal to reduce work, and that was in respect of advising a lower rate of response to the constant stream of government consultation documents that arrived in the office. Additionally, it is interesting to note that the idea was raised of undertaking some form of practical demonstration of small-scale community enterprise (an idea that was to make its mark in the 1980s) but, for the time being, it was decided not to move ahead on this front.

Inevitably, in the face of a continuing high level of activity, the problem of priorities refused to go away. Returning to the issue at the end of decade, the Chairman of the Council, Peter Self, felt that the Association was 'bursting out of its clothes',[28] and that to avert the danger of getting too much involved in the daily round of planning activity and not taking initiatives itself, what was needed was 'a sense of vision and strategy rather than a tactical programme.'[29]

Underlying the sense of concern about the range and volume of activities was the knowledge that the Association was consistently under-resourced. It always had been, but the question that now arose was whether it had the reserves to break into new territory. In pointing to the challenges of the decade, Ash also warned that 'financially speaking the Association lives dangerously.'[30] It continued to live dangerously throughout the 1970s, with a mid-term assessment that 'we are surely near the limits it is possible to be in advance of the practice of our times.'[31] As well as revenue expenditure, the Association was also forced to draw on capital to enable a move in 1971 from King Street to more spacious offices in Carlton House Terrace. The Association was barely solvent, but, defiantly, it was claimed that 'the country cannot yet afford to be without the TCPA.'[32]

One problem was that the upsurge of activity and expenditure was not matched by a corresponding increase in membership subscriptions. The work of the environmental education unit brought in its own special category of membership, but, that apart, total numbers actually declined during the course of the decade – from about 1500 to 1350. Taking account of corporate membership (the major source of subscription revenue), individual affiliations totalled less than

1000. Grants from charitable trusts and other bodies, coupled with private donations, accounted for most of the Association's revenue. Additionally, that the Association was able to sustain a high level of activity on such a slender resource base was due in no small measure to the strong commitment of the professional staff (which, in that period, included Colin Ward, Tony Fyson and David Lock, as well as the Director, David Hall), and the voluntary contribution of expertise and enthusiasm from a small corps of members. A feature of the Association is that it has always been able to call on the services of leading politicians, practitioners and academics of the day, and, as a scan of the lists of who was on the various committees reveals, the 1970s were no exception. Amongst the politicians are the names of Anthony Crosland, Arthur Blenkinsop, William Deedes, Bryan Gould and Evelyn Dennington; practitioners such as Andrew Thorburn, Colin Buchanan, Michael Dower and Desmond Heap; and academics including Peter Self, Derek Diamond, Peter Hall, William Robson and Robin Best.

A small organization with a wide network of influence is how the Association has always seen itself, and in 1974 a benchmark to measure its standing was provided with the celebration of its seventy-fifth anniversary. Colin Ward wrote an evocation, *Say it again, Ben!*, to mark the event,[33] and the journal invited words of recognition from a variety of dignitaries. Amongst these was a former Secretary of State for Education who had come into contact with the work of the environmental education unit, Margaret Thatcher, whose words – bearing in mind her profound influence on planning in the 1980s – are recalled in full:

The Town and Country Planning Association has always advocated the benefits which could accrue from enlightened planning. In this it has been in the forefront of public opinion. Most of us accept that a large number of planning mistakes have been made from the best of intentions; therefore we have to learn lessons not only from the distant past but sometimes from areas planned comparatively recently. Above all we are more conscious now that planning must be directed to facilitate communications between human beings.

Some of the best examples of beauty, proportion, and symmetry are still to be found in the past. Part of our job is to ensure that the best designs of the present are available to people of ordinary means.

I am particularly glad that we no longer bulldoze everything to the ground in order to rebuild. Some of the older buildings mingled with the new can give that feeling of continuity, stability, and confidence which each generation needs if it is to make its own distinctive contribution to the future. I congratulate you on attaining your seventy-fifth birthday.[34]

Another cause to look both backwards and ahead came, first, with Osborn's ninetieth birthday in 1975, followed three years later by his death. With a record of campaigning for the Association dating back to before the First World War, his death was very much the end of an era. As one of the leading figures in British planning in the twentieth century (although, like Howard before him, he remained the 'quintessential amateur')[35] observations about Osborn's work were equally about the issues in planning in that period. The Association itself remained loyal to the issues for which he had campaigned, and which were integral to its own history, but was now embarked on a wider course of action. Osborn himself stuck to his guns to the last, but reflected that he and the movement he led had failed. Living conditions in cities were in many respects worse not better, there were not enough new towns, the countryside was under duress, communities came together in protest rather than through a sharing of ideals and planning objectives had become de-humanized.[36] If this was a gloomy testimonial, it was balanced by warm tributes of achievements for a crusade that had been steadfastly pursued and, more pertinently, by the evidence of the Association's continuing work.[37]

Osborn left behind an organization that was working to capacity (if not, as Maurice Ash observed, 'stretched beyond breaking point'),[38] with committees and working parties, conferences and publications all a part of the routine business. Each year the Association organized a full programme of conferences on a variety of topical issues, together with weekend schools for councillors and international study tours (including an annual tour of the new towns for overseas visitors). The journal (edited by Derek Diamond from 1972) continued as a monthly publication, with the editorial policy and coverage encouraging more debate and a wider range of views than it had done under Osborn's former stewardship, when it had performed a more single-minded role.

As an active pressure group, no less important than ploughing its own furrow was the continuing task of maintaining links with other parts of the voluntary sector. David Hall spoke about a need to strengthen 'the third force in planning', which he believed could be achieved through greater technical and financial support (partly through public funds) for existing environmental groups and for the establishment of new groups to fill geographical and other gaps on the pressure group map. 'By helping the third force to become articulate and constructive a new confidence in what planning can do will be generated, and a new trust will be disseminated between the general

Sir Frederic Osborn (pictured here on his eightieth birthday in his garden at Welwyn) retained an unbroken belief in the value to society of good planning.

public and the authorities arising from what should be a cooperative effort.'[39]

In line with this philosophy, the Association was careful to maintain and foster links with as many groups as possible (recognizing that this was yet another call on its limited resources). Thus, in the mid-1970s, there was direct representation on the British Committee for World Town Planning Day, Committee for Environmental Conservation, Council for Environmental Education, Council for the Protection of Rural England, European Architectural Heritage

Year, International Federation for Housing and Planning, Keep Britain Tidy Group, National Council for Social Service, National Playing Fields Association, and Yorkshire and Humberside Council for Environment. In addition, close links were maintained with a wide variety of other organizations, including the main environmental professions. Maurice Ash had earlier laid claim to the Association as 'an important part of the fabric of this country and, indeed, at least a thread of the civilized world';[40] and in its continuing links with other organizations it was still weaving as many threads as possible into the national fabric.

NOTES

The Age of Dissent

1. Marwick (1982), p. 272.
2. Dennis (1970), p. 366.
3. Davies (1972).
4. *Ibid.*, p. 2.
5. Eversley (1973), p. 3.
6. In London, for instance, the early 1970s saw two well-orchestrated protest campaigns, one opposed to a Greater London Council plan for an urban motorway 'box' and the other to redevelopment proposals for Covent Garden. In both cases, the plans were subsequently abandoned.
7. Aldous (1975).
8. For the changes in planning in the 1970s, see, for instance, McKay and Cox (1979).
9. McKay and Cox (1979), p. 57.

Beyond New Towns

10. 'A new vision for new towns', *TCP*, Vol. 38, No. 1, 1970, p. 4.
11. South-East Joint Planning Team (1970).
12. Colin Ward, 'The missing half', *TCP*, Vol. 41, No. 1, 1973, p. 12.
13. TCPA Annual Report for 1976, p. 2.
14. Open letter to the Secretary of State for the Environment, *TCP*, Vol. 44, No. 12, 1976, pp. 516–519.
15. 'The end of dispersal?', *TCP*, Vol. 43, No. 2, 1975, p. 55.
16. TCPA (1977), p. 1.
17. Peter Self, 'This time, listen!', *TCP*, Vol. 45, No. 5, 1977, pp. 244–247.
18. TCPA Annual Report for 1976, p. 6.
19. *Ibid.*, pp. 7–8.
20. 'TCPA issues for Habitat', *TCP*, Vol. 44, No. 4, 1976, pp. 248–249.
21. *Ibid.*

Patterns of Choice

22. Maurice Ash joined the TCPA in the 1950s, though he had been attracted to the ideas of Howard since his school days. Of independent

means, he believed that the ideals of the Association were a cause worth supporting. He became Chairman of the Executive from 1969 to 1983, and Chairman of Council from 1983. He was also a member of the South West Regional Economic Council from 1965 to 1968. (Personal interview, 10th March 1987).

23. Minutes of TCPA Council, 20th May 1971.
24. Observation in *TCP*, Vol. 41, No. 7–8, 1973, pp. 357–358.
25. 'Association objectives', *TCP*, Vol. 41, No. 11, 1973, pp. 502–503.
26. Minutes of TCPA Council, 22nd May 1975.
27. Minutes of TCPA Council, 27th November 1975.
28. Minutes of TCPA Council, 22nd February 1979.
29. Minutes of TCPA Council, 23rd November 1979.
30. TCPA Annual Report for 1969, p. 2.
31. TCPA Annual Report for 1974, p. 3.
32. TCPA Annual Report for 1975, p. 3.
33. Ward, C. (1974) *Say it again, Ben!* London: TCPA.
34. Margaret Thatcher, *TCP*, Vol. 42, No. 7, 1974, p. 362.
35. Wyndham Thomas, 'The quintessential amateur', *TCP*, Vol. 43, No. 5, 1975, pp. 248–251.
36. *Ibid.*
37. In the February/March edition of *TCP* (Vol. 47, Nos. 2–3, 1979, pp. 91–103) eulogies on Osborn were submitted by Colin Ward, Peter Self, Arnold Whittick, Wyndham Thomas and (on behalf of the international movement) by V. R. Nielsen.
38. Minutes of TCPA Council, 22nd February 1979.
39. 'The third force in planning', *TCP*, Vol. 41, No. 6, 1973, p. 304.
40. TCPA Annual Report for 1970, p. 3.

7

1980s:

RESPONDING TO CHANGE

Although the tide of postwar politics had already started to turn in the 1970s, it is seldom that one can date political change with the precision of a single day. For it was on Thursday 3rd May 1979, with the election of the first of the Thatcher Administrations, that Britain finally decided to part company with the assumptions and beliefs on which the postwar political edifice had been built. Such has been the primacy of the leader that the following decade was shaped by ideas and policies that assumed the name of 'Thatcherism'.

It is Thatcherism that provides the unavoidable political context in which not simply the work of the TCPA but the very nature of town planning itself has been debated and, to an extent, reshaped. Like a juggernaut, it seemed at first as if the new political force would sweep away all before it, demolishing planning and breaking up the ground on which the Association had based its campaigns.

Yet the record of the 1980s was by no means one of capitulation and defeat. Far from it, for by the end of the decade a planning system remained in place and the Association had demonstrated a remarkable ability not simply to survive but to adapt to the new political and economic climate. Part of the secret of this successful response is to be found in an area of common ground where long-standing decentralists like the Association were to meet with the new ideologues who have sought to 'roll back the frontiers of the State'. It is on this common ground, amidst a complex interaction of ideas and action, of rhetoric as well as reality, that the key to the Association's history of the 1980s is to be found.

THE POLITICS OF PROPERTY

> . . . the politics of property seemed to ensure the creation of a client Tory vote closely resembling the client Labour vote of old, and in many cases consisting of the same people. (Hugo Young, 1989, p. 525, referring to the 1987 General Election)

The early 1980s was a divisive period – illustrated here by two photos taken in 1981, one at Toxteth after a night of riots, the other outside County Hall, London, where councillors and residents demonstrated against a proposed commercial development at Coin Street. (Photos by courtesy of the Hulton Picture Company)

One of the political catch phrases of the 1980s was that of 'popular capitalism', a term used to describe the intentions of successive Thatcher Administrations to incorporate more people directly in the workings of capitalist enterprise. A key to achieving this was to offer ordinary working people a stake in the property of the nation, whether it be through share ownership in hitherto public corporations like British Gas and British Airways, or simply through the transfer of council housing stock to sitting tenants. By one means or another the electorate (as Hugo Young observed in the above quote) was increasingly locked into a culture of property, a fact that is an important component in explaining the changing consciousness that characterized the decade and which has a direct bearing on the fortunes of planning. The balance shifted unmistakably from a bias in favour of the public sector to that of the private sector, from the protective qualities of the State to individual enterprise. Basic beliefs in the value of property ownership and profit-making combined to create a radically different setting for the exercise of planning than that which preceded it.

'Thatcherism' marked a sea change in British politics on a scale unknown since the great surge towards collectivism in the 1940s. In contrast to this earlier period, the tide flowed in the other direction, if not, in fact, sweeping away the whole edifice of postwar intervention at least seeking to loosen the hold of the State and to create a new climate of opinion. Ahead of her time, eleven years before her election to power the future Prime Minister proclaimed the gospel that was to be named after her: 'What we need now is a far greater degree of personal responsibility and decision, far more independence from the government and a comparative reduction in the role of government.'[1]

Margaret Thatcher made her mark as a populist, and the rhetoric of less government and more personal freedom struck a popular chord. But it is a form of populism underpinned by more than rhetoric, with a collection of political and economic ideas held together under the banner of the New Right. Strands in this banner run back to Adam Smith's classical interpretation of political economy and to the neo-classical economics of his nineteenth-century successors, to the Victorian values of enterprise and self-assertion, to notions of personal freedom embodied in the philosophy of the Austrian, Friedrich Hayek, all, in turn, interwoven with modern theories of monetarism and the extension of market principles to all sectors of social policy and decision-making. A seeming contradiction is that this neo-liberal tapestry is then set within a strong framework of order, a framework that derives its strength from centralized mechanisms of control.[2]

The contradictions of New Right philosophy worried its critics, but events have shown that it was more robust than early prophets predicted. Margaret Thatcher remained in office for nearly twelve years, 'a period [starting in 1979] which could later be defined as an era,'[3] and long enough to set in train irreversible trends in British society. Far from running out of steam, the 'Thatcher revolution' continued into a third term, and the election victory in 1987 'did not end the Thatcher era but did something more telling. It locked the Thatcher era into place, as a phase in Britain's political evolution of which the end was not in sight.'[4]

For an area of policy like town planning, an intrinsically public sector activity, the political events of the 1980s marked a fundamental challenge to both its legitimacy and institutional viability. Taken at surface value, everything that Thatcherism stood for seems to be at odds with the very idea of planning as an interventionist activity. And, in these terms, the early 1980s were indeed seen as a time of assault on sacred assumptions and uncertainty about the future. The appointment in 1979 of Michael Heseltine, a champion of free enterprise, as Secretary of State for the Environment sent ripples of concern through the planning profession. In spite of early assurances that it was not his mission to dismantle the planning system, sceptics were anxious that his fervent commitment to make it all more efficient and responsive to the needs of investors would inevitably have the effect of undermining the system as a whole. Moreover, early initiatives like the abolition of regional economic planning councils and the introduction of Enterprise Zones (which reduced planning controls in selected areas) and Urban Development Corporations (which usurped the powers of local planning authorities) were widely interpreted as the thin end of an anti-planning wedge.[5]

To some extent a premonition of doom and disaster was borne out by subsequent events. Successive measures added to the number of areas and types of development beyond the reach of normal planning procedures, a trend that is characterized by the populist title of the 1985 White Paper, 'Lifting the Burden', with its implicit threat (more rhetorical than real, as it transpired) of dismantling the 'burdensome' planning system.[6] Margaret Thatcher's personal intervention immediately after the 1987 General Election, committing herself to use the full force of radical policies to tackle once and for all the inner-city question, added to fears that the planning system would be hard-pressed to remain in place, at least in an acceptable form.

In some respects the fears were exaggerated, but, if planning was not swept away, it certainly changed. In the face of new demands, it became more pragmatic and more incremental, focusing on implementation, and responding to individual development initiatives. Successive Secretaries of State tended to make policy 'on the hoof' through appeals decisions and to rely less on structure plans as a framework for rational decision-making. The basic structure remained in place, but the incremental effects of limited initiatives combined with a reorientation of the whole ethos that surrounds planning was considerable. Perhaps, argues Andy Thornley, the real measure of change is not of the many things that planning can still do but rather of what it cannot:

> If planning is seen as preserving the best environmental heritage, promoting development in areas where the market is inactive or modifying the extreme side effects of the market, then planning could be said to be still in business. If planning is viewed as going beyond this and having some role in satisfying social needs it will need to employ non-market criteria and its ability to do so could be said to be radically constrained.[7]

This is, of course, a continuing debate, and there is a dimension to it which is of particular interest to the TCPA. Certainly, if one takes the global view, a blunting of the social edge of planning (as Thornley suggests) is inimical to the basic cause of the Association. The establishment of a broadly comprehensive planning system consistent with the wider aims of a Welfare State, was, after all, a central goal of Osborn and his fellow campaigners nearly fifty years ago. But there is also a longer decentralist tradition in the Association, a tradition that has sometimes co-existed uneasily with the tendency towards planning as a centralist, bureaucratic activity. From its very inception (evidenced in the early writings of Howard) the Association has sought to cut a fine line between the two – between the benefits of the State and collective action and the free association of individuals and a community scale of action.

Thus, while it has not been in the interests of the Association to see a weakening of the planning system as such (and the introduction in the 1980s of measures with this effect was strongly resisted), the emergence of a new situation where some of the bureaucratic overlay has been stripped away and where localized initiatives might be allowed to flourish has offered unexpected opportunities. The 'gift' came from an unlikely source (with the ideological underpinnings of the New Right a world apart from Howard's cooperative socialism of the 1890s), but, however it came about, the opportunity was too good to miss. Beyond the frontiers of the State is a land that can be settled by different peoples.

There was, for a start, the Thatcherite commitment to breaking the hold of socialist local authorities and of creating more opportunities for private and voluntary sector involvement. The former Secretary of State, Michael Heseltine, explained the philosophy in these terms: 'We can push power out beyond local government and into the hands of the people whom it is elected to serve . . . If housing estates are badly run, the cure is to give the tenants themselves more power. If public servants waste public money, let the private sector be called in to compete in saving it, while giving better service. If local authorities provide indifferent education, give more authority to schools and more influence to the parents as representatives of the pupils' needs.'[8] Although subsequently a Cabinet outcast (prior to returning to his old office as Secretary of State for the Environment, in John Major's Administration), Heseltine's view conforms closely to the approach that characterized the work of the third Thatcher Administration. In this, the Prime Minister's personal involvement in fresh inner-city initiatives served to distance policies, with a new role for the private and voluntary sectors, from the essentially public sector dominance of the past.

Another boost for the new approach came from an unexpected source, that of the Prince of Wales, who, in a series of public statements and personal commitment to community-based projects, spoke out strongly in favour of less centralized, less bureaucratic approaches to the management of our environment.[9] The Prince, like Margaret Thatcher, proved to be a populist *par excellence*, giving voice to the previously unheard needs and preferences of ordinary folk. His views on architecture were particularly outspoken, and lent considerable weight to the community architecture movement with its recognition of a need for human scale and wider public involvement in the whole building and design process.

The populists hit their target because there was already a latent pool of disaffection, fostered by the relative failures of former planning schemes and a perceived deterioration of environmental quality. The community movement of the 1970s had already warned of this trend, and it was for politicians to bring it all together. As Patsy Healey has observed, 'citizens and new right philosophers appear thus to be at one in their demands for greater individual autonomy, and more reliance on self-correcting mechanisms rather than regulation.'[10]

With the ground thus mapped out, the Association was well-placed to make its own mark. For all the contradictions surrounding planning in the Thatcher years – the rhetoric of getting rid of planning against the reality of its survival, the rhetoric of loosening the hold of government against the reality of strengthening central controls – decentralism was now very much in the public eye. Initiatives taken by the Association in the 1970s, like planning aid and environmental education, bore fresh fruit, and some of the calls of leading campaigners at last found attentive ears. Major issues, like the continuing North-South divide and the future of the countryside, were by no means neglected (and, indeed, featured high on the agenda), but it is probably the 'bottom up' approach which will be recalled as the star turn for the Association in the 1980s. The idea of giving voice to communities and of seeing a role for professionals 'on tap rather than on top' had found its moment. Thatcherism was an unlikely catalyst for the remaking of planning but that, up to a point, is how it has turned out.

A MATTER OF SCALE

> The North–South divide, the growing problems of the South, the future of the countryside and the fostering of 'bottom-up' initiatives were among the policy issues addressed by the TCPA in 1988. (TCPA Annual Report for 1988, p. 4)

The above statement towards the end of the 1980s, pointing to a balance of interests between 'macro' and 'micro' levels of activity, provides an apt summary of the dual policy focus of the Association throughout the decade. Thatcherism (as the previous section has indicated) created opportunities as well as a need to stimulate action on both a strategic and community scale.

Although this duality was consistent with the basic principles that date back to the original garden city scheme and which have been honed and recast ever since, the strategy adopted in the 1980s marks an important break with the past. Until then, the thrust of the Association's policies had been directed primarily towards issues on a regional and national level, with local considerations seen as implicit. Even the founding of the two garden cities, at Letchworth and Welwyn, was limited to the initial processes of formation and to subsequent propaganda rather than to direct involvement in the details of community organization. Policies for new towns, green belts and regional planning, and a persistent lobby for an appropriate system of national planning, characterized the level at which the Association traditionally operated. Only in the 1970s, with environmental education and planning aid, was there the start of a community-based approach as an explicit dimension of policy, a trickle that became a flood in the decade that followed.[11]

Referred to variously as a 'bottom up' or 'local life' approach, the Association's involvement at this level can be demonstrated in different ways. Undoubtedly, one important source was the Third Garden City initiative, a proposal for a demonstration garden city (detailed separately in Chapter 8). An outline prospectus in 1979 proposed a small community designed to achieve a maximum degree of independence and self-sufficiency – a concept that was consistent with Howard's original notion of a garden city, but which was also responsive to the needs and technological opportunities of Britain nearly a century after the original scheme.[12]

The initiative had various outcomes. It brought the Association into touch with potential community-builders based at Milton Keynes, the Greentown group, and with an associated world of alternative ideas. Although this particular scheme did not materialize, a different location, at Lightmoor in Telford New Town, provided more yielding ground. For there, with the involvement of an individual, Tony Gibson, who was to have a significant impact on the whole 'bottom up' approach, a self-build settlement took shape in the 1980s, attracting publicity and prizes in its wake. Moreover, Lightmoor was followed by other community projects, notably that of Conway in Birkenhead – an inner city experiment – and by another Gibson venture, the Neighbourhood Initiatives Foundation. Launched in 1988, the Foundation (formed jointly by the TCPA and the Housing Associations' Charitable Trust) acts as a catalyst for neighbourhood action, 'working from the ground up, not imposing the dead weight of impersonal, insensitive structures devised from outside.'[13]

Another dimension of the 'bottom up' approach has its origins more with the planning aid initiative that dates from the 1970s. The Association's planning aid service (also recorded in Chapter 8) flourished during the 1980s – responding to community requests ranging from local planning issues to the highly contentious question of the future of the Divis estate in Belfast – although in 1988 it was decided to 'hive off' what had become known as the London Planning Aid Centre as an autonomous unit. Another significant initiative of this period is that of the Manchester-based Community Technical Aid Centre, highlighted by David Hall as a 'heartening success' in a decade when 'moments of euphoria have been thin on the ground.'[14] Formed in 1979 at the Association's northern office, the aim was to provide free technical advice for inner-city residents wishing to carry out their own community-based projects or to prepare detailed reports to submit to the council. With grant aid and the support of the then Manpower Services Commission, a wide range of activities was possible for most of the 1980s. A reduction in external funding led, in turn, to a shift in focus, away from its traditional role of 'enabler' and towards one of implementation. Fee-charging became a new aspect of its work: 'to be charitable but businesslike is the prime aim.'[15]

Finally, a further manifestation of the 'bottom up' approach was that of *Network*, a new publication from the Association's press. Starting in 1984, the initial brief was to provide members with more information about the TCPA's activities, including the various 'local life' initiatives. When a previously-circulated planning aid newsletter was disbanded in 1986, it was this latter part of the brief which became the main task, and the magazine and newsletter was re-launched as a quarterly, with the title *Community Network*. One difference with the original version was that now the publication was designed for and sponsored by a wider network of organizations in the community architecture, design, planning and technical aid movement.[16] Each of the sponsoring organizations edits its own page of news in a cooperative enterprise that itself expresses the ideals of the movement about which it reports.

All of these were new ventures for the Association, and not without a record of achievement and external recognition. But questions were raised within the Association as to whether its coverage of community issues was not, perhaps, leading it to spread its limited resources too thinly. The Association also laid itself open to accusations that it had deserted its long-standing role of impartiality and that it was engaging in radical politics.[17] It is indeed true that community action was not favoured in all quarters in this period. No one disputed the fact that it represented a challenge to conventional patterns of lobbying for change and to the normal ways in which local authorities and central government expected things to be done. But, if the approach was novel, that was because it was popularly perceived that many of the traditional avenues for democratic representation had been obstructed by a weakening of local government and by the seeming unresponsiveness of central government to rational argument. In any case, the Association was at pains to explain that there were positive reasons for actively supporting this kind of action. It was a principled position, based on the view that a more decentralized form of society in which people would have more say over their own lives was long overdue, and that in the 1980s 'the means now exist, both in the technical sense and in the growing aspirations of so many people to play a greater part, by which such changes can be achieved.'[18]

But a balance had to be struck. Although the Association had pinned its colours boldly to the community mast, it had no wish to abandon its more strategic interests. On the contrary, it was seen to be important to keep a balance; regional and national issues were not regarded as a world apart from community initiatives, but rather as points along the same continuum. And the democratic principle of giving people more control over their own lives was by no means confined to a particular locality; it was a principle to be protected at all levels of planning.

So in the 1980s, as it had done throughout its history, the Association continued to tackle the 'big' issues. It rode the storm of the Thatcher revolution, contesting new legislation which seemed to ignore hard-won principles of democratic planning, challenging successive measures to weaken existing practices, and lamenting the loss of local government powers. But it was a hard struggle. At the end of the first year of the new political era, the Association spoke of 'deep dismay' about the situation.[19] With the early abolition of regional economic planning councils and the shift of most development control powers to district council level, the Association made it clear that 'planning would become no more than an ad hoc response to the development pressures and that the removal of regional planning would, amongst other things, mean that no solutions would be found to inner city problems.'[20]

For its first fifty years the Association had fought for the establishment of a reasonably comprehensive planning system, as the essential prerequisite for achieving a better environment in town and country, and it was not now going to preside quietly over its dismantlement. 'The TCPA is a watchdog for good planning,' it reminded those who might have thought that planning was undefended. 'It provides a voice at national level for individuals and groups with a common purpose, linking the diverse concerns of the environment movement in a broad front which has influence in the highest counsels in the land.'[21]

But the new Conservative government had its own way of doing things, and (as already indicated) successive measures, from Enterprise Zones and Urban Development Corporations which cut across local systems of accountability, to changes in development plan machinery and general development orders designed to loosen the hold of planning, all served to reinforce the Association's concerns. For the Association it was a contradictory situation. The idea of Enterprise Zones originated from one of its own influential members, Peter Hall, while a form of Urban Development Coorporation had for long been advocated as a way to tackle the problems of the inner city. But, in the way they emerged, neither was consistent with the Association's own priorities and concern to balance firm planning guidance with local democratic processes. And although some consolation could be taken from the evidence of a planning system still recognizably intact – 'the radical-right government, here as elsewhere, [having proved] that its bark was a good deal more significant than its bite'[22] – it was hardly a time for optimism. At the end of the decade, the Chairman of the Executive, John Blake, had grounds to conclude dismally that planning had lost its way, and that it was 'now under threat, as never before, both institutionally and philosophically.'[23]

Seeking to protect the machinery and constantly extolling the merits of planning was one way in which the Association's policy was directed. The other way was through involvement in substantive issues, from energy policy to inner cities, from the North-South divide to the future of the countryside, and each year saw the publication of a range of policy statements. It remained, in every sense, a very high profile campaign, alerting the public to key issues and challenging the government on procedures as well as policies.

To take but one illustration, there is no other organization that has campaigned so consistently on the issue of regional planning. In the 1930s and in the 1960s this was particularly high profile, and in the 1980s, with most of the apparatus dismantled but with obvious regional disparities, the banner of the 'North-South divide' (as the issue was now termed) was lifted again. It is an all-embracing issue that carries within it the conflicting problems of, on the one hand, regional decline and what can be done about it, and, on the other hand, congestion and problems of affluence in the rest of the country (notably in London and the South East).

A report published by the Association in 1987 pointed to the divisive effects of the economic restructuring process that had been underway over the previous decade, reinforcing a profile of 'two nations' – one characterized by high wages and a high level of skills, and a concentration of power and decision-making, and the other by low wages and a low level of skills, dependent on and peripheral to the South East.[24] What had to be done, recommended the Association, was to reverse these trends, and this would not happen without government intervention in a variety of ways, directed within a coherent framework of regional policy. Various proposals were made, from enhancing the role of northern airports (especially Manchester) to assessing the impact and potential of the Channel Tunnel, and from improving the infrastructure of information technology in northern cities to overhauling training arrangements. There were also firm proposals to improve the machinery of regional government, including the formation of development agencies or enterprise boards. But two years on a new report by the Association showed that progress in bridging the divide had been negligible, that most of the proposals had not been taken up, and that certain issues (like the flow of information to and within peripheral regions) were becoming crucial in the context of a post-industrial economy.[25]

The other side of the coin is the overcrowded and, in many ways, intolerable, aspects of life in the South East. In an important discussion paper, 'Riding the Tiger', David Lock put the case for a new strategic plan to guide development.[26] Departing from convention, the proposed plan would be produced by a partnership of governmental, private and voluntary sector interests, and would contain radical initiatives to counter the problems of overdevelopment and spiralling land values. Although the paper was not presented as official TCPA policy, the intention was to stimulate public debate on an issue that the government was refusing to tackle in anything like a coherent way.

A major recommendation in the Lock proposals was for a fresh programme of new cities and country towns, an objective that remains close to the philosophical heart of the Association. Although

there is no governmental support for the revival of a public programme of new towns, few opportunities are lost by the Association
to restate the case. At the Tenth Ebenezer Howard Memorial
Lecture in October 1988, Geoffrey Steeley (County Planning Officer
for Hertfordshire) called for a revival of Howard's concept of a sub-
regional cluster of garden cities, termed the social city.[27] Steeley
argued that the concept was already in evidence in his own county,
and that further social cities should be encouraged in other parts of
the region.

Responding to the call, David Hall repeatedly argued that new
settlements will provide an important component of future regional
plans, particularly in the 'Greater South East'. Far from being a
concept of the past, abandoned by successive governments, 'there is a
greater need for garden cities and new settlements, especially in the
South East of England, than at any time since the heyday of the postwar new towns programme.'[28] It is not that a population increase is
anticipated, so much as the evidence of up to 1.5 million new houses
that will be needed by the end of the century and the undesirability of
fitting these into existing urban boundaries. But the location of the
new settlements cannot be left to chance, with private consortia
making their own bids in isolation from a wider strategy. What is
needed, argues Hall, is a coherent strategic planning policy for the
region, produced by a partnership of local and central government.

At the end of the 1980s, it was an argument with a depressing
familiarity about it, the case having been won before in the 1940s and
again in the 1960s. Nothing better illustrates the observation that
progress in planning is by no means inevitable, that there are periodic
losses as well as gains, and that campaigns have to be waged to
recover ground as well as to win it for the first time. Nor does anything
better illustrate the 'vigilante' role of the TCPA, seeking to protect
planning from the incursions of new generations of politicians who
are either unversed or hostile to ideas and beliefs that had once been
part of a seemingly enduring consensus.

'KEEPING THE TORCH ALIGHT'

> In due course, planning will inevitably come into fashion again.
> Until it does, it is important that the torch is kept alight. That is
> the task – the prime task of the Town and Country Planning
> Association. (John Blake, TCPA Annual Report for 1987, p. 3)

The imagery of keeping the torch alight is resonant of the best
evangelical traditions of the Association, recalling the days when the
garden city pioneers saw themselves as missionaries for their cause.
There is an underlying sense of salvation, of good versus evil, of

something that is essentially pure and right pitted against the forces of darkness. It is a rallying call, consistent with nine decades of campaigning for beliefs and ideals that were always one step ahead of their practical realization and which were, more often than not, under threat from governments that refused to share in the same fervour for planning. To that extent, moral self-belief is nothing new. Yet, in the 1980s, in the face of a constant assault on planning, the claim to act as the 'nation's watchdog for good planning' was especially justifiable.[29]

The repercussions of this vigil were not simply to have an external impact, in terms of mounting different campaigns and seeking to

The demolition of some tower blocks in the 1980s (like this one at Hackney) symbolized the gains as well as losses for the ideals espoused by the TCPA. High-density housing had always been vigorously opposed.

influence events. No less significant for the Association were the internal implications. Both the aims of the organization and its ability to finance and manage itself came under the microscope in what proved to be an exhaustive and, at times, traumatic process of soul-searching. It was a testing period in more sense than one.

Like so much of the Thatcher era, certain trends were already underway before her election to power in May 1979. Planning had been under duress for some years previous, attracting a growing public disaffection for its failure to deliver the kind of environment that people wanted. To add to this, for the Association the retreat from a State new towns policy had removed a central plank from its campaign platform. All of which contributed to a diversification of the Association's policies and priorities, and a search for a new role. The crisis for planning in the Thatcher years intensified a problem that was already latent.

With hindsight, the definition of the problem is clear enough. The Association, for long preoccupied with regional and national policies, was now adding to these a portfolio of community and local issues. In organizational terms, could it operate at both levels or should it concentrate on just one or the other? This was not an abstract question, for, at the start of the 1980s the role of the Association and what it stood for was unclear to its own members as well as to outsiders, and, to make matters worse, involvement in a widening range of interests was imposing serious strains on the limited resources of the organization.

Successive attempts were made to address the problem, with a need to concentrate the efforts of the Association in pursuance of clearly-defined aims seen as being central. In November 1982, staff and Executive members spent a weekend in Dorking discussing what should be done. Rob Cowan (at that time the Planning Aid officer) circulated a paper that analysed the problem of diversification and called for the adoption of a simple aim for the TCPA that would be easily understood by the public. 'Without a focus, the Association cannot project any distinct image, and without an image it cannot attract the support it needs.'[30]

What, though, should be this simple aim? If the answer remained elusive there was, at least, a strong feeling that the newly-acquired 'bottom up' approach should be enhanced to shape the Association's future. It was recognized that 'the Association's image may not be all that it should be', and that this new emphasis would not be to everyone's liking, but it was concluded that 'the appropriate strategy should be to show how [the new ideas] relate to the basic principles which the Association has always advocated . . . an evolution from the Association's past policies and values rather than seeming only to be offering a bright new package of ideas and values.'[31]

The fruits of the Dorking weekend emerged a little over a year later, following further discussions and committee ratification, in the form of what was published as *A New Prospectus: Policy direction for the next 20 years.* In this it was explained that while traditional objectives of the Association remained very much on the agenda, new circumstances surrounding planning called for additional activities:

> The Town and Country Planning Association has therefore added a further dimension to its work in relation to these urgent needs of society today. We believe that the new approach to how we shape our living environment must consist of three vital elements:
>
> (1) MORE LOCAL INITIATIVE – to give people the power to improve their own local environment.
>
> (2) MAXIMUM DECENTRALISATION – to ensure that environmental decisions are never taken at a higher level than is clearly necessary to secure some wider objective, and that decisions at all levels are community-focused.
>
> (3) A STRONGER BUT MORE FLEXIBLE PLANNING FRAMEWORK – to re-orientate the planning system to provide a stronger framework for achieving vital long-term objectives, while allowing more freedom for local choice, variety and experiment.
>
> All three elements are aimed at creating a much stronger localized approach to decision-making, so that people can be actively involved in shaping their own environment. Such a fresh approach will have profound implications for communities and democracy, and for the planning system.[32]

This was a powerful endorsement of the community-based approach, but it was by no means the end of the debate. In the face of continuing resource problems and a widening base of activities, another weekend meeting was arranged for members of the Executive Committee and staff, this time at Exeter in April 1986. It was called by the then Executive Chairman, Mary Riley, to review recent work and to consider whether new directions of policy and activity were appropriate.[33] The mission of the Association was still very much on the agenda.

A belief in the basic philosophy of the organization was reinforced, but there was clearly some concern that the Association was still casting its net too wide. Priorities to emerge were those of pursuing the local life approach, helping the disadvantaged, and lobbying for constitutional reform to enable the first two objectives to be realized.

Energy policy, local government reform and inner-city policy remained high on the list of what needed to be done, as did strategic planning issues and new towns and communities. 'Thus the Association should not lose its mainstream concern for securing an effective planning system and the right planning policies. It was just that a different kind of planning was needed.'[34]

So, through to the second half of the 1980s, the Association was unwavering in its dual mission, operating at the level of the community as well as in its more strategic domain. Faced with a decision to prioritize it had effectively opted for both. But, as events have shown, it was not really to be a free choice. For most of the decade, financial crisis was never far away, and the wide range of activities which over-extended the organization was constantly called into question. As early as 1981, Maurice Ash (who was then Chairman of the Executive), spoke of the Association being 'close to the abyss', with an annual deficit of £15,000 amounting to three-quarters of the reserves.[35] Not so close to the abyss, it would seem, to heed the advice of a future Executive Chairman, John Blake, who urged on the leadership a review of its multiple responsibilities, recommending that the environmental education and planning aid functions be 'hived off' into independence.[36]

Instead, at that time the main response to financial crisis was to institute immediate expenditure savings, which included redundancy for one of the planning aid team. This action, and a loss of morale in a difficult period, for planning generally as well as for the Association, encouraged some of the staff (more radical, through the nature of their work as community activists, than had traditionally been associated with the TCPA) to lobby the Executive and to publicize their case with a 'press leak' to the weekly newspaper, *Planning*. 'Crisis brews behind TCPA's Nash facade' was the heading of an article that questioned the Association's real commitment to 'grassroots activities', and which suggested that it was 'no longer the force in the land it once was.'[37] Subsequent letters to the newspaper from Maurice Ash and the Deputy Director, Kelvin Macdonald, sought to correct errors of reporting and to argue that the real crisis was that of planning itself.[38]

The latter observation was true enough, in that the difficulties facing planning in the 1980s inevitably impinged on the work of the Association. Morally, the case for its continued work in promoting planning remained strong, in some ways strengthened by the difficulties confronting it, but moral fortitude does not pay the bills. In spite of a short-term recovery, with a surplus in the accounts recorded between 1982 and 1985 (in the latter two years by the most slender of margins), the structural and continuing nature of the problem was exposed by a deficit of nearly £50,000 in 1986. John Blake quoted from the auditor's report, warning that the situation was 'financially unsound and risky' and that the organization was 'very close to the edge'. Liquid assets at the end of June 1987 had fallen to just £1,136, against an annual expenditure level of more than half a million pounds.[39]

This time there could be no prevarication. An emergency plan was introduced, marked by the words 'retrenchment and reorganisation'.[40] Immediate economies were made and a tighter system of financial control was adopted. To redress the liquidity problem, an endowment fund was started (totalling £83,000 by the end of 1988) and sponsorship income was increased. Within two years, the situation had eased, although – given the scale of annual turnover and the uncertainty of much of the Association's income – it was by no means totally resolved.

Part of the 'rescue package' was to bring forward changes in office practice and management and committee reorganization, some of which had been mooted for several years and which had evoked varying responses. 'The TCPA is a fun place to work where staff have a great deal of freedom and appear generally to enjoy what they are doing,' was the view of an American management consultant who visited the organization in 1981.[41] But he also added that the staff were 'over-worked and under-paid. The office space is inadequate and poorly organized. The accounting system is inadequate . . . The organizational structure is clumsy and antiquated, [and the] office management over the years has been a too casual operation . . .'[42]

Even in advance of this report, changes were being introduced, including the appointment of a Deputy Director (first, Kelvin Macdonald and then Chris Gossop) to share the burgeoning workload and to assist with the internal organization. Following the 1986 financial crisis, a Management Sub-Committee was formed to spearhead and monitor the necessary changes, in advance of a more 'root and branch' approach to the whole management and policymaking structure of the organization. After ninety years, the cumbersome dual committee system of a separate Executive and Council was finally replaced in 1989, with the merging of the two into a single Council with a reduced membership of not more than thirty-six members (who have become the new Trustees of the organization).

In other respects, the Association continues in a way that is consistent with its history. It has never been able to sustain (nor particularly to seek) a mass membership, and its ninetieth anniversary arrived with a membership total of about 730 individual and student members and about 450 corporate members – numbers which would not have looked out of place at any time since its inception. What has always mattered more than sheer numbers is the contribution to the work of the organization of a small number of activists, and the networks of influence that can be achieved through a membership drawn from a wide spectrum of political, commercial and professional interests. The Association has always managed to attract leading planners to its ranks, and the 1980s were no exception. During this period, for instance, it enjoyed the support of Derek Diamond (for nine years Editor of the journal and then Treasurer of the Association in its most difficult years); Mary Riley, Chairman of the Executive and an ardent advocate for the 'local life' approach; and her successor, John Blake, who represented the TCPA at the lengthy Sizewell Inquiry and who, internally, was closely involved with the various rescue plans for the organization.

Through individuals and affiliations, linkages with other bodies have always been central to the Association's activities, and at few times were these more necessary than in the 1980s, when so much was at stake. In spite of its internal difficulties this aspect of the Association's work was undiminished. In 1988, for instance, it was formally represented on no less than twenty-two environmental and community organizations, in Britain and overseas, and another sixteen were listed where links were maintained without formal representation.[43] The role of the Director, David Hall, has been particularly important in this area of networking, with an active and continuing programme of maintaining and developing new contacts in Britain and in the international planning community.

In many respects, in organizational terms, the decade closed on a more buoyant note than that on which it opened. It might be that the main force of the storm has passed. At the beginning of the 1990s the financial situation of the Association looks a little more stable, and the purpose of the Association more focused. The 'bottom up' approach has been integrated into the general work of the organization, while the operational side of it has been 'hived off' to autonomous bodies.[44] Issues of national importance – regional planning and countryside policy, the future of the planning system and the case for a new generation of garden cities – entirely consistent with the Association's background, again head the agenda and are attracting considerable interest and support. The 1980s was a testing decade, but one detects at the end of it a renewed 'spring in the step' that not so long ago seemed improbable.

NOTES

The Politics of Property

1. Margaret Thatcher, quoted in Peter Riddell, 'An instinct, not an ideology', in Owen (1987), p. 5.
2. An exploration of the basic philosophy and the contradictions between

centralist and decentralist tendencies is provided in Dunleavy and O'Leary (1987), pp. 72–135.
3. Young (1989), p. 135.
4. *Ibid.*, p. 518.
5. See, for instance, Griffiths, R. (1986) 'Planning in retreat? Town planning and the market in the eighties'. *Planning Practice and Research*, No. 1 and Thornley, A. (1986) Thatcherism and simplified planning zones. *Planning Practice and Research*, No. 1; and Thornley (1991).
6. 'Lifting the Burden' was a White Paper issued by Lord Young, Minister without Portfolio, *et al.*, Cmnd. 9571, London: HMSO. In it, an answer is given to Lord Young's rhetorical question, 'Do we need the present town planning system?', with the words, '. . . in many ways it has served the country well and the Government has no intention of abolishing it.'
7. Thornley (1986), p. 22 (see note 5).
8. Heseltine (1987), pp. 132–133.
9. The Prince's views are always widely reported, but the widest audience was reached in a television programme, 'A Vision of Britain', BBC 2, 22nd October 1988.
10. Healey (1989), p. 2.

A Matter of Scale

11. The community focus dates from the start of David Hall's leadership and his espousement of this cause as an essential part of the TCPA's strategy for better planning.
12. TCPA (1979) 'A Third Garden City: Outline Prospectus'.
13. TCPA Annual Report for 1988, p. 15. See also leaflet, 'Neighbourhood Initiatives' (undated), published at Lightmoor, explaining the project.
14. David Hall, in a personal interview, 22nd June 1987.
15. TCPA Annual Report for 1988, p. 17.
16. The original sponsoring organizations were the TCPA, the Association of Community Technical Aid Centres, the RIBA Community Architecture Group, the London Planning Aid Service and Manchester CTAC.
17. For instance, in a personal interview (17th February 1989) with Wyndham Thomas, former Director of the TCPA, a critical view of the community approach was taken, suggesting that the Association had, perhaps, rather lost its way.
18. TCPA Annual Report for 1985, p. 2.
19. TCPA Annual Report for 1980, p. 9.
20. *Ibid.*, p. 10.
21. Statement of TCPA aims and objects, from Annual Report for 1984, pp. 2–3.
22. Hall (1988), p. 361.
23. TCPA Annual Report for 1988, p. 3.
24. TCPA (1987).
25. TCPA (1989).
26. Lock (1989).
27. Geoffrey Steeley, 'The path to real reform', *TCP*, Vol. 58, No. 2, pp. 49–51.

28. David Hall, 'The case for new settlements', *TCP*, Vol. 58, No. 4, pp. 111–114.

'Keeping the Torch Alight'

29. The phrase was adopted in a redefinition of aims in 1984.
30. 'A future for the TCPA', discussion paper by Rob Cowan, submitted to TCPA Executive Committee, 24th October 1982.
31. 'The future of the TCPA', proposals arising from the weekend discussion at Beatrice Webb House, 5th–7th November 1982, p. 5.
32. TCPA (1984) 'A New Prospectus: Policy direction for the next 20 years', p. 5.
33. In an interview with Mary Riley, November 1989, the importance of the Dorking and Exeter meetings was stressed. The 'bottom up' approach was seen to be at the very heart of the Association's traditions, but needed to be constantly reaffirmed.
34. 'TCPA Meeting of Executive Committee and Staff, April 25th–27th, 1986, Crossmead Conference Centre, Exeter,' p. 4.
35. Maurice Ash, confidential note to TCPA Executive and staff, September 1981.
36. Letter from John Blake to David Hall, 19th June 1981. The rationale for this course of action was 'to enable the main thrusts of the Association's activities to be directed into fresh pastures.'
37. 'Crisis brews behind TCPA's Nash facade', *Planning*, 16 October, 1981, p. 3.
38. Letters to *Planning* from Maurice Ash and Kelvin Macdonald, October 1981.
39. Special Meeting of the Executive Committee, 24th September 1987. Speaking (in a personal interview, November 1989) of the financial crisis at this time, Derek Diamond (then the Honorary Treasurer) pointed to an interesting contradiction between the ideological commitment to a 'bottom up' approach and the very heavy reliance on government grants to support it.
40. Speaking in 1989 (at the Annual General Meeting), John Blake described the strategy in these terms.
41. Arundel Research Corporation (New Mexico), 'Survey of the operations of the Town and Country Planning Association', August 1981, p. 1.
42. *Ibid.*, pp. 1–2.
43. TCPA Annual Report for 1988. The organizations in which the TCPA was formally represented were the Association of Community Technical Aid Centres, Community Technical Aid Centre, Council for Environmental Education, Divis Planning Group, Environment Council, European Environmental Bureau, Freedom of Information Campaign, Green Alliance, Habitat International Coalition, International Year of Shelter for the Homeless Trust and Overseas Group, Laird Enterprise Trust, Land Use Society, Lightmoor Council of Management, National Council of Voluntary Organisations, National Development Control Forum, Neighbourhood Initiatives Foundation, Planning Aid for

London, Poplars Working Group, RTPI Development Control Panel, Streetwork, Tidy Britain Group and Transport 2000.

44. Notably, these new arrangements include the formation of the Laird Enterprise Trust Association, the Neighbourhood Initiatives Foundation and Planning Aid for London.

8

CAMPAIGN PROFILES

The previous two chapters have shown that in the 1970s and 1980s the Association's activities were diversified to embrace a range of community-based or 'bottom up' initiatives. This shift in emphasis closely reflected changes in the role and status accorded to town and country planning amongst the public and politicians alike.

Participation and commuunity action shifted the balance between the professionals and the general public, and the TCPA saw a role for itself in facilitating the process. It was a populist role, and various activities were initiated. Of these, four are high-lighted in this chapter. There was, first of all, the education venture, based on the formation of an environmental education unit to spread a general message of environmental awareness and popular involvement, starting in schools and colleges. Secondly, there is the continuing story of planning aid, where professional advice and expertise is made available to assist the community to achieve its own goals. Thirdly, this period includes the evidence of an active role in public inquiries, with an eye on flaws in the democratic process as well as on the issues themselves. Finally, we have another continuing story in a revival of interest in starting new communities, an aspiration that dates back to the very formation of the Garden City Association in 1899.

ENVIRONMENTAL EDUCATION

> I must content myself by concluding in suitably old-fashioned terms with my view that environmental education is dynamite. (Maurice Ash, addressing the conference of the International Housing and Town Planning Federation, Liverpool, May 1972)

For most of the 1970s and into the 1980s environmental education marked an important area of activity for the Association. The roots of this initiative are to be found in the growing interest in the idea of public participation in planning in the 1960s, and in the commitment of a new Director.

Making the most of Skeffington

When the Labour Party was returned to office in 1964 Richard Crossman, appointed as Minister of Housing and Local Government, inherited a backlog of delays in the approval by central government of the development plans produced by local planning authorities. He appointed a Planning Advisory Group to report on ways in which the process of planning and the preparation of development plans could be hastened.

Pending changes in the structure of local government it was recommended to the Minister that a committee should advise the appropriate Ministries in England, Scotland and Wales, appointed in March 1968 'to consider and report on the best methods, including publicity, of securing the participation of the public at the formative stage in the making of development plans for their area.'[1] The Chairman of the Committee was the late Arthur Skeffington, a Labour Member of Parliament who was at the time Joint Parliamentary Secretary for the Ministry of Housing and Local Government. The importance of the Skeffington Report, *People and Planning*, delivered to the then Minister, Anthony Greenwood, and to his Scottish and Welsh equivalents, William Ross and George Thomas, in 1969, lay not so much in its recommendations, as in the way it legitimized the activities of local interest groups.

It had been all too easy in the past for planning committees to dismiss objectors to development plans as self-appointed guardians of the public interest responsible to no one but themselves. By contrast the Skeffington Report (illustrated by a well-known graphic artist, David Knight) was intended as a popular presentation of the right of the public to be heard. The point could not be missed that this was a government-sponsored document giving status to the efforts of a whole range of unofficial bodies to involve citizens in the planning process.

Among these 'unofficial bodies' was the TCPA. When David Hall was interviewed for the post of Director in 1967, after Wyndham Thomas had been appointed as General Manager of Peterborough New Town Development Corporation, the members of the Executive Committee were conscious of the need for someone who would maintain the stress on regional planning, but who would also steer the Association into new areas where planning was drifting.[2] A further theme quickly emerged, that of participation or public involvement.

Anticipating Skeffington's findings, the Association's National Conference in October 1968 took Planning for People as its theme and produced an enlarged double issue of its journal to explore the theme of Children and Planning. Introducing it, F. J. Osborn wrote that:

Specially inspiring is the evidence that the children themselves are taking a hand, not only in the study of towns and countryside, but in personal participation in works of improvement, and that so many devoted teachers realize the value of this both as a factor in present education and a promise for 'all our future'.[3]

The Skeffington Report, published in the summer of 1969, made specific educational proposals. Discussing the role of local authorities, it was observed that the same council would often be both local planning authority and local education authority, and it was consequently recommended:

> that where the authorities are the same, the closest possible liaison should be kept between these two departments in order that knowledge about the physical planning of the community may be made available as part of the outward-looking curriculum which has been recommended in several reports on education; where the authorities are different, liaison is even more important. Lessons on such subjects will come to life most vividly where children feel involved.[4]

The Committee was here touching upon a notorious characteristic of local government departments, shared with central government, the statutory undertakers, and indeed educational institutions: to be departmentalized is to be compartmentalized, and to work in isolation. There are not many examples at any level of government or of management generally where this issue has been effectively and permanently solved, however many sessions of liaison committees have been held. This pious Skeffington recommendation did, however, provide an official justification for an activity which several local authority planning departments adopted and have continued to this day: that of employing a member of staff specifically to work with teachers and schoolchildren. Several key figures in the TCPA's educational activities, for example Anne Armstrong and Graham Russell, were employed for just such a function.

The Report also urged that education about town planning should be 'part of the way in which all secondary schools make children conscious of their future civic duties,' that it should be 'part of the liberal and civic studies within places of further education,' and that the training of teachers should include 'a similar emphasis on civic studies, including the philosophy of town and country planning.'[5]

The phrasing of these recommendations invited the comment that whenever a social issue is perceived to be important, whether it might be road safety, sex education or race relations, the cry goes up that

the schools should do something about it, and should add indoctrination on this or that particular topic to their already overcrowded
curriculum. It also leads to the significant criticism that environmental education, while 'potentially a way of helping young people to
understand that human exploitation can also be effected through the
manipulation of spatial arrangements', could also become 'merely a
way of indoctrinating them into a belief in the need for planning and
planners.'[6]

Nevertheless, the Skeffington proposals and the evidence that led
to them enabled the newly appointed TCPA Director, David Hall, to
legitimize environmental education as a field where the Association
could make its mark and gain support. He convened two meetings in
November 1969 and May 1970 to bring together key figures in the
world of environmental education to discuss the contribution that the
Association could make. Several of the people attending were subsequently to make important contributions to the Association's incursions into the world of education.[7] It was emphasized that, even
though Britian was one of the most urbanized of all nations, environmental education had an automatic rural bias, and that the particular
focus of any activities by the TCPA should be to establish the claim of
the urban environment as an area for local school investigation.

There were thus, it was concluded, three aspects of a useful role in
education. One was the publication of an education bulletin and of
teaching materials, another was the creation of town trails similar to
the nature trails already in being in the countryside, and a third,
argued by David Hall and Keith Wheeler, was the hope that the
Association could eventually 'sponsor the setting up of an urban field
centre for use by schools.'[8]

An analysis made by the Association's then information officer,
Pat Blake, showed a continuing rise in the volume of inquiries
received from teachers and students in schools and colleges, not only
about the new towns, a topic on which the TCPA was, almost by
tradition, considered the best source of information, but on every
kind of urban issue: housing and redevelopment, transport, conservation, the inner city and changes in employment patterns.

The Educational Beehive

Armed with the Skeffington recommendations, the opinions of the
educators and the evidence of a growing demand for guidance and
sources of information, the Association sought funding for the first
two years of an environmental education unit, and this was obtained
by a grant from the Joseph Rowntree Memorial Trust and the
Elmgrant Trust (one of the charitable undertakings of the Dartington
Hall trustees). It was assumed that the education unit would become

self-supporting after two years. The successful applicants for the task were Colin Ward and Anthony Fyson, both of them teachers in inner London. Both, literally, left the classroom on a Friday in the Spring of 1971, and started work at the TCPA on the following Monday. This was the day when the Association opened its new offices in Carlton House Terrace after many years in King Street, Covent Garden. In the intervening weekend, they had been helped by members of the Executive Committee to fix carpets and arrange furniture.

The education officers had the kind of mixed experience their new employers thought desirable. Before training as a teacher, Ward had worked for many years for several firms of architects and planners. Fyson, a geographer, had worked as a planner for an inner London local authority, before teaching in a new town and in central London. They had a further advantage. Both were political radicals but could not be identified with any political party. Fyson had been a VSO volunteer in Fiji and was active in his local environmental pressure group. Ward had edited the monthly *Anarchy* from his kitchen table all through the 1960s.[9] Both were harbingers, and perhaps were appointed as such, of a change in the TCPA climate in the 1970s.

Eight years later Maurice Ash was to write:

> But, even so, how could he [Ward] have reconciled his views to those of planners, who presumably believed in centralism and that Big Brother knows best? For, make no mistake, Colin never changed his views. Indeed, he advanced them more effectively . . . But I do believe that Colin's impact upon the thinking of the TCPA has been considerably and entirely beneficial. In reality, I suspect Colin Ward never had any difficulty in reconciling his point of view with that of the TCPA . . . Social engineering is not enough, and planning has dangerously overreached itself in supposing that it is. Thank you, Colin, for showing us that our seeds were otherwise![10]

On the day that the education duo started work, a one-time clerical employee of the Association, Rose Tanner, who at the time worked for the pacifist weekly *Peace News*, called in to see old friends, and was instantly drawn back into TCPA activities as the secretary of the education unit, then as assistant education officer, returning as bookshop manager and then as editor of the *Planning Bulletin*. She was not the only member of the TCPA staff to return continually over many years as funds became available. Industrial psychologists use phrases like 'the span of autonomous decision-making' to describe the satisfaction of such jobs.

Ward and Fyson had no doubts about this satisfaction. They had planned during the previous term to produce a monthly *Bulletin of Environmental Education* (*BEE*), the first issue of which would be sent to every secondary school in Britain and to all teacher-training institutions. It would be in a humble, loose-leaf, build-it-up-yourself, format, as a basis for informed urban environmental teaching.[11] Their approach had to be circumspect since there were already several organizations among teachers in this field. Quite apart from recently established bodies concerned with General Studies and Liberal Studies, there were well-founded organizations like the Geographical Association and the Historical Association. The National Association for Environmental Education had evolved from the Rural Studies Association, a body founded at the time when it was regretted that the rural school so seldom recognized rural interests and the prospect of rural employment in its curriculum. It has been painstakingly prodded forward into a broader view of the environment by a handful of dedicated teachers.[12] The then Society of Environmental Education had recently been founded by another group of teachers and teacher-trainers, anxious to redress the anti-urban bias. It eventually wound itself up, but not before its key figures had become valuable friends of the new TCPA initiative and had renewed the life of yet another existing body, the Council for Environmental Education, which had been founded as a coordinating organization at the time of the 'Countryside in 1970' Conference, and which fulfils this role to this day.[13]

In this specialized world, and to the confusion of the uncommitted teacher, *BEE* was barging into the territory of a whole series of initials: NAEE, SEE and CEE. Could it possibly have any distinctive role of its own?

The approach of the TCPA's education unit, while not contradicting that of any other organization or group addressing itself to teachers, had several distinctive features. The first was the claim that environmental education was not a subject, but an aspect of every subject in the school curriculum. Some teachers had worked for years to develop 'O' and 'A' level examinations in Environmental Studies, in the belief that to gain general acceptance in the subject status race, it was necessary to have an 'academic top'. Ward and Fyson claimed that only a handful of pupils would sit for such an examination and that it was more important to stress the environmental aspects of every subject on the timetable, 'from RE to PE' as they used to say.

The second was the insistence on what became known as an *issue-based* approach:

Years of work in this field have confirmed our original conviction that our task was *not* to encourage teachers to give lessons on the principles of town and country planning, or the legislative basis governing their application, but to encourage education for mastery of the environment, aiming at a situation where the skills to manipulate the environment are accessible to all people, not merely to an articulate minority. If the aim of environmental education is not to make children the masters of their environment, what else can it be for?[14]

In the search for an approach to the environment which really engages the ordinary child in school it was normal to advocate a study of the locality as the starting point. But in the very first issue of *BEE*, Michael Storm remarked that there was no other area of the school curriculum with such a gap between universally accepted policy and actual practice, and no area which so readily produced an inevitable disillusionment for the teacher. He continued:

Despite a considerable experience of orthodox 'local study' in history, geography and social studies, pupils are ill-equipped to understand the *processes* at work in their society, affecting their environment. The treatment of local themes in such a way as to interest young people requires much thought, much preparation – and a degree of sophistication which is often lacking. Quantities of information, whether presented didactically or 'discovered' by field observation or from local documentary sources, are not sufficient to guarantee effective 'involvement'. Too often, it appears, programmes of local study set out to deal with the question: 'what should people know about their locality?' An apparently minor alteration of this question to *'what issues are currently alive in this area?'* would in fact occasion a complete reconsideration of the programme. In the first place, this question implies that there could be no standard approach or content to local studies, since themes will vary according to locality. Yet wherever the school is situated, a problem-oriented approach to local study is possible.[15]

The same point was made in the content of political education by Bernard Crick, who declared that 'Civic education must be aimed at creating citizens. If we want a passive population, leave well alone.' He was arguing for the need in school to accept conflict and to avoid presenting *the* system and *the* consensus as some kind of universal truth:

If politics is the recognition and tolerance of diversity, so must be a political or civic education . . . To stress deliberately 'what we have in common' and to underplay differences is both a false account of politics and a cripplingly dull basis for a political education.

'Consensus' is not something to be invoked like spiritual cement to stick together something that would otherwise be broken apart; it is, on the contrary, a quality which arises to ease the continued co-existence of those who have been living together. It is not prior to the experience of a political community; it is a product of that experience, and therefore cannot be meaningfully taught until a person understands however generally and simply, the actual political problems and controversies of his or her community.[16]

Ward and Fyson, and the growing band of contributors to *BEE*, seized upon statements of this kind for several reasons. An approach based on the acceptance of conflict was closer to the realities of town and country planning than one which assumed that environmental decision-making was a question of professional expertise with an assenting public relying on a consensus that denied the existence of land-use conflicts. At the same time such an approach laid to rest the often-expressed fears that the classroom would be used for the indoctrination of one particular attitude to the politics of planning. Most important of all, the 'issue-based' stance called for active learning rather than passive teaching, and consequently for a different *style* of teaching and learning.

The Association's educational activities were, in this respect, riding the crest of the wave of educational innovation that marked the 1960s, in a climate immeasurably more buoyant and self-confident than that of subsequent decades. Apart from the experiments, both in teaching methods and in the curriculum itself, undertaken by individual teachers and schools and by the subject associations, the body called the Schools Council for Curriculum and Examinations (funded jointly by local education authorities and by central government, but independent of both) had promoted a whole series of curriculum development projects, some of which were highly relevant to the TCPA's approach. The Humanities Curriculum Project introduced a teaching method based on the pupils' examination and discussion of 'evidence' with the teacher adopting the role of a neutral chairman: while the Integrated Humanities Project sought to end the separation into 'subjects' of history, geography and language in the early years of secondary education. For the later years and examinations the History Project advocated modules of local history, world history and a specialized topic like the history of technology or medicine. It also involved the direct examination and evaluation of 'evidence', and the development of 'empathy'. Its recommendations live on in the requirements of the GCSE examinations introduced in the late 1980s. The same is true of the very influential Geography for the Young School Leaver project.[17]

These apparently 'official' initiatives strengthened the hand of the individual teacher in school, and there were at the same time un-official trends that favoured the *BEE* approach. One was the move-ment subsequently known as 'de-schooling' that led groups of former teachers to set up 'free' schools or 'alternative' schools with a strong emphasis on the use of the local environment itself as a teaching resource.[18] The other was a growing environmental consciousness in its several forms: consciousness of the crisis of consumption, energy, resources and pollution, realization of the errors of the housing and planning policies of the previous decades, and a belief that environ-mental responsibility was a personal and social, as well as a govern-mental and professional concern. All these factors guaranteed a band of allies in schools and teachers' colleges, and a very warm welcome for *BEE* in the educational, general and specialist press. '*BEE* asks sharp, probing questions', noted *The Times*, and *The Daily Telegraph* saw it as 'an apt reminder that environment, as Lord Butler would say, is the art of the possible'. *The Guardian* saw it as 'certainly the best teaching resource material available in this field. It has a rare quality in not only reducing the academic eco-jargon to simple understandable terms, but also in providing a wealth of ideas and practical *action* material on a range of topics from making "town trails" to "How to cope with a cyanide disposal problem",' and *The Sunday Times* found it '. . . a jolly broadsheet full of ideas. Children taught by teachers who read *BEE* could find themselves doing anything from following town trails, cataloguing the effects of a new motorway on the local environment, to putting their town planners on open trial'.[19]

Streetwork and Town Trails

Access and direct involvement were at the heart of the new approach:

> The emotional contact with poverty, unhappiness and general
> dissatisfaction with which urban studies pupils are inevitably
> confronted seems barely represented by the bland and curious
> phrase 'urban fieldwork', and I propose 'streetwork' in its place
> – suggestive I hope of the kind of community involvement
> already aimed at in the *avant-garde* theatrical world through
> 'street theatre'.[20]

The useful word that Anthony Fyson coined epitomized the central thrust of the education unit's activity. It was adopted as the title of the book the education officers wrote for teachers about their experience and the techniques they recommended. It was also adopted as the name of the organization that took over the publication of *BEE* when

The Education Unit advocated 'streetwork', the urban equivalent of fieldwork. Here children from Princess May Primary School, Stoke Newington, explore the local environment.

the TCPA relinquished it. Fyson himself wrote a book for pupils called *Change the Street*, which began with the explanation:

> This book is about streets and about the people who live in them. It is not about *important* streets, not about *famous* buildings; it is about the kind of streets most of us live in, the streets we use all our lives, and what happens to them makes a difference to us. For this reason we should show more interest in the kind of streets we have. You may not feel very concerned about such things but you can be sure that even if you pay no attention to what is happening in your district, others will. And they are likely to be people who will shape the environment in which you live for their own purposes and goals. These may not be yours. *Don't let them get away with it!*[21]

His encouragement to readers to make use of their streets was calculated. One entire issue of *BEE* was a manual, produced in collaboraton with Community Service Volunteers, on how to organize a carnival.[22] The classroom equivalent of these techniques for securing active involvement and participation, is improvised drama, role-playing exercises, simulations and academic games. Often the secret was to oblige participants to adopt a role which was the opposite of their stance in real life.[23] *BEE* provided a forum for teachers, over a wide subject spread, involved in devising this kind of activity. At the same time, Tony Gibson of Nottingham University School of Education was experimenting with primary and secondary school pupils and with local community groups to develop materials and techniques that could make residents' participation in neighbourhood planning effective.[24] Some years later he was using his 'Planning for Real' techniques at the TCPA's Lightmoor and Birkenhead projects.

Keith Wheeler, meanwhile, was developing the first educational town trail. Nature trails were burgeoning, and there were, of course, guided tourist walks which almost universally ignored or deplored twentieth-century aspects of towns as well as the sensory aspects of our perceptions of the environment. Like Ward, he looked back to the inspiration of one of the earliest supporters of the Garden City Association, the Scottish biologist Patrick Geddes.

Geddes, Wheeler explained,

> must be regarded as the founding father of environmental education. He wanted teaching to be centred round, as he called it, 'heart, hand, and head, the three H's', and not the 'three R's'. He therefore developed an occupational approach to learning, not as vocational training, but to further the growth of the whole personality by taking part in the work of farmer, fisherman, explorer, and so on. He eschewed competitive learning which he believed only added fuel to the warring capitalist world. He wrote: 'Education must be transmuted into growth-helping, and all teaching must begin with: Look and see, and then go on to: find out and do'. Geddes insisted on the relationship between education and environment, not only because it was in the real world of place, work and society that the young human obtained a proper education, but also because an understanding and sympathy for environment would lead to an improvement of the environment.[25]

With his colleague Bryan Waites, and with the help of Konrad Smigielski, then Leicester's City Planning Officer, and Gerald Mitchell of the Planning Department, Wheeler produced the Leicester Town Trail, published as a special number of *BEE*, and several times reprinted. With its wealth of suggestions and its environmental appraisal sheet, this was immensely influential and was followed by literally hundreds of urban trails and led to a new level of sophistication in environmental interpretation.[26]

The TCPA issued Town Tracker badges for schools to dispense, and the emphasis was of course that pupils should construct their own local trails:

> Develop your Town Trail so as to study the floorscape; the street furniture; house facades; the plaques on walls. Search out the names of architects inscribed in half-hidden places; ascertain dates of buildings, collect strange patterns in brick or stone. Evaluate different ways of building houses, shops and offices; compare and contrast one group of buildings with another. Look for distant and unexpected views in the urban landscape . . . Include within your Trail the chance of experiencing a wide range of environmental 'stimuli'. For instance, listen for characteristic street noises; take part in open-air activities like a market or procession; breathe in the air and take note of the variety of smells that can be experienced.[27]

The propagation of learning experiences like these in *BEE*, together with the innumerable visits to schools, colleges and conferences by the education staff, put the TCPA at the centre of a network of people exploring new approaches to environmental education, interpretation and action. There was, for example, Brian Goodey (then of the Centre for Urban and Regional Studies at Birmingham, later of Oxford Polytechnic), a geographer who almost singlehandedly had introduced into planning education in Britain the American developments in perception studies and cognitive mapping typified by the work of Kevin Lynch,[28] and who now had the chance to pursue the same themes with school teachers. There was a wide range of teachers already exploring the use pupils could make of cameras and cassette records in interpreting the environment. Tony Francombe of Milton Keynes and Gordon Boon of Wolverhampton were examples, while Bill Pick of Leeds was using similar techniques to examine children's own environmental perceptions and preferences.[29] The architect Jeff Bishop (then of Kingston Polytechnic, later of the School for Advanced Urban Studies in Bristol), besides his work in the field of environmental psychology, was exploring in primary and secondary schools techniques by which children could become environmental designers, thinking in three dimensions.[30]

BEE had become a forum for this range of new, experimental and active approaches, and the means by which, once a month, accounts of 'How we did it' were put into the hands of subscribing schools.

They fitted together into an attitude that Patrick Geddes would have understood in the earlier years of the TCPA, since 'He anticipated by some fifty years the idea that the average citizen has something positive to contribute towards the improvement of his environment. Geddes was convinced that each generation had the right to build their own aspirations into the fabric of their town. In order to achieve this a basis of civic understanding had to be created through education. Geddes canvassed schools, societies, and associations and attempted to draw them into making surveys and plans of their locality; creating play-spaces, planting trees, and painting buildings. He seized on any vehicle to expose people to situations in which they had to make judgements.'[31] The most forthright statement of this position in *BEE* came from a much-reprinted article by Simon Nicholson, arguing for an environment of 'loose parts' susceptible to rearrangement and redesign by its citizens, and resenting that the creative urge had been hijacked as their own preserve by the professionals: 'Creativity is for the gifted few: the rest of us are compelled to live in the environments constructed by the gifted few, listen to the gifted few's music, use the gifted few's inventions and art, and read the poems, fantasies and plays by the gifted few. This is what our education and culture conditions us to believe, and this is a culturally induced and perpetuated lie.'[32]

The Urban Study Centre Movement

It was Tony Fyson who first explored the idea that the TCPA should sponsor the setting up of an urban field centre for use by schools. There had, in fact, been an explosion of rural centres, thanks to the activities of the Field Studies Council. They were run, not only by that Council but by bodies like the Youth Hostels Association, and increasingly by local education authorities and by individual urban schools. They were praised for a dozen reasons and their existence had succeeded, where earlier arguments had failed, in making fieldwork an examination requirement in school examinations. Fyson found that the Field Studies Council itself had considered and rejected the idea of an urban study centre on account of its cost as long ago as 1955,[33] but that a London teacher trainer, John Higson, was again urging the establishment of such a centre. They joined forces to set up a Council for Urban Studies Centres with a remarkable list of 'the good and the great as members'.[34]

Slowly, urban studies centres were started. They were very different in their origins and activities. Some arose from the work of local education authorities' advisers; some from finding a new use for a preserved building without a function; and some came from local environmental bodies, linked with Heritage Centres for visitors. The one closest to the hearts of the Association's education unit, fulfilling the dreams of the advocates, was and remains the Notting Dale Urban Studies Centre in West London. Its success was, paradoxically, a result of its absolute independence, a result of its origins with Harrow School. In the late nineteenth century that school, like other 'public' schools and university colleges, had established a foothold in poverty-stricken urban areas by establishing a boys' club. In the totally changed atmosphere of the 1970s, the sale of an unused sports ground in suburban Wembley enabled the then Head of Economics at Harrow, John Rees, to offer a job and funding to whoever would take on the task of setting up the Notting Dale Urban Studies Centre.[35]

The job went to Chris Webb, a former London teacher (and now Chief Education Officer for Islington), and he initiated a variety of activities which fulfilled every hope that the TCPA had expressed. Local and visiting school children explored the area, with its broken-down streets and desolate tower blocks, and formulated recommendations. These were sometimes acted upon and the Urban Studies Centre became the focus and instigator of neighbourhood change. It retained, of course, its function as a resource for local and visiting schools, and the same has been true of the dozens of urban studies centres up and down Britain. In the continually constrained educational climate of the 1980s they had to argue and cajole local authorities and funding bodies in order to survive, and have done so with more tenacity than well-wishers dared to expect. The administrative costs of the Council for Urban Studies Centres were initially met by the Elmgrant Trust and subsequently by a small annual grant from the sum set aside by the Department of the Environment for the support of unofficial bodies. The Council's progress has been recorded in a series of reports[36] and there was a time at the end of the 1970s when it seemed that official support for urban studies centres would be forthcoming, since a study commissioned by the Environmental Board recommended that the Department of the Environment should itself fund a sample selection of urban studies centres.[37] The Environmental Board was wound up by the incoming government in 1979, and the Department of Education and Science has never shown an inclination to provide any grant aid to urban studies centres. Yet when Her Majesty's Inspectorate visited some of the forty-one such centres in the 1980s they found them to be 'providing a valuable service in education in enhancing understanding and concern about the urban environment' and commented that there was also 'a need for some more permanent basis for funding and hence staffing.'[38] The same issue was to plague the Association's educational activities.

Art and the Built Environment

Ward and Fyson were continually involved in addressing meetings, seminars and 'workshops' of teachers, and one Saturday morning Ward found himself addressing a course for art teachers at West Dean in Sussex, an invitation accepted simply because he had an idle curiosity about the house, left to the nation by Edward James, patron of the surrealists in the 1930s. Unknown to him at the time, his audience included Ernest Goodman, headmaster of the Manchester

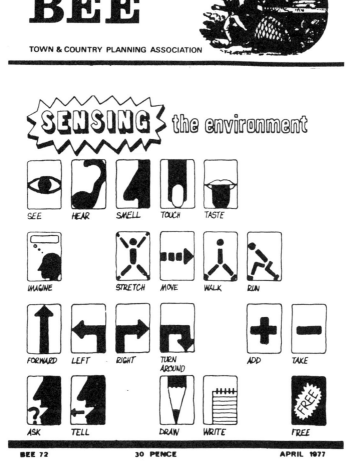

The TCPA/Schools Council project, Art and the Built Environment, reached hundreds of schools with a sensory approach to the neighbourhood. Brian Goodey wrote *Sensing the Environment* as an issue of *BEE*.

High School of Art and Ralph Jeffrey, one of Her Majesty's Inspectors for Art. He was subsequently approached with the suggestion that he should propose to the Schools Council a curriculum development project with the title 'Art and the Built Environment'.

The idea was instantly adopted by the TCPA. Not only would it pay part of the education unit's salary costs, but it was also an absolute vindication of its non-subject-bound approach to the environment, built around individual pupil perceptions that had always been advocated by the Association's education staff. A proposal was made, and wound its way through the hierarchy of committees in the Schools Council for a two-year project to be called Art and the Built Environment which aimed, through using trial methods and materials in a group of 'trial schools':

a) to enlarge the students' environmental perception and enable them to develop a 'feel' for the built environment;
b) to enhance their capacity for discrimination and their competence in the visual appraisal of the built environment;
c) to evolve generally applicable techniques and materials for achieving these aims;
d) to disseminate these in a form suitable for teacher training and guidance.[39]

The project was to be directed part-time by Ward and the project officer, seconded by the ILEA to the TCPA, was Eileen Adams, Deputy Head of Art at Pimlico School in London. She was the obvious choice since she had developed there the Front Door project, an environmental exploration instigated by Ken Baynes, Head of the Design Education Unit at the Royal College of Art,[40] which had been the basis of a series of 'radio-vision' programmes devised for the Schools Broadcasting Council by Colin Ward.[41] *BEE* was the vehicle for disseminating the project, and once again the leaders in the field produced special issues which would serve as manuals for teachers in the schools officially taking part in the project, but which would at the same time draw in teachers, whatever their subject, wherever *BEE* was read.[42] An independent evaluation commissioned by the Schools Council showed that, by the Council's standards, it was remarkably successful,[43] and it was extended by a further year (1978–79) at the TCPA and was then taken over by the Royal College of Art (1980–82). When the teachers' handbook associated with the project was eventually published Eileen Adams and Colin Ward felt able to claim that the approach it propagated had become 'a self-perpetuating activity involving students and teachers in working with architects and planners and with the direct support of local education authorities and the design professions.'[44]

This remains true, but by the time the Schools Council project was coming to an end, when it was expected that the work in schools would take on its own momentum, which it did, the climate of education was changing. When the project finally ended in July 1982 a concluding three-day summer school, conference and exhibition was held at the Royal College of Art. This was the very month when the TCPA severed its connections with its education unit, and when the government announced its intention of closing down the Schools Council. In a long speech Colin Ward evoked the sentiments of another early supporter of the Association, the architect William Richard Lethaby, who was the founding principal of the Central School of Arts and Crafts and was the first professor of design at the Royal College of Art:

Lethaby did have a remark to offer us in our present dilemmas. In 1916, in the middle of the First World War, he gave a lecture on Town Tidying, which has stayed with me ever since I first read it in the middle of the Second World War. Lethaby said, 'For the earlier part of my life I was quieted by being told that ours was the richest country in the world, until I woke up to know that what I meant by riches was learning and beauty, and music and art, coffee and omelettes; perhaps in the coming days of poverty we may get more of these.' I know this sentence by heart and I repeat it to myself whenever I hear any politician of right or left talking about education. The cry has been going up for years, 'back to basics', implying that the collapse of British manufacturing industry is a result of this educational sabotage. Basic things for me are what they were for Lethaby: learning and beauty, and music and art, coffee and omelettes . . .

I am much more worried about the profoundly anti-educational atmosphere that surrounds the young than I am by cuts in the expansion of educational spending. Part of the reason is that in the boom decades after the war, education and the rewards it brings, were oversold. Every additional bit of expenditure, every increase in student numbers at the upper and more expensive end of the system, every new development in educational technology, was a step towards some great social goal, and would yield results all round. But it has not delivered the goods . . . But every contracting industry has its casualties. The Art and the Built Environment project began its life, not in an academic organisation, but in the education unit of a poverty-stricken voluntary organisation, the Town and Country Planning Association. This very month, the TCPA has felt obliged to cut the umbilical cord of its education unit and its journal *BEE*, and they are starting a new life of their own as *Streetwork*. I hope that teachers who have valued *BEE* will continue to support it. And the Schools Council itself has received its death sentence. Well, so what? you might ask, and I too, have been one of its innumerable critics. But what the Schools Council did was to buy a little *time* for an essentially time-consuming activity – the dissemination of ideas and methods which were there already, in and out of school, among wider circles of teachers . . .[45]

A Change in the Climate

. . . financial problems forced the Association to make Anne Armstrong, Liz Hurst and Graham Russell – the staff of the Education Unit – redundant in the middle of 1982 . . . The decision to end the work of the Education Unit within the TCPA was a hard one to take and the support for the work of the unit from other bodies in the field of environmental education was very apparent. It is no exaggeration to say that there would not have been the development of urban environment education that there has been in this country but for the Association's work in this field. (TCPA *Annual Report,* 1983)

In 1979 contributors to the hundredth issue of *BEE* stressed that its influence was more than local. An American high school teacher was reported as saying that 'The only way we get any ideas in environmental education is to look at *BEE* when it comes out' and tribute was paid to the work of Anthony Fyson and Keith Wheeler through bodies like the Council of Europe and United Nations agencies in ensuring that 'one of *BEE*'s biggest successes has been in encouraging and directing the development of environmental education in Europe.'[46] Editorial comment was less euphoric. It referred to 'the astronomic rise in printing and postal costs since we first put *BEE* on the market', and to the effect of cuts in educational spending which were already manifest in the mid-1970s: 'Our circulation is no longer increasing. Every downturn in educational expenditure has its effect on our subscription list and there aren't any upturns. Often the decision to continue or abandon a subscription rests with a hard-pressed school librarian who has to make invidious choices among the commercially produced and the hopelessly uncommercial journals which the school buys.'[47]

That year Colin Ward left the TCPA to become a full-time writer and in the following year Anthony Fyson left to become Director of the Centre for Environmental Interpretation in Manchester and subsequently Editor of *The Planner*, while Rose Tanner became manager of the TCPA bookshop. The work of the Education Unit was taken over by one full-time worker, Liz Hurst and two part-timers, Anne Armstrong and Graham Russell, who were also employed as education liaison workers in local authority planning departments. As the economic climate worsened both for the TCPA and schools in the 1980s, the three staff members as well as three placements funded by the Manpower Services Commission were made redundant. To ease this painful situation a small grant was obtained to set up a new charity, Streetwork Ltd, based at the Notting Dale Urban Studies Centre, funding for the Council for Urban Studies Centres having been obtained by the TCPA from the DOE for the last time, and the work of running it contracted out to its former staff now forming Streetwork. Both sides tried to make the best of this messy separation.[48]

The Association's involvement in environmental education at school level had come to an end. Asked about the implications of this, several years later, Anthony Fyson said:

When we started work in 1971, Colin and I asked each other how long it would last (for while the *BEE* could be self-supporting, there was really no way that it could also pay the wages). We agreed that seven years was a realistic timespan. The truth is that it's much easier to set something in motion than to keep up the hard work. We were travelling endlessly, at a local, national, and in my case, international level. This was both time-consuming and expensive. The important thing is that everything we initiated still exists, in the worst possible education climate.[49]

Ward's views were similar. In 1975, long before the advent of the Thatcher government, he wrote in *BEE*:

In March the Council for Urban Studies Centres convened a conference, largely for local government officers in education and planning departments, with the aim of refuelling the campaign to get such centres started. Now anyone with the slightest degree of cynicism in their nature would say that a worse time to call such a conference could not be imagined . . . Education departments (as *BEE* knows to its cost) have been desperately looking for little luxuries to cut out of their budgets . . . If we are moving towards a poor Britain (actually of course we are fantastically rich) then environmental education, however, we define it, is going to be one of those things that will still expand and grow. The environment is so rich as an educational resource that we can no longer neglect to make use of it.[50]

Fourteen years later his view was that 'Everything we started still exists, simply because we were the vehicles for a few good and educationally sound ideas: town trails, urban studies centres, CUSC and *BEE* are all still alive. I'm just sorry that they aren't still bringing credit and invisible earnings to the TCPA. But I do feel that Tony and Rose and I helped move the Association's outlook towards a popular and populist stance.'[51]

PLANNING AID

In spite of all the efforts to make public consultation an effective part of the planning process, most people feel that their influence on plans for the future, even on very local matters, is very marginal. (TCPA, *A New Prospectus: Policy direction for the next twenty years*, 1984, p. 3)

The 'popular and populist' stance of the TCPA that Colin Ward and others contributed to was further strengthened by the parallel initiative of planning aid. As with environmental education, planning aid had its origins amongst the changing perspectives of the 1960s.

For all the interest amongst politicians and professionals in rational methods of planning and government in that decade, and a continuing belief in science and technology to win the day, it was in the 1960s that the lie was called. Certainly, in the field of town and country planning, the mood of certainty that had surrounded plan-making in the immediate postwar period was shown to be ill-founded. The idea of rational planning was one thing, but the real test was whether or not it actually 'delivered'. A consensus in planning could last for only as long as the 'planned' could see benefits arising out of the process. And in the 1960s (as shown in Chapter 5) – in the face of a growing perception that planning was not simply failing to eradicate deprivation in the city, but was actually, in some cases, adding to local problems – doubts turned to anger. No longer were ordinary people, the so-called 'non experts', prepared to sit back and let the professionals and politicians make all the running. For the future, planning was to be more participatory.

Questioning outcomes also served to expose the highly political nature of the process. Far from being neutral, critics pointed to the layers of values and preferences that surrounded particular decisions and schemes; the idea that there were winners and losers in the planning process rapidly became a part of the conventional wisdom. The Skeffington Report fuelled the debate with its tacit acknowledgement of a plurality of interests, and the need to close the political gap that had opened up between planners and planned – hence the general thrust of the report in favour of participation.

Interestingly, the Association was attached to both the 'old' and the 'new' approaches. It had over the years identified closely with traditional methods of rational planning, yet it had also consistently championed the interests of those who stood to gain most from environmental improvements. Strains of Fabian orthodoxy, with its reliance on the State as the main agent of change, were mixed with the radicalism of liberal causes and a belief in individuals and communities to force the pace of reform.

In fact, the Association, sensing a change in the wind, was keen to provide evidence to the Skeffington Committee, favouring a more open and participative approach, and in due course welcoming the publication of the report in 1969. With a sense of history and new opportunities, it was ready to embrace an approach to planning that was later described by one of its officers as a 'popular movement leading to people taking direct action to control and transform their surroundings.'[52]

The arrival of David Hall as the TCPA's new Director in 1967 coincided with the beginning of a process of 'quiet, respectable radicalization',[53] with younger people joining the policy-making Executive and with closer links created with community groups. Such changes were timely, for in the aftermath of Skeffington the crucial question was no longer one of *whether* the public should be involved in planning but rather one of *how*.[54] It was within this context that the idea of planning aid was explored.

The term *planning aid* was itself an American import, where it had been introduced as one concept amongst many in the flowering of community movements towards the end of the 1960s. Deschooling, local rights centres, community work and advocacy planning were different manifestations of a new style of grassroots activism that was becoming more evident in American cities. Particularly in the heady days of 1968 such activities were part of a counter-culture, challenging not simply the rights of professionals to tell others what to do but also the very legitimacy of the State. 'Power for the people' was the new urban watchword.

According to David Lock, planning aid was first seriously discussed in this country at a crowded meeting in the TCPA's offices (then in King Street, Covent Garden):

It was in 1969 and the discussion had been focusing on practical problems facing the public who wished to participate in the planning process, particularly in the context of public inquiries. Someone referred to the legal aid system and said that what was needed in planning was some kind of planning aid, principally to ensure that money was available to groups that wished to take part in such inquiries.[55]

In contrast, the existing system of providing assistance to people affected by planning issues was piecemeal, relying as it did on a variety of bodies for which this was not their primary task.[56] Local authority planning departments, the National Council for Social Service, Councils for Voluntary Service, the Civic Trust, Citizens' Advice Bureaux and Law Centres all played a part, but all within limits.[57] Additionally, the TCPA itself continued to offer an Information Service (something it had done from its earliest days as a campaigning body), but this was under pressure in the face of a growing volume of demand for advice and information from the public.

A case existed for something along the lines of planning aid, and, given its radical overtones, it is interesting to note that the case was very soon to be taken up by a future President of the Royal Town Planning Institute, Jim Amos.[58] For Amos (with direct experience of inner-city problems as Liverpool's City Planning Officer) planning aid should be an enabling service that would 'help the inarticulate, disorganised and disadvantaged groups in the community to claim their rightful place in the planning process. . . .'[59]

Amos returned to the theme in 1971, this time in his presidential address to the RTPI:

It would do much to make the planning process more democratic and sensitive to its effects if a free planning advice service could be made available to those most in need.[60]

In spite of Amos's personal commitment, it was to be the TCPA which was to turn the idea into reality when, in 1972, it decided to incorporate its Information Service within a more far-reaching Planning Aid Service. Initially, it was anticipated that the latter would deal specifically with enquiries and requests coming directly out of the workings of the planning process. When the Association's Information Officer left the organization, the opportunity was taken to create a new post of Planning Aid Officer. David Lock was appointed to the post in November 1972, and the new service opened for business in January 1973.

Pioneering Planning Aid

The brief of the Planning Aid Officer was to give information to those who requested it on all aspects of planning, to give advice on the practicalities of organizing community groups, and to make full use of existing opportunities for public involvement in the planning process. Lock was joined later in 1973 by a second member of the unit, Angela MacKeith.

Initially, the Planning Aid and Environmental Education units shared the same room at Carlton House Terrace; both were pioneering experiments and gained from this proximity and exchange of ideas and early experience. Together they represented the main thrust of the Association's new populist approach.

The launch of the unit was well-publicized nationally, and within months some 2,500 leaflets had been mailed to carefully targeted group like Citizens' Advice Bureaux, community action group leaders, local politicians, planners and social workers. The leaflet attracted 'a great many letters and phone calls to the Planning Aid Officer,'[61] suggesting that planning aid was indeed filling a perceived gap.

In spite of this early volume of activity, the theory and practice of planning aid was still at a formative stage, with at least three possible models in currency. One was that of advocacy planning (favoured amongst activists at the time in the United States), relying as it did on the altruism of volunteer planners to identify and commit themselves to a group's cause rather than simply to provide technical advice. A second model (more favoured by the RTPI) was based on the example of legal aid, with the aim of increasing access to professional expertise.[62] Finally, there was the less circumscribed model of 'bottom up' planning, which sought not merely to involve but also to empower communities to participate in decisions affecting their everyday lives.

Inevitably, with so much in the melting pot, much of the early work of the TCPA unit was marked by a degree of pragmatism. It was, partly at least, a question of getting involved, and then of reflecting and learning from experience. A measure of involvement is that of the number of cases handled by the unit – some 700 in its first year, doubling in 1974 and thereafter remaining fairly constant at about 1,000 cases each year until the end of the decade. Initially, a majority of cases arose from a variety of urban and inter-urban motorway projects, though within a year it was housing issues that headed the list.

Within the Association the unit had the dual advantage of relative independence combined with institutional support. David Lock was able to attend policy-making meetings, and thus to ensure that planning aid secured a place on the main agenda throughout the 1970s. Finance was provided by the Association itself, and through grant aid (renewable annually) from the Department of the Environment.[63] The uncertainty attached to the latter fuelled Lock's recollection of this period as one characterized by 'the stimulation of being perpetually broke.'[64]

By the end of its second year of operation, and in the light of experience gained to date, a new approach was developed. Lock decided on a strategy for the unit of prioritizing and encouraging the 'servicing of self-help, rather than acting as advocates in any capacity.' This strategy thus encouraged the making of networks and contacts with residents' and tenants' associations, in order to match their needs with the availability of skilled professionals. Networking was an important part of this process, not only to bring various groups into touch with professionals but also to mobilize as much support as possible from the latter. Partly through his own work and representation on the RTPI's own planning aid working party, Lock went to some lengths to secure 'bridge building with the profession'[65] and to seek to allay fears that the TCPA was undermining professional integrity.

In similar vein, it was also important to maintain good relations with planners in local authorities. Inevitably, however, there would be times when conflicts could not be reconciled:

> There were a lot of County Planning Officers sitting in the TCPA Executive or in the Council. They were very supportive of the service until, of course, we turned up on their patch to give planning advice. Then they were on the phone complaining to David Hall that we were stirring up trouble. There were several resignations from the Association because of the planning aid service we provided.[66]

The fact is that it was not easy to create a synthetic model of planning aid that met the needs of both practising planners and of community activists.[67] Planning aid remained at a formative stage, and, in any case, a degree of conflict is inherent in the process. Perhaps, though, at least the nature of planning aid that was being developed was becoming a little clearer. Clearly, within the Association the service offered accorded neither with an advocacy nor a legal aid role. Instead, it was inclining more towards a model of fostering community self-help and autonomy by the provision of planning information and education. This implied a tendency to move away from a client-based approach in which casework arose 'from all sorts of individual clients ringing up for planning aid as they would a plumber', and to focus instead on making available resources for those most in need.[68]

New Orientations

In 1975 Angela MacKeith left, to be replaced by Rob Cowan (who had previously worked at the Planning Exchange in Glasgow). In due course (in 1978), Cowan succeeded Lock as Planning Aid Officer and was to make his own distinctive contribution to an evolving model of aid. Cowan's arrival also coincided with an upsurge in community-based protests against a variety of inner-city development proposals. A notable example is that of a long and bitter campaign by local residents in opposition to plans to redevelop Tolmers Square, Euston. Another example is that of the unit's involvement in support of a campaign to prevent the redevelopment of a site at Moncrieff Street, Peckham, where the unit 'took action beyond giving advice' and drew the Association as a whole into a national campaign against prior demolition and unilateral property clearance.[69] As the next section of this chapter will show, it was also to be the response of the Planning Aid Unit to a call for assistance from a local group in opposition to British Nuclear Fuels at Windscale, which led not only to the Association's representation at a major public inquiry but, in turn, to the emergence of national energy policy as a key area of its work.

For Cowan, planning aid was not 'a dispassionate professional service [but] all the indications are that the most effective and significant planning aid work at present is being done by people who are committed to the cause for which they are providing help.'[70] He made the case for a more politicized model, 'because the various parties involved have different amounts of political and economic power.'[71] Only through redressing the effects of such imbalances could planning become a democratic activity.

This reinforcement of a move towards a more active involvement in community initiatives called for a 'multi-disciplinary approach to situations involving complex interrelations of people, problems and skills.'[72] It was a recognition that a range of professional skills needed to be available to help groups in particular campaigns. In spite of this commitment, Cowan recalls that:

> Overall, we were still helping far too much the well-articulated, well-resourced individuals and residents' associations. The inarticulate and the underprivileged needed it more, but we were not adequately resourced to provide this. We were spread extremely thin.[73]

Indeed, this and other features of the service provided by the unit[74] were revealed in a comprehensive evaluation commissioned in 1979 by the Department of the Environment.[75] An analysis of the case files showed that during the unit's first six years of operation it was not primarily serving the needs of less advantaged groups, but that its services were 'provided to those who were already reasonably well able to manipulate the system.'[76] There was also a marked geo-graphical concentration of cases in the South East, especially within

Greater London itself; and the number of cases in localities 'populated by lower socio-economic groups' was relatively small.[77]

In response to these findings, attempts were then made by the unit to encourage the formation of local planning aid groups in the provinces. By the late 1970s a number of such groups had been formed, most notably in Manchester and Birmingham, but also in Central Scotland, the North East and South Wales. The spread of planning aid in this way amounted to a vigorous programme of networking – setting up such groups in the first place and combining them into area networks. It had the overwhelming advantage of locating skills where they would be most needed, and where local knowledge was in itself an essential resource. This new approach also had implications for the nature of work in the London-based planning aid office. Now the emphasis was on putting people in touch with local experts rather than the core staff undertaking the casework itself. In this way the volume of work that was possible was greatly extended.

Following the election of the first Thatcher Administration in 1979, planning aid yet again took a fresh turn. A combination of anti-planning political rhetoric and a shift in powers from local to central government was matched by something of a local backlash in the form of a radical brand of municipal socialism. In particular, from 1981 until 1986 the Planning Aid Unit found allies especially amongst Labour councillors in the Greater London Council. Many of these councillors had themselves engaged in local community campaigns and were also sensitive to women's issues, racism and black unemployment. The Brixton riots of 1981 simply added to growing concerns about the plight of London inner-city neighbourhoods.

All of this had a significant impact on the workings of the Planning Aid Unit. In direct terms, the unit gained financially in 1982 through the award of a Greater London Council grant, used to set up a separate London Planning Aid Service. Indirectly, its position was strengthened by the supportive context of Britain's major municipality openly espousing policies of 'people's planning' and participatory democracy.

Thus, the record shows that in the early 1980s not only did planning aid become more aligned with community campaigns but also that its activities were increasingly located in London's inner-city areas. A combination of factors – including the effects of public spending cuts, and the introduction of the first of the Urban Development Corporations – contributed to a considerable increase in the demand for planning aid information and advice services. Over a ten-month period, from May 1981 to March 1982 some 1,500 cases were handled, of which more than 500 were from the Greater London area alone. Many of the latter were cases in areas of gentrification or were directly linked to the effects of economic recession. Factory closures, for instance, led, in turn, to a related decline in local services, in the private as well as public sectors. The London Docklands exemplified this process, with community protests directed not only towards the effects of closures but also against the influx of new uses for a higher-income market.

Requests for planning aid from residents, amenity and community groups in London were intensified, and the unit was commissioned to prepare reports and submissions for public inquiries, such as that in 1981 on the redevelopment of Hays Wharf. Other activities included a new brief for community education, with a number of courses prepared for local groups to provide information on the planning process. The unit also produced a number of leaflets, and assisted other organizations with their own publications. Its own *Planning Aid Newsletter* was concerned increasingly with issues such as community technical aid centres, self-build housing, planning aid and adult education, and inner-city issues in general.[78]

By the time that Cowan's period with the unit ended in 1982, the nature of planning aid had shifted still further along a political spectrum, away from simply giving advice and towards an active campaigning stance. The circumstances of the 1980s, as well as the predisposition of the activists, drew the unit increasingly into the realm of planning aid as a political process, working to redress the effects of inequalities in society and challenging the autonomy of professional power.

It is also interesting to note its changing role within the Association – through providing 'a constant touchstone' to show what was happening on the ground.[79] Planning aid was 'bottom up' planning personified, and issues like Windscale and Moncrieff Street bridged a wide gap between local and national networks. The unit therefore performed a valuable function in offering direct experience and in helping to refine the concept of 'bottom up' planning, to which the Association attached so much importance in this period.

Planning Aid goes Mobile

In spite of constant financial difficulties, by 1983 the unit was itself handling over 1,000 enquiries each year and, at the same time, coordinating the work of up to sixty volunteers in the field. New networks were formed, including the London Planning Aid Service, and the unit was also involved in the creation of an Association of Community Technical Aid Centres. In other cases, links were forged with regional branches of the RTPI.

Cowan left the unit in 1982, and, after a brief interregnum under Marc Dorfman, a new phase started with the appointment of Brian

Anson. Trained as an architect, Anson brought to the unit, in his own words, 'twenty years of community activism'.[80] He was soon joined by Mike Beazley, and together they formed the core of a group of 'Young Turks' calling for the TCPA to take more positive action 'to release latent local energy and initiative from the bottom up'.[81]

In Anson's view, the Planning Aid Unit was crucial to the TCPA's commitment to the task of increasing opportunities for individuals and communities to exert a real influence on decisions affecting their own environment. Thus, the role of the unit was seen to be one of community action, rather than one of providing information. It could not be:

> . . . run on a shoestring from the end of a telephone from an office in London. During the first decade of operation enquirers were helped to find their way through the maze of the planning system. But this gave little scope to change the system, to give communities greater decision-making power so that they wouldn't need planning aid.[82]

To some extent, Cowan had already led planning aid in this direction, but, working as a team, Anson and Beazley were determined to take it further. A hallmark of their approach was to break the metropolitan mould and to travel elsewhere in Britain 'looking for business':

> We mapped out all the enquiries the unit had received and there was an incredible bunching in the South East. We made the decision then to go outside that region.[83]

Over a nine-month period between September 1983 and May 1984 the pair travelled extensively around the country. New tactics were developed, like 'acting as a catalyst' and 'going into a place cold'. The former was based on a recognition that the main task was not necessarily to build a network 'but rather to act as a catalyst to enable the network to build itself;' the latter referred to arriving at a new location unannounced and building up contacts by 'operating at street level'.[84]

An important boost for the new approach was the purchase in May 1984 of a VW camper van for planning aid work:

> And with the idea of the van we began thinking of this notion of penetration into areas where trains or even buses couldn't go. And it would enable us to carry material – planning aid literature, TCPA material.[85]

Mary Riley (then Chair of the Association's Executive) helped to secure the necessary funds for the purchase of the van, and some of the annual grant from the Department of the Environment was used to fit it with a computer, projector, display units, a library and a telephone. The van acquired a place, symbolically as well as practically, at the very heart of Anson and Beazley's style of planning aid. Not only did the unit become mobile, but it had its impact on the general work and orientation of the TCPA itself:

> We had definitely taken the TCPA out on the road . . . And at all times we were the living example of the whole philosophy of the TCPA, the bottom up approach.[86]

As it toured around Britain – covering some 4,000 miles by early 1985 – the van also helped to attract publicity for planning aid. New contacts were developed, for instance, in North Wales, where the Welsh Language Movement sought advice on planning implications of second homes and, in turn, introduced a cultural dimension to the work of the unit.

This early phase of mobile planning aid was characterized by forays into neighbourhoods to see what was at issue rather than carefully prepared campaigns, combining promotional work with street level 'surgeries'. Inevitably, this sort of approach encouraged complaints from the public about a particular local authority, but, in time, Anson and Beazley sought to rebut accusations that all such work was necessarily confrontational. Indeed, they saw an important role for planning aid as a means of bridge-building between the planners and planned. Creating cooperative networks was thus an important goal.

The Divis Flats Camapign

Undoubtedly, one of the most eventful forays of the mobile unit was into the troubled city of Belfast. Perhaps it was inevitable that any planning issue there could not be detached from a wider nexus of sectarian conflict, and that political controversy would be endemic. This was certainly the case with the issue identified by the unit.

It all started in April 1983, when Marc Dorfman visited Northern Ireland and held talks with the Director of the Northern Irish Federation of Housing Associations, and with community groups on both sides of the sectarian divide. The Federation already had links with the Belfast Community Technical Aid organization, and was encouraged to develop contacts with the TCPA's Planning Aid Unit in London.

The ground was laid, and two years later Anson and Beazley made an eight-day visit to Belfast, beginning with an inner-city housing estate known as the Divis flats. Described by Anson as having 'all the ills of any UK ghetto plus a few problems that none of them suffers,[87] a dominant feature of the estate was the constant presence of police and security forces – including a helicoper landing pad on top of one of the blocks, constant surveillance and other signs of military activity.

The Divis flats had been built by the Northern Ireland Housing Trust between 1966 and 1972, and consisted of twelve seven-storey deck access blocks and a nineteen-storey tower (which housed the helicopter pad). In social terms, the flats became a refuge in 1969 for many people whose houses had been destroyed by fire; and in the 1980s up to 80 per cent of the residents were said to be unemployed. Structurally, it bore all the hallmarks of the poor quality systems building that afflicted many housing developments dating from that period, with pockets of incurable damp, rampant mould and fungus, 'flashback' of sewage into flats and infestation of vermin. As if all this was not enough, it resembled a military fortress more than a place in which to live.

The estate was frequently described as 'the worst housing in Western Europe'. It was an environment of unmitigated harshness and by the mid-1980s the estate's residents' association had been fighting for a decade to get the whole complex demolished. In David Hall's words: 'In the TCPA's 30-year campaign against high density housing, we never thought that the worst could be as bad as this.'[88]

Acknowledging the gravity of the situation, the Department of the Environment and the Northern Ireland Housing Executive agreed to demolish two blocks and to refurbish the rest. Total demolition was ruled out on the grounds of high costs and the lack of suitable land for rebuilding.[89] Two blocks were duly demolished in Summer 1984.

It had been hoped that the Divis Residents' Association would accept this partial response to the problem, but this was not to be. Instead, the Association cited an earlier government report which admitted that 'the physical environment within the Divis complex is regarded as disastrous for the residents.'[90] The time for compromise had passed, and the Residents' Association was prepared to accept nothing less than the total demolition of the estate, coupled with a programme for rebuilding and relocation of tenancies. In all of this, provision was demanded for the active participation of residents with a view to creating a decent neighbourhood environment.

But the gap between the two sides was wide – the housing authorities believing that enough had been done, and the residents calling for much more. It was into this deadlocked situation in June 1985 that the planning aid workers found their way. At the end of their visit they returned to London, and immediately launched an appeal fund to publicize the plight of the residents and the conditions they had

View of part of the Divis estate, and press conference at Carlton House Terrace, London (with David Hall in the Chair).

witnessed in the Divis. Some of the money raised in this way was used to mount an exhibition of photographs, while the rest of it helped to meet the costs of inviting sixteen of the residents to attend the opening of the exhibition in November 1985.

It was a telling event, the stark images of life in what was described in the exhibition as 'this environmental junkyard' and the disturbing presence of embattled residents generating media interest and the attention of politicians. Given the political implications of such an event, for the TCPA this was a challenging test of its commitment to community causes. In fact, the response was entirely positive. The exhibition itself was held in the TCPA's London premises; Mary Riley urged a 'bottom up' solution to the problem of the Divis; and a policy statement was issued in support of the Residents' Association and with an offer to assist in the preparation of a plan for the redevelopment of the estate.[91] Arrangements were also made for the exhibition to be shown at a number of venues elsewhere in Britain and at the 1986 International Habitat Conference in Berlin.

Understandably the exhibition and the TCPA's stance drew its share of hostile criticism. The Association was accused of being 'wholly superficial' in its approach to the problem, and of damaging its 'reputation for professionalism'.[92] Moreover the Department of the Environment saw fit to withdraw the grant it had provided for more than a decade for planning aid activities. This action, effected in July 1986, marked the end of the National Planning Aid Unit and the departure of Anson and Beazley. And so ended another phase in the planning aid story.

In fact, the sheer momentum of the Divis campaign and the passions aroused by the issue meant that this was not yet the end of the TCPA's involvement. The London Planning Aid Service continued, and one of its workers, Andy Roscoe, gave what time he could to supporting the cause of the Divis residents. He organized an exhibition to mark the first anniversary of the 'Demolish Divis' campaign, and another delegation arrived from the flats to tell of limited progress. A trust had been formed to raise funds to enable an architect/community worker to be employed to help the residents prepare their own plans for redevelopment. Later in 1986, the Northern Ireland Housing Executive announced that it would demolish the rest of the complex, but the timescale remained vague. Beyond that, a Divis Planning Group continued to meet regularly during 1987 and 1988, with a view to contributing to a plan for the estate, but its effectiveness was hampered by a lack of adequate funds and by difficult relations with the Northern Ireland Housing Executive.

The Divis issue had taken planning aid to the sharp edge of urban campaigning, and in the end it led to the unit's own downfall. It was also the toughest test for the TCPA of its real commitment to 'bottom up' planning and to radical community politics. Looking back on this period one can see that neither the planning aid officers nor the TCPA's policy-makers were found to be lacking; and yet one cannot escape a feeling that perhaps the Association was being drawn a little too far from its role of greatest strength, as a pressure group for planning rather than through direct involvement in community politics. Only in the latter stages of this period (in negotiations with the

RTPI) did it veer more to this former role, seeing itself more in the nature of a professional adviser than as frontline activist.

London Planning Aid Service

The issue that was negotiated with the RTPI was that of a combined planning aid service for London, independent of each organization, to provide free consultancy to groups and individuals unable to afford professional fees. In addition to its work at a national level, the Association had since 1982 (with the support of the Greater London Council) been running its own London planning aid service (LPAS). It was actually bettter resourced than the national enterprise, and although it was located in the Association's offices it enjoyed considerable autonomy in its day-to-day work. Policy was monitored through a joint steering committee, with external as well as internal representation.

Meanwhile, in the previous year, 1981, the RTPI had set up its own London planning aid service, based on a model of providing free consultancy and professional advice where this was needed. The approaches of the two organizations were, thus, rather different – the RTPI unit adopting a 'legal aid' model, as opposed to the more interventionist approach that characterized the TCPA's work. In the words of one of the latter:

> The service has never seen itself as merely an advice and information service – important as those functions are. LPAS (London Planning Advice Service) has always articulated the more progressive strands of thought in planning practice, particularly where they emanate from the community and voluntary sector in which LPAS is rooted.[93]

The London branch of the TCPA's planning aid work stemmed from the large volume of casework for the capital that the national unit had always attracted. Within a broad remit to encourage public participation in London's planning, and to give specialist advice in response to requests, it was very soon decided to concentrate on particular types of work. Instead of 'issues that concern only the individual'[94] the focus would be on the community, and not just any community but specifically those 'poorer, deprived areas and communities in London.'[95] With this orientation, the service was to become 'extensively involved with local and city-wide community organisations, on cases that needed longer term technical support, community development work and/or the development of new planning techniques and solutions.'[96]

In its early years, the new London service was rather over-

shadowed by the higher profile work of the national unit. Carole
Tyrell, who joined the former in 1984, recalls rather ruefully:

> When I turned up, the unit was in this very gloomy balcony
> [above the room used by the national team], with bits of paper
> everywhere, and some very old fashioned desks. There was not
> a very exciting aura about LPAS. National Planning Aid seemed
> to have a very exciting time going around the country in their
> van for two weeks at a time.[97]

Staffing of the service was balanced between a small core team of
full-time workers, and a network of volunteers in various parts of
London. From a total of thirty-two volunteers in 1982, numbers
increased to over one hundred in 1986. The political setting for the
growth of the service was that of Ken Livingstone's leadership of the
Greater London Council and the promotion of the idea of popular
planning, a strategy that was matched by the activities of a number of
inner London Labour-controlled boroughs. Running counter to priorities at central government level, equality issues relating to gender,
race and disability were high on the local political agenda. A Leftist
brand of radicalism was in the air, and the young activists in the
TCPA office warmed to the challenge.

Amongst its various activities, the London planning aid workers
established a 'women and planning' project, based on the experience
of casework that showed the kinds of difficulties women experienced
with the planning system. The project was supported with a Greater
London Council grant to enable the publication of a manual on the
subject, produced as a cooperative task in conjunction with various
women's groups and volunteers. Another initiative was to set up a
black and ethnic minority advisory group, and, in turn, an appointment was made to enable specialist advice on issues in black and
ethnic communities.[98]

Both in its range of issues and in the volume of casework, the
London service was clearly responding to real demands. A review of
its own work showed that about 40 per cent of staff time was spent in
direct contact with local groups.[99] By the middle of the 1980s it was
dealing with just under 1,000 cases each year, of which about one-
third required a long-term involvement (the latter being issues arising
from town centre redevelopment, traffic schemes and the use of
derelict land and buildings).[100] Concerned that it was being drawn
too closely into the continuing work of community groups, the staff
team in 1985 and 1986 chose instead to encourage the formation of
locally-based planning aid groups. One such group was that of the
Lambeth Planning Resource Centre. As part of its brief to support

local groups, the unit was also productive in its output of planning aid pamphlets and manuals, an activity that had become 'a mini growth industry' in itself.[101]

At a wider level, the unit became involved with issues affecting the whole of London, not least of all in supporting a vigorous but unsuccessful campaign to oppose the abolition of the Greater London Council. It also added its voice to calls for a Londoners' Rights Bill, and (following the Greater London Council's demise in 1986) supported the TCPA's lobby for some form of strategic planning to fill the vacuum left in the capital.

But with its main source of support gone, there was a sense in which the work of the unit after 1986 was becoming reduced to 'a series of rearguard actions'.[102] To add to the problems, delays in receiving continuing grant aid in 1986 contributed to a serious cash flow situation for the TCPA, at the very time that it was seeking to deal with a financial crisis in the organization as a whole.[103] Perhaps inevitably thoughts turned to the future of the remaining planning aid unit, and its position in relation to the parent body.

Several options emerged. The planning aid workers themselves mooted the idea of finding their own premises and becoming totally independent.[104] Another option that emerged was David Hall's suggestion to hold discussions with the RTPI London planning aid operation, with a view to a merger. Both options encouraged a wider review of the aims and nature of planning aid, and for most of 1987 a lively debate ensued.[105]

The way ahead proved to be along two tracks. In an attempt to secure greater accountability and financial rigour, Hall sought from the Association's planning aid team a clearer statement of its aims and methods of working.[106] At the same time, talks were opened with the RTPI to pursue the idea of a merger of the two operations.[107] The RTPI option was, however, far from straightforward, and there were some misgivings on either side about such a move. Even as late as 1988, it was apparent that some within the RTPI were critical of the TCPA's unit, which had resulted in 'high profile political positions'.[108] In turn, the TCPA was resistant to the RTPI team's view that in a merged organization responsibility for casework should be in the hands of a professional planner.

In spite of a difficult negotiating period, an agreement was eventually reached that a new combined service should be created, under the name of Planning Aid for London. This duly started in October 1988, and was constituted as an autonomous body with the following aims:

> . . . to provide free, independent, professional advice on the full range of town planning and environmental problems to

community groups, residents' associations and individuals
unable to afford consultants' fees.[109]

It was a compromise arrangement and for the TCPA it might have
semed that in fifteen years the development of planning aid had come
full circle. The brief for the new organization was not unlike that of
the unit that had been formed in the first half of the 1970s.

To note the apparent return of planning aid to its roots is not in any
sense to infer a judgement. If it might seem that it trimmed some of its
aspirations this has to be seen in the context of a less favourable
political climate, and in the light of experience gained in the intervening period. The very formation of a new unit was in itself evidence of
a continuing commitment to planning aid, and the bulging files of
casework could testify to the volume of demand for its services. At
the same time, the model that was adopted certainly appeared very
different to the more confrontational approach developed a few years
earlier for the Divis campaign and to deal with political issues of race
and gender.[110]

Reflections

For the TCPA the various phases of planning aid proved to be a
revealing test of its own changing philosophy. The fact that planning
aid was nurtured under the auspices of the Association is evidence of
the organization's commitment to a new brand of 'bottom up' planning. There is no doubt, however, that at various times tensions
surfaced. For while, on the one hand, involvement of communities in
the planning process was entirely consistent with its own long-held
beliefs, some of the methods of radical protest were less so. As David
Lock has observed, this was not, by and large, how the Association
normally operated:

> The Association has always been a small body; it is not a very
> democratic body; and historically it was most successful as a
> pressure group. The strength of its pressure group politics was
> always by the sheer force of personality and argument of one or
> two key individuals, who brought to bear their case on one or
> two key individuals in government.[111]

There is an open divide between pressure group politics by persuasion and direct community action, and planning aid exposed the
breadth of this gulf. The TCPA was drawn to the very edge of
traditional pressure group politics, but was it really equipped to cross
the Rubicon? Again, it is Lock, the first Planning Aid Officer, who
can offer an incisive observation:

The Association, frankly, was trying to cope with too many issues of too varied scales. On the one hand, it was trying to maintain interest in, and articulate an intellectual appraisal of, strategic planning. It was trying to hang on to that long established tradition. On the other hand, it ws also trying to handle day-to-day grassroots community affairs. And I really think that this gave the Association indigestion over the years. It was never designed as a popularly based movement. It was and is a self-appointed small pressure group. That is its strength and its only legitimacy.[112]

In the end, events probably turned out for the best. In 'hiving off' the planning aid unit, the Association was following a precedent set not only by the recent example of the environmental education unit but also by the much older practice of devolving responsibilities for the building of the first garden cities at the beginning of the century. Thomas Adams, one of the Association's pioneers, had noted as long ago as 1903 that the prime duty of the organization was to educate others.[113]

Moreover, the Association has retained a continuing interest in planning aid, through its support for community technical aid centres (discussed in the previous chapter) and through the publication of the community magazine, *Network*. It holds fast to the importance of 'planning from below', although it has to be concluded that planning aid *per se* is no longer so central to the mainstream work of the Association.

PUBLIC INQUIRIES

Very few political, social or economic issues can be simply resolved by the application of analytic knowledge or specialized research methods. In almost all cases public policy-making will continue to rest upon 'ordinary knowledge', social learning, and existing interactive decision-making systems. (Dunleavy and O'Leary, 1987, p. 309)

In addition to extending access to planning through environmental education and planning aid, the Association for over twenty years played an important role in the public inquiry process. Several major inquiries in the 1970s and 1980s concerned matters about which the Association had strong views. At the same time, they provided an opportunity for the Association to pursue its long-standing interest in the workings of the democratic process and, more specifically, in the way in which public participation in decision-making is best achieved. Through this work, the TCPA was led into a range of associated activities: holding pre- and post-inquiry conferences, giving evidence to government committees, commenting on proposed procedural changes. Some of these activities are described below and should be seen as an integral part of the Association's work on major public inquiries. This multiplicity of roles is perhaps best illustrated by the Sizewell public inquiry which took place between 1983 and 1985 and investigated a proposal to build a nuclear power station in Suffolk. The TCPA's involvement in that controversial issue forms a significant part of this section.

Policy and Process

In the late 1960s and early 1970s two factors in particular boosted the status of public inquiries. One was the public's growing awareness of and interest in environmental issues. The other was an apparent government commitment to public involvement in decision-making within the planning process. Although the Skeffington Report (referred to in previous sections) dealt largely with Development Plans it also signalled a much wider concern for more accountable decision-making in all aspects of planning.[114] One of the most important public inquiries which took place in its wake was into plans to redevelop Covent Garden, the site and surroundings of the former fruit and vegetable market in Central London. Approached by and working with local community groups, the TCPA gave evidence strongly objecting to the state of the proposed redevelopment, the loss of so many fine buildings and the consequent breaking up of a community. In 1975 the government announced that a new plan should be prepared, taking account of local opinion. Two hundred and forty buildings in the area were hastily listed as being of architectural or historical interest. This was a turning point in a national redevelopment versus rehabilitation argument and, quite rightly, the Association claimed some credit for that decision.

But outright victory for the TCPA at major inquiries has been rare. After two inquiries into a site for London's third airport, the Association's campaign for an estuarial site was supported when the government selected Maplin Sands in Essex. But the result of the third inquiry (1982), at which the Association again gave evidence was to promote the expansion of the existing Stansted airport – a decision which fulfils none of the TCPA's objectives concerning regional planning and decentralization. However, it is to some extent because major inquiry decisions are at times set aside that the Association realized the value of taking its case beyond the narrow confines of the actual hearing. This is illustrated by its activities around the public inquiry into the Greater London Development Plan which took place in the early 1970s. After holding a conference, 'Whither London?', the TCPA published the papers presented in a booklet entitled *London Under Stress: a study of the planning policies proposed for London and its region* (1971) in an attempt to draw in a wider public. Its evidence to the inquiry dealt essentially with the GLC's weak approach to the decentralization of development. It was prepared by a specially convened 'London Group' of members, and was also published as *Region in Crisis: an independent view of the Greater London Development Plan* (1972).

In 1977 the Association became caught up in an inquiry which was altogether of a different order. This was the Windscale inquiry, held to hear objections into a planning application from British Nuclear Fuels Ltd to build a plant for reprocessing irradiated thermal oxide fuel at Windscale (now called Sellafield) on the Cumbrian coast. It was during the 1970s that many pressure groups began to see nuclear power as a major environmental threat and, despite its many short-comings, the Windscale inquiry was the first official focus in the UK for public opposition to this source of energy. The TCPA eagerly grasped the chance to make known its growing interest and concern in energy policy in general and nuclear power in particular.

Its initial involvement in the inquiry was accidental, having been alerted to the proposal by a local Cumbrian group seeking pro-fessional advice from the TCPA's Planning Aid Unit. At this point, it seemed likely that the reprocessing plant would go ahead on the local planning authority's recommendation. The TCPA was quick to exert pressure on the government to 'call in' the application and hold a public inquiry. More specifically, the Association urged the setting up of a Planning Inquiry Commission, a wide-ranging form of public hearing provided for in the 1971 Town and Country Planning Act. It also requested financial help for participants. Both requests were rejected.

As with its evidence to the Greater London Development Plan inquiry, the TCPA published its case on the Windscale proposal. The introduction to that book, *Planning and Plutonium* (1978), summar-izes the problems which the Association had faced. It lacked time, it lacked money, and it queried the logic of studying one part of the nuclear fuel cycle which was inextricably linked to the whole. Be-cause of the haste in which the inquiry was convened and the hurried way in which it was conducted, the Association's case was fragmented and hard to follow. So unfair was the process that at one point the TCPA considered withdrawing. Moreover, the absence of an overall national energy policy into which the proposal could be fitted meant that there was no way of assessing the need for the plant.

Despite such difficulties, the TCPA presented a wide-ranging case, its evidence covering the effects of exposure to low level radiation, nuclear proliferation and the economics of nuclear power. Most of its witnesses were eminent experts in their fields. None of them could be paid for their services. Since the adversarial nature of such inquiries demands that parties are either objectors or supporters, the Association was, of course, firmly in the former camp. Yet, in fact, its Executive Committee had not (and has not since) passed an 'anti-nuclear' resolution as such. Its position at the Windscale inquiry was described as one of 'honest doubt': there were too many uncertainties for the project to be sanctioned at that stage and the government was urged to delay a decision until more was known about both the implications of the proposal and its relationship to national energy policy. For the first (and last) time, the Association was represented by Counsel. In early 1978 permission was granted for the reprocessing plant.

The Windscale inquiry taught the Association a considerable amount about the inadequacies of the public inquiry process. It also seems to have led to its involvement in a new dimension of the nuclear power debate. In his Postscript to the published evidence, Maurice Ash sums this up when he says that '. . . as a moment's pause for thought may suggest, it is an incredible question that the Inquiry was asked to answer: as to whether plutonium is not too lethal, both socially and physically, too dangerous to use? There is little that is not subsumed in the mere asking of that question, concerning our ways of understanding the world and the life towards which these lead.'[115] Finding a place and a means for debating the non-scientific aspects of nuclear power became an additional task for the TCPA.

In an effort to make the Windscale inquiry's contents more widely known, another book was published which listed and classified the issues raised by all the parties, proponents and opponents.[116] As a direct result of the experiences of a truly major inquiry (the Windscale inquiry lasted 100 days) two policy statements were also produced. The first, 'Energy Policy and Public Inquiries' (1978), stemmed quite obviously from the Association's concern over the absence of any overall energy strategy. The expectation at that time was that a planning application would quickly follow for the construction of Britain's first commercial fast breeder nuclear reactor, while the then National Coal Board was proposing to work coal reserves in the Vale of Belvoir. Underlying the TCPA's ideas for formulating and implementing a national energy policy was the desire to secure public involvement in policy-making. On the specific proposal for the fast reactor, the published statement recommended a two-stage hearing with wide terms of reference covering the general principles of nuclear technology, consideration of alternative sites and environmental impact analysis. Mindful of the complexity of the issues brought together in the nuclear debate, it concluded that a

High Court Judge (as at the Windscale inquiry) 'is probably not appropriate for the purpose (of chairing the hearing) in view of the likelihood of such a person's experience being based on having to assess hard provable facts relating to past events rather than seeking a balance of advantage between uncertain consequences postulated from a combination of qualitative and quantitative evidence and opinion.'

The second post-Windscale policy statement was entitled 'Financial Help for Objectors' (1979) It pointed out the basic injustice of a system which offered no financial help to those who made representations out of a concern for the public interest rather than for private gain or self-interest. At the Windscale inquiry, British Nuclear Fuels Ltd had spent five times as much as all the objectors put together. Plainly, an inspector, however careful, could not redress such an imbalance. Therefore, it was suggested that a proportion of the money required by objecting parties should come from central government, and different ways of organizing this were put forward.

But funding for objectors did not find favour. Neither did the fast reactor proposal materialize. In June 1979 a Conservative government came to power and by the end of that year had launched the largest ever programme of thermal nuclear power stations. Announcing this in the House of Commons, the then Secretary of State for Energy, David Howell, said that his understanding was that 'even on cautious assumptions, it would need to order at least one new nuclear power station a year in the decade from 1982.' Subject to safety clearance, the first one would be a pressurized water reactor (PWR), an American-designed reactor fundamentally different from the existing British gas-cooled reactors.[117] It was also the type of reactor which had gone so disastrously wrong at Three Mile Island, Pennsylvania in March 1979. In 1980, Sizewell in Suffolk was named as the site for the first PWR.

Sizewell

From 1980 until 1986 the TCPA maintained a high public profile in the nuclear debate. Although the actual Sizewell inquiry, which ran from January 1983 to March 1985, was the focus, the activities in which the Association became involved ranged far beyond that event. Looking through the papers of that period, it comes as a surprise to learn that a small voluntary body with many other demands on its resources achieved so much. It is clear that the Association saw the Sizewell proposal both as a turning point in this particular environmental debate and as a crucial issue in the democratic process.

One of the starting points was the suggestion from a member local authority that the Association should undertake independent research on their behalf into selected subjects in the energy, and particularly nuclear, field. After wider discussions, sixteen member local authorities showed interest in this idea and funded a programme of research coordinated by the Association. This ultimately formed the basis for a case presented at the Sizewell inquiry by the TCPA, supported by thirteen local authorities.[118] Without this considerable injection of money, the presentation of the case would obviously have been greatly diminished.

That so many local authorities from different parts of the country and of all political persuasions should have come together under the umbrella of the TCPA says much for the independence of the Association. The impetus for the project was twofold. First, the inquiry's terms of reference included 'the Central Electricity Generating Board's requirement for the power station in terms of the need for a secure and economic electricity supply and having regard to the Government's long-term energy policy'.[119] On the face of it, this appeared to be precisely one of the matters which the Association had repeatedly said should be open to public debate. Such a discussion seemed particularly important to many local authorities in view of the fact that a nuclear programme on the scale proposed would effectively rule out expansion of electricity generating from other fuel sources. Local authorities in coal-mining areas were anxious that the TCPA should investigate this, and present evidence to the inquiry on its social and economic implications. Secondly, a recent Government committee had recommended that subsequent inquiries into nuclear power stations (i.e. post-Sizewell) should be 'site-specific and need not re-open the wider issues of principle . . .'[120] Possible recipients of future stations such as Northumberland and Cornwall County Councils who wished to comment on matters of principle felt obliged, therefore, to participate in the Sizewell inquiry.

By the end of 1981 the TCPA had formed its own Sizewell Working Party. This included some who later gave evidence at the inquiry, some who had been involved in the Windscale inquiry, and some from other bodies which were also planning to attend the inquiry. Within the Association those most involved were undoubtedly David Hall, the Director, and John Blake, then Vice Chairman of the Executive.[121] Duplication of evidence by objecting parties had been a constant criticism at the Windscale inquiry and the TCPA wished to avoid repeating this mistake. Throughout 1982 and the first part of 1983, a loose-knit body known as Sizewell Coordination met on Saturdays at the TCPA's London offices to exchange information on the content and progress of their cases. Association representatives attended all fourteen meetings and provided the necessary secretarial support service. One outcome of the meetings was to reveal areas of the CEGB's case which were likely to be challenged at the inquiry. It was in this way that the TCPA's own case was enlarged to include the question of the disposal of nuclear waste. (Although this additional work was limited to the cross-examination of CEGB and government witnesses, it is interesting to note that it led to significant changes being made in the way in which nuclear waste is both defined and measured).

As well as piecing together an increasingly complex case – a task made more difficult by the fact that four of its technical witnesses lived in the USA – the Association also used the long run-up to the Sizewell inquiry to pursue its aim of achieving financial help for voluntary bodies. Even the CEGB appreciated the inherent problems of a one-sided debate and was willing to establish a fund for objecting parties – if the government would approve the proposal. But the government would not. At the Sizewell pre-inquiry meetings held in 1982 the TCPA put forward the case for funding. The Inspector, Sir Frank Layfield, was well aware of the problems described, having himself represented the Association at the Windscale inquiry. But, although he wrote to the government asking them to reconsider the provision of financial assistance for Sizewell objectors, the response was essentially no different to that which the Association and others had already received: the statutory provisions governing inquiries were themselves designed to safeguard the public's interest.

It was at the final pre-inquiry meeting, when it was clear that no government money would be forthcoming, that the TCPA requested that the Inspector be provided with his own Counsel, as one way of helping to redress the balance. Speaking for the TCPA, John Blake explained that those who could not afford legal representation would suffer particularly when it came to cross-examination of the opponent's technical witnesses.[122] On 19th January 1983, just after the start of the Inquiry proper, the government announced that it had agreed to a request from the Inspector that Counsel to the Inquiry be appointed. Among his tasks would be the pursuance of matters 'on the inquiry's behalf, which appeared not to have been fully covered by earlier questioning'. No official reference was ever made to the TCPA's earlier submissions on the matter but the lateness of the appointment indicates that it was not an idea which either the Inspector or the government had originally entertained. The TCPA is probably correct, therefore, in taking credit for what was unquestionably a very material improvement in the lot of objecting parties.

A third strand to the Association's involvement was its more academic study of the inquiry process; a continuation of its long-standing concern for the way in which major public inquiries are conducted. This work was partly funded by the Nuffield Foundation, with the subsequent report forming the basis of several post-inquiry papers and meetings.[123] Incidental benefits of this full-time presence at the inquiry were that the journal of the TCPA was able to carry monthly reports of the two year hearing, while students and school-children visiting the proceedings could be offered a small educational service.

On the inquiry floor, the TCPA played the largest role of all objecting parties: it fielded most witnesses, carried out most cross-examination and raised most procedural points. All this was made possible because of the large amount of time given freely by expert witnesses and by the outstanding work of John Blake, who acted as lay advocate (while also holding a senior position in local govern-ment). In terms of content, the Association challenged the CEGB's assumptions regarding energy demand, arguing that the Board had assumed an unrealistic increase in electricity's share of the market while underestimating potential savings from energy conservation. It questioned the contention that the nuclear plant would produce significant cost savings over coal and oil. (Events since then have proved the accuracy of this assertion.) On the safety side, it was sceptical of the high level of confidence placed in the integrity of the pressure vessel and concluded that the CEGB's assessment of the risk of a loss of coolant accident was over-optimistic. It was the only objecting party to cover the matter of decommissioning of the plant, reminding the Inspector that after a maximum life of thirty-five years the two reactors would remain, radioactive and a risk to human life, on Suffolk's Heritage Coast until well into the 22nd century. It was also alone in raising questions on the storage of nuclear waste.[124]

In pursuing its interest in the conduct of the inquiry, the TCPA made more use than any other party of the regular Tuesday morning sessions at which the Inspector allowed parties to raise procedural difficulties. One such matter which the Association fought for was the right of objectors to read aloud their proofs of evidence, as the CEGB had already done. In its subsequent *Sizewell Report* (1985) the TCPA in fact recommended that all proofs of evidence should be taken as read: at the inquiry it was making the point that both sides should be treated in the same way. As John Blake pointed out, 'objectors are already working at a considerable disadvantage at this inquiry and we urge therefore that they should not be placed at yet further disadvan-tage.' This was an argument which the Inspector could not counter although later he again reversed his decision and large amounts of the evidence of objecting parties do not appear on the official inquiry transcript.

Throughout the long Sizewell inquiry the Association sought to keep in the minds of the Inspector and the proponents the difficulties being encountered by a small voluntary body because of the huge imbalance of resources. These disparities were particularly obvious on the inquiry floor where the CEGB and its supporters had the services of large teams of barristers and solicitors while the TCPA and most other objecting parties had no legal representation. It was, however, as a result of this situation that the Association began to reconsider the role of legal representation and to doubt seriously the value of the judicial process at this type of public inquiry. Whereas the judicial system is designed to determine guilt or innocence, public inquiries have the quite different purpose of enabling evidence to be heard and evaluated with a view to reaching 'a balanced decision'. Sizewell witnesses were interviewed for the Association to obtain their views on the inquiry process. One problem noted in using the judicial process was that the selective nature of cross-examination – designed to demolish a case by attacking its weakest parts – at times gave a misleading picture of the totality of the evidence. Moreover, a considerable amount of the evidence at the Sizewell inquiry was of a qualitative nature, not susceptible to the traditional forensic cross-examination of the courtroom. Other witnesses pointed out that some barristers had clearly been out of their depth during the presentation and discussion of highly scientific and technical evidence, and unable to carry out the cross-examination required. Moreover, everyone was agreed that the judicial format positively discouraged public participation.

The full reasons behind the TCPA's decision to reappraise radically the issue of legal representation at major public inquiries are set out in its *Sizewell Report*. While fully supporting the use of public inquiries, the report recommends that witnesses should give evidence in their own right without legal or other representation, and that inspectors should have their own team of barristers to question all parties from a neutral standpoint when appropriate. This recommendation went to the heart of the TCPA's concerns over major public inquiries: if implemented, it would materially reduce the judicial element of the hearing, making it immediately more understandable to the public. By putting all witnesses on the same footing, it would be a much fairer system. It would also substantially reduce the costs of large inquiries. Such a restructuring would, in the TCPA's view, lead to a shorter, fairer and more comprehensible way of dealing with major planning proposals.

In 1986 the TCPA had an opportunity to test out its new proposals for major public inquiries when asked to give evidence to a Government Select Committee investigating the planning appeals and public inquiry system. Although the evidence presented was wide-ranging, reflecting the Association's long involvement in these fields, the questions from MPs focused largely on the major inquiry. There was particular interest in the TCPA's view on the wisdom or otherwise of separating policy and site-specific considerations; the justification of including certain technical matters (such as the safety of nuclear reactors which are subject to a separate regulatory process) in an inquiry's terms of reference; the funding of objectors and the problems of legal representation.[125]

The subsequent report of the Select Committee was, from the Association's point of view, encouraging. It reiterated the TCPA's important message that national policy was, on occasions, an appropriate matter for determination at public inquiries. In such cases, it recommended the use of either the Planning Inquiry Commission – which the Association had called for ten years earlier over the Windscale proposal – or a single major hearing which covered both policy and local site-specific issues. It also recommended that a more inquisitorial approach be adopted which may involve the appointment of inspector's Counsel. Lastly, it asked the government to devise a scheme for giving financial assistance to objectors where policy matters were under consideration 'and not [to] expect them to bear the costs of submitting evidence themselves'. To the Association, the report heralded the much needed reform of the major public inquiry process for which they had been campaigning in so many different ways for over a decade.[126]

While the Select Committee was taking evidence the TCPA also had a series of meetings about its *Sizewell Report* with the Department of the Environment. In the event, both courses of action proved disappointing. The government's response to the Select Committee (1986) rejected most of its recommendations. It did not favour the two-stage inquiry, it was 'not convinced' that inspector's Counsel was generally necessary, and it repeated the view that there was no good reason why objecting parties should be financed from public funds. The DOE witheld its letter of response to the TCPA's own report for several months, until the government's response to the Select Committee had been published. Although it agreed with some of the Association's less substantial recommendations, and incorporated them in its Code of Practice for major inquiries, it felt unable to take up some of the more innovative suggestions . . . To deny:

> [inquiry participants] the opportunity of presenting their case as they saw fit could be seen to offend the principle of natural justice. We sympathise with the general concept of trying to move from the adversarial to the inquisitorial approach, but we are not convinced that it would be appropriate to remove the long-standing right of legal representation.[127]

These were, of course, predictable responses from a government which was actively seeking ways of speeding up the decision-making process. They were, however, depressing for those who had been so bound up with this aspect of the Association's work; doubly depressing in the light of the government's decision to proceed with what has become known as 'Sizewell B'. Not surprisingly, some members questioned the value of pursuing so energetically causes which were clearly of no interest to the government. A more cynical approach is perhaps discernible in the part which the Association played in the Dounreay public inquiry which followed close on the heels of the Sizewell inquiry. This involved a planning application submitted by the UK Atomic Energy Authority and British Nuclear Fuels Ltd to build a commercial plant for reprocessing fast reactor fuel at Dounreay, an existing nuclear research site on the northern tip of the Scottish mainland. Here was a proposal which, in the TCPA's eyes, illustrated perfectly what it had been saying for so long about the problems of having no national energy strategy: it bore no relation to any CEGB programme and indeed the UK had no commercial spent fast reactor fuel in need of reprocessing. The proposal was in fact the result of a joint agreement entered into, without any public debate, in 1984, between Britain, France, West Germany, Belgium and Italy to

Windscale, Sizewell and (in this photo) Dounreay were all landmarks in the TCPA's energy campaign policy of the 1980s.

collaborate in the development of a fast-breeder system. The reactors would probably be in mainland Europe and the fuel sent to and from Dounreay by sea and air.

The TCPA realized that, in many respects, the environmental implications of the Dounreay proposal were more serious than those of any previous British nuclear establishment, with plutonium, one of the most lethal of materials and the chief ingredient of nuclear weapons, possibly to be treated as a commodity in trade and commerce. The Association pointed out that the need for the public to be involved in any decisions involving a so-called 'plutonium economy' had been clearly spelt out some ten years before by a Government Royal Commission.[128] Despite its own severely de-pleted resources, the TCPA urged the government to ensure that the application was subjected to close scrutiny including full public disclosure of the scheme of which it was apparently a part. As well as wide terms of reference, they asked (again) for financial assistance and an accessible venue for the inquiry. John Blake travelled to Dounreay for the first pre-inquiry meeting to represent the Association.

The response received made it clear, however, that none of the above requests would be met. The inquiry was held at Dounreay during 1986 and dealt only with local environmental matters. The TCPA submitted a written statement: three sides of paper summariz-ing their position but hardly doing justice to the depth of their reservations. Central to their concern was that approval for the reprocessing plant would effectively pre-empt the outcome of any future inquiries into fast breeder reactors. Thus, this highly contro-versial technology could become part of the country's energy pro-gramme without any of the detailed discussion called for in the 1976 Flowers Report.

It was to be three years before a decision, in favour of the proposed development, was forthcoming. Objections were largely overridden, but not without continuing controversy about the way the inquiry had been conducted as well as about the development itself. At least, in procedural terms, some consolation could be found in the Secretary of State's recognition that in future major inquiries a case might be made to him for the appointment by the government of a Counsel to probe evidence on behalf of objectors – a concession in line with the Association's own pleas for the democratization of the process.

Recent Issues

In addition to energy issues, and continuing its long-standing interest and involvement in the creation of new settlements, the Association also submitted written evidence to three inquiries into new townships in the south of England, proposed by a consortium of private developers. The first, at Tillingham in Essex (1986), was opposed on principle because of its location in the Green Belt, although the Association also took the opportunity to call for the ploughing back of profits into the local community – an ideal enshrined in its earliest writings. This application was subsequently refused, largely because of its location in the Green Belt. The next two proposals, at Foxley Wood in Hampshire (1988) and Stone Bassett in Oxfordshire (1989), were also, in due course, refused. In its written evidence to the inquiries, the Association explained that it had consistently advocated new settlements as a means both of relieving development pressures in existing urban areas and of providing more pleasant surroundings in which people could live and work. It called for a balanced mix of households, settlements sufficiently large to support a good range of social and community facilities and a high standard of landscaping and housing design. It also pointed out that many families do not have their own car and that job opportunities should be planned as an integral part of the settlement.

In 1986 the Association entered the Channel Tunnel debate, campaigning again on the procedural aspects of the decision-making process as well as the detailed issues at stake, although it did not object in principle to the proposals. Strong representations were made concerning the decision to by-pass the public inquiry process through the Hybrid Bill procedure, which offers little opportunity for participation by bodies like the TCPA whose own land is not directly affected, and which presents even greater barriers for the lay person than the inquiry system. Additionally, the terms of reference were restrictive and did not allow the Association to demonstrate how the Channel Tunnel might benefit the country as a whole, as opposed to its immediate impact in Kent and the Greater London region. (This coincided with the TCPA's work on the so-called North-South divide and its calls for a more geographically balanced national economy.)

In mid-1987, the Association was plunged back into the nuclear debate with the CEGB's submission of plans for a second pressurized water reactor, at Hinkley Point in Somerset. The decision as to whether to participate in the inquiry, which took place in 1988 and 1989, was a difficult one. As will be clear from the above, the TCPA had repeatedly sought to make use of the public platforms which the inquiry process provides. Moreover, since Sizewell, there had been changes in many parts of the nuclear cycle, meaning that that inquiry could not be seen as a once-and-for-all investigation of nuclear power. However, some of those who had worked on the Sizewell case were unable or unwilling to make the same commitment again while others felt there were new, more promising battles to be fought.

Within this context and led, again, by John Blake, then Chairman of the Executive, the Association found a way of covering what it considered to be the most important issues, although in a much scaled-down fashion. This time, the TCPA was particularly interested to explore two apparently contradictory aspects of the energy debate: firstly, the government's decision to privatize the energy supply industry and, secondly, their insistence that a minimum of 20 per cent of the country's electricity should be generated by non-fossil fuels. In the light of the CEGB's admission that there are no economic advantages attached to nuclear power, and since no other non-fossil fuels look capable of meeting the 20 per cent quota, the TCPA sought an explanation for the CEGB view. As at Sizewell, it pressed the point that, on the basis of the available evidence, the environmental risks of nuclear power are unjustified. Through cross-examination rather than evidence, the Association repeated the concern it has constantly expressed in public about nuclear waste: that, in the absence of any real progress on solutions to the long-term storage of high-level waste, it is highly irresponsible to add to the already large problem – a problem set to increase significantly as the country's elderly nuclear power stations are closed down.

In the closing weeks of the inquiry came the government announcement that the nuclear power industry would not be privatized: when the true figures were revealed, commercial interests were plainly unwilling to invest in an enterprise where the economic record – past, present and future – appeared so poor. As a consequence, the subsequent decision on Hinkley in September 1990 reflected a degree of ambivalence. On the one hand, planning consent was granted for the development; yet, on the other hand, whether or not it is actually built will await upon the outcome of a government review of the role of nuclear power in electricity generation, due to take place in 1994. For the campaigners against nuclear power, this delay might be no more than a temporary reprieve – an opportunity to reappraise the situation at a time when nuclear power is now widely accepted as a crucial environmental issue.

NEW COMMUNITIES

> One small Garden City must be built as a working model . . .
> (Ebenezer Howard, 1898, in Howard, 1946 edition, p. 159)

Of all its recent ventures, a commitment to the vision of a fresh generation of new communities marks something of a return to the very origins of the Association as a promoter of garden cities. But the new communities revival was not a question of trying to reinvent the past, so much as one of seeking to adapt well-tried principles to modern circumstances. For the Association the exercise proved to be both a challenge and a source of inspiration.

A Third Garden City

During the 1970s, the Association had attracted some innovative individuals into its fold, and it was to be from what one of this group, David Lock, refers to as 'the direct development lobby' (including also Colin Ward and Tony Fyson) that the new communities initiative stemmed.[129] Sharing with the Director, David Hall, a common belief in 'bottom up' planning they also believed that the time was right for a practical demonstration of those very principles that had led the original garden city lobby more than three-quarters of a century previously into the business of new settlement formation.

Colin Ward was to play a key role in the early stages of the 'revivalist' movement, and if there is a single date to mark the start of it all it is that of his presentation of an imaginative paper, 'The Do-it-yourself New Town' at a conference in 1975.[130] In this, Ward argued for a new concept of building communities, in which the residents themselves would be involved directly in planning, designing and building their own homes and neighbourhoods. The role of local authorities would be limited to that of site provision and basic services. His ideas were formed against a background of sensing that while the official new towns programme was running out of steam, at the same time there was evidence of a lively 'alternatives' movement in which self-reliance was an important feature.[131]

Over the coming year or so, Ward's proposal, through exposure in various publications and at events (such as that to celebrate the seventy-fifth anniversary of the formation of Letchworth) gradually gained wider support. Within the Association its adoption was assisted by the creation of a new special interest committee, the Ecology and Development Group (EDG). It was the EDG which in 1977 considered the possibility of the TCPA involving itself in creating a new community of the future;[132] an idea that was reinforced in the Association's Annual Report in 1978, in which it was noted that the garden city idea was ecologically sound.

Various innovators were attracted to the EDG, bringing to it a mixture of technical and 'alternative' ideas. Amongst these were James Robertson (author of *The Sane Alternative*), Tom Burke (from Friends of the Earth) and Herbie Girardet (active in the counter culture of the 1960s, and an advocate of self-reliant new communities). Meanwhile, on the Association's Executive there were a few who lent their own support to this kind of approach – notably, Maurice Ash (who started the Green Alliance in 1978) and Tom Hancock (who had devised a craft villages scheme).

Support within the Executive grew as it became increasingly evident that the mainstream new towns programme was being run down, and in 1978 a New Communities Committee (NCC) was formed. Its brief was 'to consider and report . . . on any matters relating to the planning and development of new communities, with particular reference to New Towns and settlements in the present and future, and to the appropriate types of development agency for building them.'[133]

In progressing new ideas, a seminal event proved to be that of the Association's Annual General Meeting in May 1978, at which the then Chairman of Milton Keynes Development Corporation, Lord Campbell of Eskan, issued a direct challenge:

Is not one of the tasks facing the TCPA to recapture the public's imagination and demonstrate how the 'Garden City' . . . is a civilising and civilised form of settlement, in which the quality of life that can be enjoyed will give shape to the present confusion of economic, intellectual and even spiritual forces that surround us at present? I should have thought the time was ripe for a new programme of action by the Association . . . A new demonstration of first principles is needed: could not the TCPA campaign for the building of a small country town set in its own belt of market garden land? . . . such a project could take on to the next century the ideas that the TCPA gave to this one.[134]

He further suggested that Milton Keynes Development Corporation (MKDC) should be approached to provide two grid squares – approximately 500 acres – of its undeveloped land, for such an experiment (a suggestion that is considered in the next section).

Meanwhile, responding to the general challenge, in the following year the Association published an Outline Prospectus for a 'third garden city'. The brief was for a new settlement:

on a human scale; a basically co-operative economy; a marriage of town and country; control by the community of its own development and of the land value it creates; and the importance of a social environment in which the individual can develop his own ideas and manage his own affairs in co-operation with his neighbours.[135]

The Prospectus proposed a settlement size of at least 10,000 people on 500 acres. Land would be purchased at as near as possible to its existing use value, to be owned and managed by the community. There would be a great variety of housing styles and tenureship; with maximum energy conservation incorporated into all aspects of the

Images of Third Garden City. (Illustrations by Rob Cowan in Outline Prospectus, 1979.)

community. Economic activities would be small scale, environmentally conscious and geared to the needs of the community and the job satisfaction of employees; with an emphasis on co-operative, craft and self-employed activities. There was to be a high level of self-sufficiency in food (meaning a high priority for agriculture and horticulture); and the community would be designed to minimize the need for car journeys by prioritizing other modes of transport. Welfare and other facilities would be funded from increased land values and rates, emphasizing a community based approach and local autonomy.

Following consultation, David Hall concluded that 'Nearly everyone commends the Association's decision to accept Lord Campbell's challenge to produce ideas for a third garden city, and most people commend the Prospectus itself . . .' adding that the Prospectus generated 'much argument . . . to support opposite points of view about particular aspects.'[136]

Along the way, the TCPA abandoned the title 'third garden city' in favour of 'new communities'. Kelvin Macdonald, then Deputy Director and in charge of the project, explained that in Howard's original plan, restructuring existing urban areas was to have been carried on simultaneously with the construction of garden cities. He continued:

> The results of the new communities project . . . would be
> valueless if they perpetuated . . . past mistakes by
> concentrating solely on the creation of new places on greenfield
> sites . . . A 'new' community could come about as much through
> management, through changing structures and institutions and
> through Patrick Geddes' 'conservative surgery' as through the
> building of visionary settlements. Indeed, the value of such
> settlements, apart from their worth to their few inhabitants,
> would lie solely in the lessons they could teach those seeking
> changes in their own area.[137]

How, though, were such ideas to be turned into action? Towards this end, the Association obtained a grant from the Joseph Rowntree Memorial Trust. A series of working groups were then formed to discuss different aspects of new community formation. The topics were: housing, employment, farming and landscape, personal services, utilities, communications, community structure, and finance and development. A ninth group – on inner cities – was set up subsequently to consider how to apply the new community principles to inner-city locations. The groups each met four times between February and June 1981 and involved 120 experts on the various topics.[138]

The first draft of a report on the findings was circulated in the Spring of 1982. Macdonald wrote:

> . . . one theme began to emerge naturally within each separate
> section of the report. The theme is that of localising power and
> localising people's ability to take action. This is not a new idea.
> It is fundamental to the moves for greater worker control, to the
> search for ways to achieve greater self-sufficiency in food and
> energy; and in the slow progress towards setting up a more local
> tier of government with real powers and responsibilities. The
> report tries to add a new dimension to the theme – not in terms
> of theory or rhetoric – but in showing some practical ways to
> develop localisation.[139]

The report was not completed, but instead, one of the working group members, Tony Gibson, took on the production of a book based on the draft report and the work of the groups. The book was finally published in 1984, entitled *Counterweight: the neighbourhood option*.[140] Although it referred to the report as its 'basic source', it was rather more a development of Gibson's own ideas about neighbourhood regeneration.

Alongside the Rowntree meetings, in 1981 the TCPA ran another competition for new communities. It was called the Future Communities Competition, and an exhibition of the same name was held at the Institute for Contemporary Arts in London. To accompany the exhibition, a programme of public talks was arranged, all with the aim of spreading the idea of new communities.

Greentown

In stimulating public discussion the TCPA was simply exercising its traditional role as a pressure group. But Lord Campbell's call for action in 1978 had also served to revive another traditional role played by the Association – that of an active promoter of practical schemes. Such a role had been played many years previously at Letchworth and Welwyn, and now the Association was invited to return to the stage of community formation. This time the locus of interest was to be a few miles to the north of the first garden cities, within the existing new town of Milton Keynes. For Lord Campbell accompanied his general exhortation with a specific invitation to investigate the feasibility of using some land within the new town for the third garden city experiment.

Apart from Lord Campbell's personal enthusiasm for the project, there were other factors that favoured such a venture. A few years earlier, the Assistant General Manager of the Development Corporation for Milton Keynes, Don Ritson, with an architect colleague, Neil Nigson, had entered a competition that was held as part of Letchworth's seventy-fifth anniversary celebrations.[141] Their winning entry was for a form of new community development, using derelict or underused land for a variety of purposes. It was proposed that planning regulations within the development area should be relaxed to facilitate a process of resident involvement and control. Underlying the scheme was a notion of achieving a lifestyle of self-reliance through smallholdings and various craft or other self-employed trades.

The possibility of such a scheme being undertaken at Milton Keynes was enhanced by the then government's decision to wind down the new towns programme, and the consequent concern of Development Corporations to achieve as much as they could within a limited life span. It was against this background that Ritson joined the TCPA's working party on Ecology and Development, in which ideas were exchanged with the likes of Colin Ward and David Lock.

Ritson's 'insider' role at Milton Keynes was crucial to the identification in 1977 of an actual site – known as Ashland – where such a development might take place. Although the proposal enjoyed the support of the Development Corporation, the local Borough Council was less enthused; ostensibly it questioned the feasibility of the site, though Higson's view was that local opinion was concerned at the prospect of a 'hippie ghetto'.[142] Either way, the opposition was sufficient for the Department of Environment to forestall development of this particular site.

In spite of uncertainty surrounding the exact location for an experiment, the Development Corporation decided to explore the idea further, authorizing its officers to enter into discussions with the TCPA. The Association responded with an outline prospectus to show how such a proposal could evolve, but the difficult question (one which persisted in the years ahead) was to decide what its own role should be. One option that was considered was to take a direct role through the formation of a development agency; an alternative approach was to work in a purely advisory capacity, with the development being undertaken by an independent agency. At that stage, the Association was keen to formulate an approach that would not be specific to this one location, but which could be applied elsewhere – on inner-city as well as greenfield sites.

Progress was slow, and in 1979 David Lock (who had by then moved from the TCPA to a post in the Development Corporation) decided to move things along by seeking to arouse public support in Milton Keynes. An opportunity arose in August of that year, with the staging of a festival of alternative technology and lifestyles (the Comtek Festival) in the city, and the gathering of participants who might well have been expected to support a new community project. Lock himself displayed copies of a draft prospectus at the Festival, and, with Tom Hancock and Herbie Girardet, made a presentation (based on the TCPA's third garden city ideas) under the banner of 'Alternatives in Milton Keynes'.[143]

It proved to be a timely intervention, and on the following day sixty enthusiasts met to discuss the proposal further and, in due course, to form a group of prospective developer-residents, the Greentown Group.[144] A temporary secretariat was elected, a group affiliation fee to join the TCPA was raised, and the Group committed itself to early negotiations for land to enable the development to proceed.

Thereafter confusion reigned. The different parties involved in the process held often conflicting views on fundamental issues affecting the proposed development. Most of the Greentown Group had an idealized vision of land being released at existing use value for purchase or for rental at a nominal rate. Above all, it was axiomatic that all development would be controlled by the prospective residents themselves, without intermediaries. David Lock, however, saw the way forward as being through the formation of a trust company to act as the development agency with a brief from the Group. He was anxious to make rapid progress, whilst Lord Campbell, with his sympathies for a project of this sort, was still Chairman of the Corporation. But Lock's approach aroused suspicions within the Group, with a fear that control over development would be lost to external bodies.[145]

In turn, the Development Corporation had its own problems. In spite of its Chairman's support, there were other members who were less than enthusiastic about the whole scheme, and the idea of releasing land at existing use value was ruled out at an early stage. Along with the TCPA, the other main agent in the process, it recognized control as an important factor, and both favoured the establishment of an independent development agency. It was thought that the best arrangement would be for residents to be in partnership with the agency, but not until the site had been purchased, planning permission obtained, and funds secured.[146] Additionally, the TCPA (while supporting the project) was cautious in its decision not to negotiate with the Greentown Group until 'an agreement is reached with MKDC'.[147]

The latter condition proved to be a source of contention, calling into question the extent of trust between the different parties. Greentown Group members were wary of the TCPA's motives, and when the Association published its Third Garden City Prospectus the Group responded with its own 'Third Garden City in Milton Keynes'. In this latter document some important points of difference were highlighted. In particular, it was noted that the TCPA's proposals 'do not make enough provision for participation in the planning and implementation process by the prospective residents.'[148]

There were also differences regarding desirable densities and the ideal size of development. The Greentown Group favoured a lower density than the TCPA (ten people to the acre rather than twenty) with a view to encouraging greater self-reliance in food and energy production. It was also keen to go ahead with a lower population target, ideally in the region of 250–300 to enable everyone to participate in planning and developing the community. This was broadly in line with the Development Corporation's own preference for a small demonstration project on about 25–30 acres.

But all this was abstract as compared with the 'realpolitik' of negotiations, with the Development Corporation and the TCPA proceeding without the Greentown Group's direct involvement.

Ostensibly, the Association took on the role of 'honest broker', undertaking to represent the interests of the embryo residents group and to secure an appropriate site. Given the differences between the various parties this was a less than satisfactory situation, and it was not until May 1980 that the Greentown Group was accepted as an equal negotiating partner in its own right. At its first meeting, the Corporation declared that the TCPA, in association with the Greentown Group, should set up a development company as soon as possible, with a view to starting to build in the following Spring.

In August 1980 the Corporation identified a site of 34 acres in the Crownhill neighbourhood. But instead of marking progress towards the realization of the project, the allocation of this site proved to be a contributory factor to its abandonment. The fact was that for the TCPA the site was deemed to be too small in itself, and the Corporation was asked to agree to the release of adjoining land as well in due course; in response the Corporation, sensitive to local opinion, said it was 'most unlikely' to do so.[149] Following a meeting in November 1980, Lord Campbell worte to David Hall to confirm that additional land would not be forthcoming, adding that 'the Association must now decide whether to proceed on the basis of the offer made or withdraw.'[150] Faced with this ultimatum, a decision was taken by the Association's Executive in February 1981 to withdraw.

So ended a protracted yet unproductive phase in the Association's return to the business of community formation. Three agencies with different sets of interests and expectations had come together in a joint venture, and the outcome was, effectively, one of stalemate. There were lessons to be taken from the exercise, not least of all in respect to the need to reconcile professional advice with local autonomy.

This was not, however, the end of the Greentown experiment. The Development Corporation agreed to continue discussions with the community group, and, although the TCPA was no longer involved in a developmental capacity, it continued to lend support to the Greentown Group's claims. Members of the Group were invited to participate in the Association's Rowntree working parties; a small grant was awarded to assist the Group in its work in framing development proposals; and it later intervened in support of a planning appeal against a decision to refuse a mixed-use development at Crownhill.

For the most part it was left to the Group to press its own claims. Two reports – an Interim Report (in December 1980) and a Development Proposal (in August 1981) – were prepared, not least with a view to persuading the Corporation that it could perform the tasks of a reliable development agency.[151] Although the reports were well-argued, they were not enough to conceal problems that were evolving within the Group itself. The lengthy process of negotiations was taking its toll, with many of its members drifting away or simply losing interest in the absence of progress.[152] Moreover, changing external circumstances were not helping the situation, with the Corporation under growing pressure to capitalize on its assets. Crownhill was a prime residential site, and the idea of using it for a low-density, mixed-use development was beginning to look increasingly unrealistic in a market of rising land prices in the 1980s.

As a last-ditch attempt to salvage something from the experience, those who were left in the Greentown Group decided to reduce their claim to that of a 6-acre site for a self-build residential scheme. Abandonment of the mixed-use proposal, with its self-reliant element, served to appease the Borough Council. But the Corporation seemed by then to have lost what little confidence it still had in the Group's capacity to develop the site. Negotiations were finally brought to an end in April 1986 (more than a decade after Ritson and Higson had first promoted their vision of a new community), on the grounds that the Group had failed to present a convincing financial management strategy.

In an article in *Town and Country Planning*, the Group refuted the reasons advanced by the Development Corporation:

> We had produced almost everything the Development
> Corporation wanted: detailed plans, specimen house designs,
> costings, management and tenure proposals. The important
> missing ingredient was firm financial backing – but this was
> extremely difficult to secure without a firm commitment to the
> project by the Corporation. We told the Development
> Corporation that we had a strong expectation of being able to go
> on to obtain finance, with the aid of experienced consultants, if
> our final drawings and other proposals were to be accepted.[153]

The remaining Greentowners felt that they had been led into a 'Catch 22' situation, where finance could not be raised without the support of the Development Corporation, which the latter would not give in the absence of some guarantees from the Group. There was also an underlying suspicion that the Development Corporation wanted to free itself of the experiment, on the basis that it might have secured a figure in excess of £150,000 per acre for conventional housing development on the Crownhill site.

Acrimony and accusation marked a sorry end to a potentially bold experiment. In the end, each of the parties came away with little but experience. In the business of new community formation, however, experience is a valuable asset, and there is no doubt that the TCPA

went into its next venture all the stronger as a result of its involvement
with Greentown.

Lightmoor

As with Greentown, it was an overture from an aristocratic Chairman
of a new town Development Corporation, in this case Lord Northfield at Telford in Shropshire, which led to the next community
experiment. In April 1980, Lord Northfield wrote to David Hall to
suggest the possibility of developing one of several sites that were not
suitable for a conventional scheme. Informal talks followed, and in
due course Telford's Chief Planner, Martin White, joined one of the
Rowntree New Communities working parties at the TCPA's offices.
It was at one of these that another participant, Tony Gibson, offered
a vision of how such a community might evolve. White and others
were duly impressed.

Gibson had himself been invited to join the working party on the
basis of work he had done at Nottingham University's Education for
Neighbourhood Change unit, concerning public participation in community planning. There he had created a series of adaptive display
techniques, organized as planning workshop games, to enable non-
experts to communicate with professionals about plans for their
neighbourhood. His philosophy was one of achieving neighbourhood
regeneration through devolving decisions to the people who live in
the area, and through making good use of what was already within a
community. Additionally, Gibson possessed the necessary personal
skills to motivate others and to find ways through the maze of
bureaucratic obstacles that invariably serve to impede the kind of
experiment which relies on 'people power'. He was to become the
key figure at Telford and also at a parallel experiment at Birkenhead
(considered in the following section).

Building on the contacts that had been established since Lord
Northfield's original invitation in 1980, TCPA representatives made
fresh visits in the light of Gibson's presentation, with a view to
examining the feasibility of the proposal. A test site was chosen for
the study, and in November 1981 it was reported that there was a
significant measure of consensus about how to use such a site.[154] Over
the coming months various site options were considered, the outcome being the choice of one that was known as Lightmoor.

It was not the most auspicious of locations for a new community.
Sited on the edge of Telford, it was pock-marked with the debris of
old coal workings and a pylon line did little to add to its amenity
value. In normal circumstances, it is doubtful whether it would have
been developed at all. Moreover, with only 22.5 acres for immediate
use (though with the promise of more becoming available in due

course), it was smaller than the TCPA would have liked. But the support of the Development Corporation was crucial, and Gibson's sense of vision helped to counter some of the more obvious shortcomings inherent in the site.

A steering committee prepared the financial ground for the appointment of Tony Gibson as the TCPA's Development Officer, and in January 1984 the Lightmoor project was officially launched. It rested on an agreement between all parties that the new community should be designed to recognize neighbouring development, rather than be built in isolation; and that it should not be about escaping from society but rather about addressing and seeking to overcome some of its problems. For the TCPA, Lightmoor was expected to carry to fruition at least three essential principles enshrined in its Third Garden City idea. It:

> must reflect the ideas and preferences of the people who join it; as far as possible it should be self-contained, embracing a combination of homes, home-based enterprises and community facilities; and the community as a whole should benefit from any improvement in the value of land which results from the development of the scheme.[155]

One of Gibson's first tasks was to gain local support for the project. This was important not only to reduce possible opposition (as had occurred at Greentown) but also as a source of recruitment. Gibson attended local events, taking every opportunity to promote the project. He involved local schools through the County Education Adviser, organized mock planning participation exercises for the site, gained the confidence of the local parish council, and mounted an exhibition and local competition about the scheme.

Gibson also had the task of establishing a formal Steering Committee to oversee the project until the community could arrange its own legally constituted development and management structure. This committee had the immediate tasks of obtaining planning permission, negotiating the transfer of the site from the Development Corporation, and progressing financial arrangements and recruitment. Membership was drawn from the two local authorities (Shropshire County Council and Wrekin District Council), the Development Corporation and the TCPA.

A priority for the TCPA was to set up a land holding company to acquire the site at existing use value, and then to transfer the land to residents as the development progressed. The Association was also keen to be closely identified with the project at grassroots level rather than simply to be seen as a remote body, and to this end an existing building on the site, The Poplars, was earmarked for a resource centre.

Having secured the support of the local authorities, the business of obtaining planning permission was less fraught than it had been in the case of Greentown.[156] More complex was the task of deciding on the best system of land tenure, and of securing finance on the most favourable terms. Gibson was always very keen to negotiate a group mortgage, and it was through his persistence and ingenuity that a deal was struck with the Nationwide Building Society. 'The trick was that along with the land at its existing low grade agricultural use value there would be a development value which would accrue to the new community and which could be the decisive factor in persuading the building society that there would be enough collateral to fall back on if the experiment misfired.'[157]

Although the group mortgage was not an inclusive arrangement (so that householders had to obtain individual mortgages as well) it was enough to provide basic services for the first phase of development. Every member contributed equally to this loan repayment, but costs were kept to a minimum through voluntary 'sweat equity'. As well as private ownership arrangements, the TCPA was also keen to introduce a rental scheme to widen access. Over a period of three years, negotiations led to the formation of the Lightmoor New Community Housing Association.

At the same time as tenure and finance were settled, Gibson sought to identify a group of prospective Lightmoor residents. He invited local people to visit the site, and describes how he used to sit on a wall on Sunday afternoons outside the derelict Poplars, waiting to receive anyone who showed an interest.[158] Media coverage also led to enquirers from other parts of the country, though especially from the West Midlands and the North West.

By the Summer of 1984 a core of prospective residents had formed and began to meet regularly. Gibson saw his role as being to facilitate these early meetings, prior to the group organizing them itself. He discouraged the formation of a residents' association as such, since he feared that such a move might pre-empt the selection process for the first phase of settlement. Instead, he advocated open meetings, alternating weekly between business and social events. At the business meetings, Gibson introduced participatory planning exercises to encourage ideas on the future of the community, and he invited various speakers on a range of community development topics. The social events were no less important in helping participants to get to know each other and to build confidence.

It was not, however, simply a question of getting any group of people together; a fundamental issue for all parties was to get the 'right' balance. For the TCPA it was important to create a community that would be accessible to a wide social catchment, avoiding any taint of exclusivity. In turn, the Development Corporation was anxious to assure local residents in nearby districts of Telford that Lightmoor would not become a haven for 'drop-outs'. Given the history of this type of community experiment (including even the now genteel Letchworth, widely ridiculed before 1914 because of its 'cranky' associations) an element of social manipulation was perhaps inevitable. Yet there was a potential contradiction for a body like the TCPA in espousing a 'bottom up' approach while having views on the composition of the group.

This contradiction, argued Gibson, could be resolved pragmatically by encouraging only those 'best suited' to join:

> What kind of people might find themselves at home with each other and with the possibilities that Lightmoor opens up? In the first place it will be people with commonsense plus a bit of imagination; down-to-earth people who like breaking new ground and who know a bit about managing for themselves without expecting to batten on the rest of the community. They will be people who enjoy a bit of company every so often but also like to feel that their home is their castle. People who don't mind joining in to make decisions and tackle problems or opportunities together, but who are ready to respect each other's independence and privacy.[159]

Aspiring new members, he argued, 'would need to have a "track record"': some evidence of their abilities to develop a livelihood on site.'[160]

The selection of who should participate was only one of the early problems. As with Greentown, another issue that very soon surfaced was that of who was in charge. To what extent should 'outside' bodies like the TCPA, Telford Development Corporation, and even Tony Gibson determine events, over and above the interests of residents? Prospective residents questioned:

> . . . the idea that any other party than the prospective residents themselves should have a decisive say in the administration of the scheme. What was the point of setting out to ensure that the community was its own developer if all these 'entrenched bodies' were to monopolise the decision-making?[161]

In response, Gibson explained that until the prospective residents were identified there had to be a set of founding fathers (and mothers) to sort out the possibilities and perhaps allay local doubts – but he agreed that now was the time for the voting power of these

The building of Lightmoor.

entrenched bodies to be subordinated to that of the settlers them-selves:

> The prospective residents considered the problem rather anxiously . . . and worked out a modification of the original legal document which would allow for an earlier transfer of majority voting power. When they put this proposal up to the

then steering group . . . it was agreed *nem con*. They found they were pushing at an open door.[162]

This principle of direct resident involvement in the management of the community was reinforced when the Lightmoor New Community Company was formed in April 1985 to supersede the Steering Committee. Within that company, the rules provided for a majority representation of residents to take effect progressively as the community grew.

With some of the ground rules established, thoughts then turned to details of design and construction. An attempt to find an architect able to comprehend the concept of a self-build community failed, and, instead, each house was designed on an individual basis. By the Winter of 1984 the first family had moved onto the site. Living (with four children) in a second-hand caravan, the family seemed to Gibson to epitomize the pioneering spirit of the whole venture, and he used the example to publicize the project and to encourage others to commit themselves. Given various problems associated with finalizing details of the group mortgage and with servicing the site, it was not, however, until January 1986 that the building of Lightmoor actually started.

In the first phase (subsequently named Leasowe Green), nine houses were built for private ownership, followed by five on a rental basis. Construction was by a mixture of self-build (mainly on a part-time basis), with some assistance from outside contractors. An emphasis was put on energy efficiency, although the cost of integrating new technologies to maximize this proved restrictive in most cases. A distinctive feature of the construction process was the joint effort in undertaking some of the communal tasks, such as the preparation of the land for services. In spite of plans to encourage community-based enterprises, a majority of the residents found employment outside the community. Furniture design, household joinery and a small building firm were the exceptions in the first phase. Only 9 acres were used for new building, together with a half acre site for the resource and community centre, the rest being left as a conservation area.

In some ways, Lightmoor evolved in a way that might have appeared on the surface to be little different to any other private estate development. But there were important differences, not least of all in a sense of idealism that drew some of the occupants to the site. The following perceptions of some of the pioneer residents are illustrative:[163]

* We saw an article in *The Observer* about alternative living and this place was mentioned. My wife was brought up on a

kibbutz and we felt the community spirit was missing in Walsall. There's a sort of natural selection among us, a certain dissatisfaction with suburban life. Already the community here is very supportive.

* There's an in-built support network as soon as you arrive. It's like having an old extended family. We're all individuals but we're all committed to making this work.

* It is the kind of joint sharing which has helped to cement the community, starting with digging the trenches for the drains. Lightmoor is not an insouciant rural idyll fuelled by idealism and feelings of loving kindness. We have to learn good neighbouring, the sheer amount of time an organisation requires to be helpful, self-sufficient and neighbourly is quite enough to sort out the pioneering sheep from the goats . . . In Lightmoor the social structure is as carefully built as the drains.

A second phase of development is planned (its start delayed as a result of further negotiations with the Development Corporation, and then by the business of obtaining planning permission), but The Poplars has been used, as intended, as a focus of activity within Lightmoor and as a base for outreach work. To the extent that the residents have assumed greater control over the development of the site, the importance to the TCPA of this outreach work (under the auspices of the Neighbourhood Initiatives Foundation, organized by Tony Gibson and Margaret Wilkinson) has increased.[164] Although the Foundation 'continues to have a finger in Lightmoor'[165] (with Margaret Wilkinson as the Development Officer for the second phase), most of its outreach work is organized on a national basis. The title of a conference arranged in 1989, 'Breaking the Deadlock – Releasing the Energy', reflects the attempt in a variety of neighbourhood settings to 'make things happen'.

For all this, however, the story of Lightmoor itself remains central to the TCPA's recent history, exemplifying as it does a new concept of 'planning from below'. Thus, the selection of Lightmoor in July 1987 for the Charles Douglas Home Award for the best entry in *The Times*/RIBA Community enterprise awards was a significant event. In making the award, the Prince of Wales said that:

What has struck me particularly about this year's winners is the success of local communities in raising resources for their own projects. This is best demonstrated in the Lightmoor New Community in Telford, the most outstanding entry this year. The Lightmoor community managed to forge a working relationship between those who are often at loggerheads in a 'Them and Us' situation. But their professional helpers remained firmly on tap, not on top. This to my mind is the secret of the whole business – the appointment of enablers who can help local communities to work their way through the cat's cradle of bureaucracy and achieve the best possible solution to a particular local problem.[166]

In response, David Hall explained that the significance to the TCPA was that 'We believed the Lightmoor project could be the model for thousands of other people wanting to make a better environment for themselves either on green field sites or in the inner cities.'[167]

And that is the real significance of Lightmoor for the Association – as a model for numerous developments elsewhere. The whole object of the exercise was to explore new ways to mobilize people to participate in the planning of their own communities. Pioneered as it was in the 1980s, at a time when traditional ways of getting things done were in question, it has proved to be a timely initiative. Lightmoor in itself remains a modest experiment, but it was never intended to be an isolated development. To the extent that it has won national acclaim, to the extent that it provides a working model of community architecture and planning, and to the extent that it has led, in turn, to a variety of further neighbourhood initiatives, the experiment has worked.

Conway

At the same time as its involvement with Lightmoor, the TCPA was also supporting another, rather different, type of community initiative. Generally referred to as Conway (the name of the district in Birkenhead where activity was centred), it was different on a number of grounds. For one thing, instead of a greenfield site (which had been the case in Milton Keynes as well as Telford), this was an existing neighbourhood with a population of about 1400. The experiment was not, therefore, about building a new settlement so much as neighbourhood regeneration. And, in contrast to the growth potential of the new towns of Milton Keynes and Telford, Conway was a depressed area with high unemployment, within the Merseyside town of Birkenhead. The TCPA was keen to apply its community-building principles to an inner-city location, and, in this respect, Conway offered a suitable setting.

In spite of differences, there was also a common thread. Each in its way – Greentown, Lightmoor and Conway – was conceived as a demonstration project, with an emphasis (particularly in the latter two) on maximizing resident involvement in processes of change. Thus, each was a demonstration of the 'bottom up' style of planning that became a significant feature of environmental activity in the 1980s. As well as this conceptual link, there was also a personal factor, in the common involvement of Tony Gibson at Conway as well as Lightmoor, which helps to explain how the London-based TCPA came to get involved in developments on Merseyside.

Gibson had, in fact, been working on an occasional basis in Birkenhead since December 1978, in connection with a participatory exercise that he had devised, known as 'Planning for Real'. The town had been selected for an exercise involving residents and local politicians, and Gibson was able to demonstrate how relations could be improved between officers from the local authority (Wirral Metropolitan Borough Council) and the people living in the area. As a result, Gibson was invited in 1983 by the Chief Executive of the Borough Council to follow up his initial work with a detailed survey within the Conway neighbourhood.[168]

The brief was for a survey of local resources, to include the skills and talents of the people in the area, as well as an inventory of disused buildings, waste land and scrap material from local businesses. The ultimate aim was 'to see how unused or underused resources could be put together to develop self-help enterprises to create employment, improve the environment, help the disadvantaged and restore some lost pride.'[169] Along with staff from the TCPA (which 'came to the project late but is anxious to see it as well established as the work at Lightmoor'[170]) thirty local volunteers were involved in the process.

The outcome of the study was subsequently published under the title of 'Making the most of local resources',[171] and presented to the Borough Council in August 1983. A feature of its proposals was the recommendation that use should be made of a three-storey, Victorian building in the heart of the area, as a base for new activities. The disused building (known as the Laird) was once the home of the Birkenhead School of Art. Its state of decay somehow epitomized the plight of the whole neighbourhood, and its revitalization could be seen to be symbolic as well as functional. A major investment was needed, but that could be done incrementally:

We [referring to a group of interested residents] want to go into the Laird on a trial basis, now, so that we can clean it up and do whatever is necessary to make it weatherproof and deter vandals. To meet the cost we hope to get approval for a Manpower Services Commission refurbishment scheme. If, as a result, we can satisfy the Council that we are both responsible and effective, we would like to move onto the next stage, which would be to introduce revenue-earning uses into the building.

When we have proved ourselves, and the building's revenue-earning capacity, we want to proceed with a longer-term plan of conversion which would be funded by a loan from the Nationwide Building Society on the security of the building, supplemented by a package of grant aid from several interested bodies.[172]

The Borough Council responded to the request by agreeing to the use of the Laird, leaving the residents – who formed themselves into a group that was subsequently named the Laird Enterprise Trust Association – to find the necessary finance. The Manpower Services Commission was one obvious source, and the TCPA, while it could not provide direct funding, was committed to supporting the project through assistance with grant applications, publicity and political lobbying. In the early stages of the project, towards the end of 1983, goals were clearly defined and prospects looked promising. However, future progress was marred by a series of mishaps and misfortune.

For a start, anticipated funding from the Manpower Services Commission failed to materialize, leaving the local group and the TCPA to make up the deficit. This led to a delay in getting the work started, and in the meantime vandalism and theft caused damage which was to add considerably to the cost of eventual renovation. As if this were not enough, fire regulations required more extensive work on the building than had been expected, so that activities were, in the first place, confined to the basement as the only free space.

On the positive side, by the end of 1984 the TCPA had obtained funds to enable the appointment of a professional project worker. The immediate task for the new appointment was to rekindle enthusiasm lost since the idea was first mooted, and to introduce the first users – amongst whom was a resident potter, a dress designer, a furniture repair scheme, an outside caterer, and the use of a specially converted room for pop group rehearsals. The adjoining Junior School painted a mural along the garden wall, a 'Planning for Real' exercise was devised to encourage local people to suggest ways of using the space around the building, and the Civic Trust agreed to fund an architectural feasibility study for the development of the rest of the building. In due course, a small enterprise advice team was established in the Laird, which it used as a base for outreach work in the neighbourhood.

As an indication of progress, in 1986 the project figured in the list of top Community Enterprise Awards and received a plaque and a money prize from the Prince of Wales on behalf of *The Times* and the RIBA. There was some satisfaction in the TCPA's view at the end of that year that 'it has been slow going, but the spade work is paying off.'[173] Optimism was shortlived, however, for continuing progress was marred by the discovery of dry rot in the building, serious enough to lead to a dispersal and relocation of the various enterprises that had been fostered. 'We have got pretty used over the past decade to never saying die,' said Tony Gibson at the end of the 1980s, as the group embarked on a search for alternative premises.[174]

It could be said that, given all the time and effort expended on the scheme, there is little so far to show for it all. The poor state of the building itself undoubtedly diverted substantial resources from more beneficial ends. But the real value of this kind of community venture is hard to assess. Simply to measure it in terms of tangible change within the neighbourhood is inadequate, if only because the kinds of problem which afflict inner-city areas such as this are a result of years of structural decline and neglect and defy easy and quick solutions. Conway is as much about changing attitudes and encouraging people to realize their own potential as it is about changing the appearance of the neighbourhood.

The sorry state of the Laird iself may have proved too much to overcome, but the fact remains that new enterprises have been started and continue to flourish, and groups of local residents have worked together in ways that might not otherwise have happened. 'Bottom up' planning is not, in its very nature, a dramatic process of large-scale change; it is more a question of sowing seeds and encouraging modest growth. Conway is indicative of both the limits and potential of this process. It raises questions as well as providing answers about the community-based approach to planning that is illustrated in each of the experiments discussed in this chapter.

NOTES

Environmental Education

1. Skeffington Report (1969), p. 1.
2. Interview with David Hall, 22 June 1987.
3. Osborn, F. J. (1968) 'Children's hour, world and prospect', *TCP*, Vol. 36, Nos. 10–11, p. 431.
4. Skeffington Report, *op. cit.*, para. 244.
5. *Ibid.*, paras. 245 and 247.
6. Reade (1987), p. 100.
7. For example, Michael Storm, then senior lecturer in the Department of Geography at Bulmershe College of Education, author of *Urban Growth in Britain* and subsequently the Inner London Education Authority's Inspector for Geography and Environmental Education; and Keith Wheeler, the Senior Lecturer in Geography at Leicester College of Education, later at Leicester Polytechnic, and subsequently Chairman of the Council for Environmental Education and the British representative on several international bodies.

8. TCPA (1970) press release, 5th May.
9. Ward (1987), p. 279.
10. Ash, Maurice (1979) 'Ward's Work', *TCP* Vol. 48, No. 7, 1979, p. 241.
11. *BEE*, No. 1, 1971.
12. National Association for Environmental Education, West Midlands College of Higher Education, Gorway, Walsall, West Midlands WS1 3BD.
13. Council for Environmental Education, School of Education, University of Reading, London Road, Reading RG1 5AQ.
14. Ward, Colin (1978) 'Education for mastery of the environment', *Space and Society*, No. 4, December, p. 73.
15. Storm, Michael (1971) 'Schools and the community: an issue-based approach', *BEE*, No. 1.
16. Crick, Bernard (1972) 'Bias' in teaching politics', *Journal of the Politics Association*, No. 1.
17. See Plaskow (1985).
18. See Ward and Fyson (1973), pp. 17–23.
19. *The Times* 16th May 1972; *The Daily Telegraph* 17th November 1971; *The Guardian* 26th April 1972; *The Sunday Times* 23rd January 1972.
20. Fyson, in Ward and Fyson (1973).
21. Fyson (1976).
22. *BEE*, No. 38, 1974.
23. Walford, Rex (1972) 'Games and the environment', *BEE*, No. 13.
24. Gibson, Tony (1979) 'Helping a community identify its housing needs', *BEE*, No. 97. See also Gibson, Tony (1984).
25. Wheeler, K. S. (1970) 'The Outlook Tower: Birthplace of environmental education', *Bulletin of Society for Environmental Education*, Vol. 2, No. 2, p. 6.
26. Goodey (1974).
27. Wheeler, Keith and Waites, Bryan (1972) 'Leicester Town Trail', *BEE*, Nos. 16–17.
28. Lynch (1960).
29. Pick, Bill and Beer, Eric (1978), 'Children's perception of their environments', *BEE*, No. 86, pp. 4–12.
30. Bishop, Jeff and Russell, Oraliam (1983), 'The building design game', *BEE*, No. 141, pp. 11–18.
31. Green (1973), p. viii. Wheeler and Ward make similar comments on the relevance of Geddes. 'Geddes argued that planning was the development of a local life, capable of improvement and development in its own way and upon its own foundations . . . not something which can be done from above, on general principles easily laid down, which can be learned in one place and imitated in another.' His book *Cities in Evolution* published in 1915 was in fact a manual for the environmental education of people rather than planners.' Ward, Colin (1982) 'The ghost of Patrick Geddes stalking Edinburgh', Lecture at the Edinburgh Winter School, School of Architecture, University of Edinburgh, 16 January.
32. Nicholson, Simon (1972) 'The theory of loose parts', *BEE*, No. 10.

33. Fyson, Anthony (1975) 'The work of the Council for Urban Studies Centres', *BEE*. No. 51, pp. 5–8.
34. Higson, John (1973) 'Introducing CUSC', *BEE*, No. 22, 1973; Report of Proceedings of the Inaugural Meeting of CUSC, *BEE*, No. 23, 1973.
35. Rees, John (1974) 'Harrow Club Urban Studies Centre', *BEE*, No. 39, 1974; and Fyson, A., Goodey, B., Bishop, J., Tilley, R., Webb, C., etc., in *BEE*, No. 51, 1975, Special Conference Issue on the Council for Urban Studies Centres.
36. Fyson, Anthony (1974) *Council for Urban Studies Centres, First Report*, TCPA: Fyson, Anthony (1976) *Council for Urban Studies Centres, Second Report*, TCPA; *Urban Studies in the 80s* (1983); *Council for Urban Studies Centres, Third Report*, TCPA.
37. Environmental Board (1978).
38. *Report by HM Inspectors on Urban Studies Centres* (1987), Department of Education and Science.
39. *Schools Council Project – Art and the Built Environment* (1976) Newsletter One.
40. Baynes, Ken (1974) 'Front Door', *BEE*, No. 34.
41. Ward, Colin (1976) 'Vernacular and suburban architecture; town centres and shopping areas; industrial architecture', BBC Radiovision – Arts and Humanities, January 14th, 21st, 28th.
42. Wheeler, Keith (1976) 'Experiencing townscape', *BEE*, No. 68; Goodey, Brian (1977) 'Sensing the environment', *BEE*, No. 72; Bishop, Jeff (1977) 'An approach to the appraisal of buildings', *BEE*, No. 73.
43. Gretton, Keith (1979) 'The Schools Council Art and the Built Environment Project: An Evaluation', unpublished report.
44. Adams and Ward (1982).
45. Ward, Colin (1982) 'Where do we go from here?' Lecture given at the Schools Council Art and the Built Environment Project Concluding Summer School and Conference, London: Royal College of Art 15–17 July.
46. Goodey, Brian (1979) 'Unfinished business in environmental education', *BEE*, Nos. 100/101, pp. 5–8.
47. Editorial Comment (1979) 'Eighty years? it seems like a lifetime', *BEE*, Nos. 100/101, pp. 2–3.
48. TCPA Annual Report for 1982, presented to the Annual General Meeting on 19th April 1983, and TCPA (1982), letter to subscribers 'We need your support to establish the TCPA education unit as a separate body'; signed by Anne Armstrong, Graham Russell, Liz Hurst and David Hall, 2 April.
49. Interview with Anthony Fyson, April 1988.
50. Editorial Comment (1975) 'Hope springs eternal', *BEE*, No. 51, p. 3.
51. Colin Ward, personal interview, March 1988.

Planning Aid

52. Robert Cowan, 'Planners, gardeners and Patrick Geddes', *TCP*, July–August 1977, p. 351.
53. Interview with David Lock, 6th December 1988.
54. David Lock, 'Planning Aid Experience', n.d. Unpublished manuscript p. 3.
55. *Ibid*, p. 5.
56. A valuable review of the early history of planning aid is provided in a report commissioned by the Department of the Environment from the University of Reading: 'TCPA Planning Aid Service: An Evaluation', March 1979. Some ten years after the first planning aid discussions it could report a continuing diversity of approach. For instance, in planning departments: 'Some seem merely to allocate responsibility to a particular officer and little more. Most provide a counter where people can discuss their query and inspect documents but these are often very inaccessible. Planning departments are often to be found in rather obscure corners of buildings, which house a range of local authority functions. The buildings are not located according to accessibility criteria and, therefore, are often discovered only after a great deal of time and effort has been expended.' (p. 23). The report also mentions that during times of 'financial restraint' it is usually the planning liaison officers who are regarded as 'a luxury which few local authorities can afford' (p. 23).
57. Additionally, aspects of planning aid were also dealt with in resource centres and housing aid agencies.
58. The RTPI, with about 70 per cent of its membership then employed in central and local government, was inherently more constrained in promoting planning aid than a pressure group like the TCPA.
59. Lock, D. 'Planning Aid Experience', *op. cit.*, p. 5.
60. Amos, F. J. C., 'Presidential Address', *JRTPI*, Vol. 57, 1971, pp. 397–399, cited in '*An Evaluation*', *op. cit.*, p. 11.
61. Lock, D. 'Planning Aid Experience', *op. cit.*, pp. 7–8.
62. University of Reading (1979), *op. cit.*, p. 15: 'The Planning Aid Working Party of the RTPI defined planning aid as ". . . the giving of planning services free (or at low cost) to individuals or groups who could not afford full fees: this would include the giving of information, or advice, or full professional services, with or without further involvement over a long period".' Planning Aid Working Party, RTPI, 'Planning Aid', Planning Paper No. 5, 1974.
63. This was essentially a grant to support 'pioneering experiments' in the voluntary sector.
64. As David Lock explained in his 1988 interview with Mehmet Ali Dikerdem, the unit 'had to hint at a new initiative each year or imply that there was a new angle on what was being done' to be eligible for a further year's funding. This also corresponded to a period of stringent public sector spending cuts undertaken by the last Labour Government of the 1970s. Interview with David Lock, 16th December 1988.
65. TCPA Annual Report for 1975.

66. Interview with David Lock, 6th December 1988.
67. *Ibid.* Lock also explained that it was usually the more senior ranking local government executives and professionals who tended to be wary of the service.
68. Thus in Lock, D. 'Planning Aid: which way ahead?' *TCP*, Vol. 44, 1976, pp. 198–200: '. . . the TCPA has never seen the provision of the planning aid service as a cosy extension to the professional practice of town planning, but much more the practice of the language of the equitable distribution of resources, opportunities and perhaps political power . . .'
69. TCPA Annual Report for 1978. The company was buying out property, moving tenants away and demolishing houses without going through the statutory planning procedures.
70. TCPA, 'Providing Planning Aid', n.d. (Robert Cowan's name and office address is on the first page).
71. *Ibid.*
72. Robert Cowan, 'A choice for planners', *TCP*, Vol. 44, 1976, p. 445.
73. Interview with Robert Cowan, 8th November 1988.
74. Up to the TCPA Annual Report for 1979, the name Planning Aid *Service* was used. From 1979 to 1984 it became the Planning Aid *Unit*, and in 1985 it was relabelled the *National* Planning Aid Unit to distinguish it from the London Planning Aid *Service* set up under the aegis of the National Unit.
75. In his 1988 interview with Mehmet Ali Dikerdem, David Lock was to quip that the Department of the Environment had spent more money commissioning the evaluation of planning aid than in providing grants for the service to expand! TCPA Annual Report for 1980: 'The TCPA and researchers were astonished and disappointed that the Department seemed to show no interest in the Report whatsoever . . . particularly as the assessment concluded that the Department of Environment's financial support for the TCPA's planning aid work had been worthwhile and good value for money.'
76. University of Reading (1979) *op. cit.*, p. 29.
77. *Ibid.*, p. 30.
78. The *Newsletter*, launched in 1980, aimed to increase the flow of information and experience between planning aid groups, aid users and planning departments. It would publicize innovative planning techniques as well as different methods of participation used in community action. In 1982 it was decided that the *Newsletter* would be published jointy between the TCPA and the RTPI. The arrangement was to cease in 1984, when the RTPI withdrew its funding. Publication stopped altogether when the financial burden became too heavy for the TCPA as well.
79. Interview with David Lock, 6th December 1988.
80. Interview with Brian Anson, 22nd November 1988.
81. TCPA Annual Report for 1984.
82. TCPA Annual Report for 1984.
83. Transcript of a conversation between M. Beazley and B. Anson on 2nd

September 1985 to be referred to as Beazley and Anson *Transcript 1985*.

84. TCPA Annual Report for 1985.
85. Beazley and Anson *Transcript* 1985, p. 11.
86. *Ibid.*, p. 15.
87. Anson, B. 'The struggle waged in Divis', *Architectural Journal*, 2 September 1987, p. 83.
88. *Network*, February 1986.
89. Letter from the Northern Ireland Housing Executive to the TCPA dated 7th October 1985.
90. Divis Residents' Association, *The Divis Report: Set Them Free*, 5th June 1986, p. 51.
91. *Network*, February 1986, reported that DRA Chairman and Secretary Frank Gillen and Fra McCann, both in the group from Divis at the exhibition, were arrested shortly after returning to Belfast, but were subsequently released without a charge.
92. Letter from Department of the Environment (Northern Ireland) dated 24th December 1985.
93. TCPA Annual Report for 1986.
94. TCPA Annual Report for 1983.
95. *Ibid.*
96. *Ibid.*
97. Interview with Carole Tyrrell and Stephen Joseph, 16th March 1989.
98. The LPAS Black and Ethnic Community Steering Group agreed with the TCPA Executive Committee that a number of the members of the latter would join the Steering Group and be assigned the responsibility of keeping the TCPA executive informed and involved in ethnic affairs.
99. London Planning Aid Service, *Submission to the GLC for continuation of grant funding for 1985–1986*, December 1984.
100. TCPA Annual Report for 1985.
101. LPAS Quarterly Steering Group Meeting Report for 19th November 1986.
102. Interview with Carole Tyrell and Stephen Joseph, 16th March 1989.
103. TCPA Annual Report for 1987. The funding requested and received by LPAS from the GLC in 1984 was £49,000, out of which salaries accounted for about £34,000. In the application of the GLC for a grant, LPAS specified the employment of one full-time Planning Aid Worker and General Coordinator, three part-time Planning Aid Workers, and two more part-timers in a self-employed capacity as Planning Rights Consultant and a Research Worker. With the difficulties experienced in receiving the London Boroughs Grant Scheme payments, the TCPA had to step in. These uncertainties corresponded to an increase in staff turnover, with Abi Sofolarin, John Johnson and Andy Roscoe leaving the Service in 1987, and Stephen Joseph joining it from the Civic Trust.
104. LPAS Quarterly Steering Group Meeting, 19th November 1986.
105. A note from the TCPA Director David Hall in August that year underlined the fact that while the TCPA continued to have overall responsibility for LPAS finances, it had no control over the Service if

anything went wrong. Besides, there was, Hall argued, a certain amount of uncertainty over LPAS' 'priorities and aims'. (Note from David Hall on Stephen Joseph's discussion paper 25th August 1987).

106. *Ibid*. While Hall agreed with the broad objectives of LPAS, defined as the provision of planning aid in Greater London, mainly to community organizations ('as distinct from individuals who are helped mainly by the . . . PAFL'), LPAS had nonetheless failed in two essential respects. He argued, firstly, that staff time allocated to recruiting volunteers, giving them cases to handle, and on keeping them with appropriate information and support had been insufficient. The pressure of casework and other demands had diverted staff time. And secondly, more care should have been shown in targeting specific areas and specific community groups in London. The service had spread itself out too thinly.

107. *Ibid*.

108. Notes on a meeting between David Hall, Tristram Reynolds and Graham Davies representing PAFL, 4th January 1988.

109. Planning Aid for London, Annual Report for 1988.

110. In private correspondence, Rob Cowan points out that the *volte face* is more apparent than real. PAFL's official aims as equivalent to a legal aid service for people unable to afford normal consultancy fees, have been carefully worded in order to allay fears that it is taking work from consultants; whereas in practice it is doing a different kind of work altogether – including pioneering participation techniques.

111. Interview with David Lock, 6th December 1988.

112. *Ibid*.

113. Thomas Adams, 'Memorandum by the Secretary as to the raison d'etre of the Association, its relationship to the Garden City Company and other matters which require consideration'. (Undated, but probably 1903) Garden City Association.

Public Inquiries

114. This report, officially entitled *People and Planning*, is usually known as the Skeffington Report after its chairman, Arthur Skeffington MP who was then Joint Parliamentary Secretary in the Ministry of Housing and Local Government.

115. This new dimension to the nuclear power debate is also referred to in Maurice Ash's article 'Energy and form: the Windscale file', in *TCP*, Vol. 45, No. 11, 1977, p. 469.

116. This book, *The Nuclear Controversy: A guide to the issues of the Windscale Inquiry* (1980), was published in association with the Political Ecology Research Group (PERG), which also played a leading part in the Windscale inquiry.

117. For the entire speech of the Secretary of State for Energy, see the *House of Commons Hansard*, 18th December 1979, Col. 287–304.

118. These local authorities were:

County Councils: Cleveland, Cornwall, Merseyside, Northumberland, North Yorkshire, South Yorkshire.

District Councils: Blyth Valley, Cambridge, Ipswich, Isle of Anglesey, Restormel, Sheffield, Wansbeck.

Also involved in sponsoring the original research were:

Shepway District Council, Strathclyde Regional Council and the Greater London Council.

119. In July 1981 the Secretary of State for Energy announced a list of what appeared to him to be relevant points for consideration at the Sizewell inquiry. They were not officially 'terms of reference', since the inspector was allowed to hear whatever evidence he wished, but were generally referred to by that name.

120. This is a quotation from the *First Report of the Select Committee on Energy: The Government's Statement on the New Nuclear Power Programme*, 1981, Vol. 1, p. 90.

121. In October 1981 the TCPA's Sizewell Working Party consisted of: Jennifer Armstrong, John Blake, Robin Grove-White, David Hall, Peter Odell, Michael Prior, Joseph Rotblat, Colin Sweet and Alice Stewart.

122. An extract from the inquiry transcript giving the detailed reasoning behind the TCPA's request for Counsel to the Inquiry is given in its *Sizewell Report* p. 57, referred to in Note 123 below.

123. Jennifer Armstrong was based at the Sizewell inquiry throughout the proceedings. Her findings and recommendations were approved by the TCPA Executive and published by the Association in July 1985 (*The Sizewell Report: A new approach for major public inquiries*).

124. The TCPA's witnesses were: Peter Odell, Michael Prior, Ronald Steenblik and Colin Sweet, on the relative economics of nuclear power and fossil fuels; Rodney Fordham, Marvin Resnikov, Steven Sholly and Gordon Thompson on reactor safety and the transportation and storage of nuclear waste; Martin Ince on the market potential of the Pressurized Water Reactor; and Stuart Crowther on the social and economic effects of a rundown of coal mining.

125. The TCPA's evidence was given to the Environment Select Committee on 19th February 1986 by John Blake, David Hall and Jennifer Armstrong. The minutes of the session, which include the evidence in full and the subsequent discussion, are available from the House of Commons Library.

126. This was the *Fifth Report of the House of Commons Environment Committee: Planning: Appeals, Call-In and Major Public Inquiries* (1986) Vol. I (181-I) and Vol. II (181-II), session 1985–86. The Summary of Conclusions and Recommendations relating to major public inquiries is in Vol. I, pp. lxxxvi–lxxxvii.

127. Letter from DOE to TCPA, 15th December 1986.

128. This was the *Sixth Report of the Royal Commission on Environmental Pollution: Nuclear Power and the Environment* (1976), Cmnd. 6618, session 1975–76, generally referred to as the Flowers Report, after its chairman Sir Brian Flowers. In paragraph 521 (p. 198) the Report is extremely critical of official attitudes towards public understanding of the implications of a plutonium economy.

New Communities

129. Personal interview with David Lock, 1988.
130. For a version of this paper, see, for instance, Ward, C., 'The do-it-yourself new town', *Undercurrents*, June–July, 1976. The paper was first presented at the Garden Cities/New Towns Forum, Welwyn Garden City, 22 October 1975.
131. In 1975 in the magazine, *Undercurrents*, Ward wrote about the 'Counter-culture planners'. He quoted extensively from the American anarchist-geographer, Murray Bookchin (1974), about a group called the Revolutionary Ecology Movement. This group was advancing 'radically new social alternatives' to the 'dehumanising urban "re-vitalisation" and "rehabilitation" projects', and attempting to 'foster community designs based on personal intimacy, many-sided social relationships, non-hierarchical modes of organisation, communistic living arrangements, and material independence from the market economy.' (Ward, C. 'Anarchist cities', *Undercurrents*, No, 10, 1975, pp. 38–40).
132. TCPA Annual Report for 1977.
133. TCPA Annual Report for 1978.
134. Lord Campbell of Eskan, 1978, address to the TCPA's Annual General Meeting, May 1978.
135. TCPA, 'A Third Garden City Outline Prospectus', *TCP*, Vol. 48, No. 7, 1979.
136. David Hall, 'Third Garden City – Progress Report', *TCP*, Vol. 49, No. 5, 1980.
137. Macdonald, K. 'The shape of things to come', *TCP*, Vol. 50, No. 6, June 1981, pp. 175–6.
138. See the progress reports in *TCP*, Vol. 50, No. 6, 1981, pp. 175–176; and Vol. 50, Nos. 11/12, 1980, p. 303.
139. Macdonald, K., 'Taking over', *TCP*, Vol. 51, No. 4, 1982, p. 89.
140. Gibson (1984).
141. Information on early developments at Greentown is drawn largely from personal interviews and correspondence with participants, obtained by Andy Wood in 1988.
142. This kind of term was used frequently in local discussion and press reports at that time. It points to a longstanding difficulty in introducing an 'alternative' type of community to an established settlement.
143. Report in *Undercurrents*, No. 35, 1979, p. 25.
144. The name 'Greentown' was derived from an article with that title, by one of the promoters of the scheme, Herbie Girardet. See 'Green Town – Alternative MK?', *Undercurrents*, No. 35, 1979, pp. 28–29.
145. A letter (dated 25th September 1979) from one of the Greentown Group, Hilarie Bowman, to David Lock expressed the suspicions of some members as to the motives for his involvement as well as that of the TCPA.
146. A 'programme of action' prepared by the TCPA suggested that it would not be realistic for an organization of prospective residents to be formed before April 1981, by which time the purchase of the site,

planning permission to develop, and funding was due to have been secured.

147. Correspondence, Hall to Lock, 2nd October 1979.

148. Greentown Group, 1979.

149. Even a presentation by David Hall at the Corporation's consultative meeting with the local authorities on October 6th 1981, failed to allay the fears of the local councils. Both the Corporation and the TCPA had to head off hostility by assuring the councils that any plan would have to be 'sound' enough for the Board of MKDC to consider implementing.

150. Correspondence, Campbell to Hall, 24th November 1980.

151. Greentown Group, Interim Report on 'Work in Progress Towards the Preparation of a Development Proposal for Greentown', December 1980; and 'Development Proposal for Greentown', August 1981.

152. At its peak, the Greentown Group had a paper membership of 250 people, but there were never more than sixty people active at any one time.

153. Boyle, G., Barac, D. and Oliver, D., 'What ever happened to Greentown?', *TCP*, Vol. 56, No. 6, 1987, pp. 176–178.

154. Reports on progress at Lightmoor were regularly published in *TCP*, and at one stage Tony Gibson wrote a quarterly column.

155. TCPA (1984) 'Lightmoor: A new kind of neighbourhood. An outline prospectus for a community with a future.

156. David Hall (in an interview with Andy Wood, June 1988) explained that the process was helped by the personal interest of the then Secretary of State for the Environment, Patrick Jenkin.

157. Gibson, T., 'Whose land is the planner's?', *TCP*, Vol. 54, No. 5, 1985, pp. 152–153.

158. Tony Gibson, in a personal interview with Andy Wood and Dennis Hardy, December 1988.

159. Gibson, T., in *TCP*, Vol. 53, No. 2, 1984, pp. 39–40.

160. Gibson, T., quoted in *The Surveyor*, 23rd May 1985, 'Building with common consent on common ground'.

161. Gibson, T., Whose Land is the Planner's?', *op. cit.*

162. *Ibid.*

163. From 'A Village of Tomorrow', *Daily Telegraph*, 27th May 1985.

164. See, for instance, the account of work in the TCPA Annual Report for 1989.

165. *Ibid.*, written by Tony Gibson.

166. Reported in *TCP*, Vol. 56, No. 9, 1987, pp. 230–231.

167. TCPA Press Release, 2nd July 1987.

168. Material for this section has been obtained through personal interviews with participants (conducted by Andy Wood in 1988) and from TCPA minutes and reports.

169. Laird Enterprise Trust Association, 'The Laird comes to Life', 1985, p. 1.

170. TCPA Annual Report for 1983, p. 6.

171. Education for Neighbourhood Change and the Jubilee Enterprise Trust Association, 'Making the most of local resources: self-help

feasibility study of the Conway area of Birkenhead', Nottingham University, 1983.

172. *Ibid.*
173. TCPA Annual Report for 1986, p. 10.
174. TCPA Annual Report for 1989, Section D. 1.

9

TOWARDS A NEW CONSENSUS?

If one has a belief in the worth of history, simply to record a particular set of events has a value in itself. Each generation has a duty to keep its books in order, and to pass on an account that is as fair and as close to the truth as it can be. This is not just to be fastidious, but to acknowledge that future decisions may be shaped by the way in which one interprets and recalls the past.

In the previous pages an attempt has been made to do just that – to piece together various fragments from a postwar archive to offer an account of what actually happened in the life of a single organization. But that is not all that is attempted. As well as providing an account of the internal workings of the TCPA, an attempt has also been made to locate its campaigning within a wider context of politics and planning. The Association has sought to influence events which, in turn, have served to shape its own actions and effectiveness.

In this concluding chapter, the first section reflects on some of the lessons of the Association's postwar campaigns. Was the organization as effective as it might have been? What can it count as its 'successes' and 'failures'? To what extent has it made a mark on the wider development of modern planning theory and practice?

This is followed by a section which reflects at a more abstract level on the role of pressure groups in postwar Britain. With an eye to the future as well as to the past, one must ask whether extra-Parliamentary activity is an effective source of influence. More fundamentally, the question is raised as to the location of political power in British society. Is a belief in pressure group politics little more than a pluralist illusion, or, empirically, does the evidence suggest that it is a real source of initiating social change?

Finally, in looking back one also has an opportunity to look forward. On the basis of what is known to date, is there a future for a campaigning body like the TCPA? Are its assumptions and policy objectives any longer relevant? On a wider level, what are the trends and changes likely to be in planning during the rest of the 1990s and into the next millennium? Is there a new consensus in the making, and, if so, how might this best be held together? Having witnessed the loss of an earlier consensus, what might be done to enhance the durability of a future one?

'SOME RUNNING EFFECT'

Things like the TCPA do have some running effect on the national situation. (F. J. Osborn, in Hughes, 1971, p. 173)

Osborn's claim about the 'running effect' of the TCPA was made at the end of the 1940s, when he, in particular, was still very much an insider in terms of the postwar planning debate and when the Association was an important focus for overseas interest in the much-admired new system. Even in that context it was a qualified claim. Osborn had experienced enough disappointments to know that 'some' effect might be the most for which one could hope, while the reference to 'things like the TCPA' is a recognition that there were other actors on the political stage (and by no means all reading the same lines).

But even with its qualifications it is an assertive statement, and one wonders whether, forty years on, the same claim could still be made. With hindsight, what effect, if any, has this one organization had on the development of postwar planning? It is, of course, an extra-ordinarily difficult question to answer – requiring the disentangling of numerous interwoven threads of influence, and an attempt to see where each starts and ends.

There is, however, a single, related question which takes one straight to the heart of the issue, and that is to ask to what extent the TCPA has achieved its own goals. What has its mission been and has it been fulfilled?

The fact is that (within a common theme of seeking 'good plan-ning') its mission has changed over the years, and there is no obvious base-line against which to measure subsequent achievement. Under Osborn's leadership the organization's name change in 1941 (from Garden Cities and Town Planning Association to its present title) was an obvious break with the past and a clear bid to represent a coalition of interests in favour of a comprehensive system of town and country planning. Principles were enunciated, and the Association was con-sulted by successive governments, but by the end of the 1940s the new planning system was certainly not equal to the stated aims of the Association. For all his acknowledgement of having 'some influence', Osborn was also in less guarded moments pessimistic about the outcome of a lengthy campaign. Not only was the machinery of planning seen to be deficient in various important ways, but, as he frequently noted, it was failing to excite the support of the general public. Where was the vision (for so long championed by the Association) to give direction to the new system?

Throughout the 1950s the Association persisted with its broad objectives of advocating 'a national policy of land-use planning that will improve living and working conditions, advance industrial and business efficiency, safeguard green belts and the best farmland, and enhance natural, architectural, and cultural amenities; so administered as to leave the maximum freedom to private and local initiative consistent with those aims.'[1] Its influence was undoubtedly exerted on some policy issues – on the framing of the Town Development Act, and the formulation of a national policy for green belts, for instance – but the decade ended with little to celebrate. In relation to the Association's aims, Peter Self's *Cities in Flood* was a reminder of how far short the system had already fallen.

Hope was revived for a while in the 1960s, with the Association's networks of political influence as effective as at any time for twenty years. Regional planning was at the top of the agenda and there were signs of a return to basic principles. The Association seemed to be once again back in the centre of a lively planning debate. A succession of regional plans encouraged a new surge of interest and affirmation for a tradition of thinking that went back to Abercrombie, if not to Howard at the end of the last century. In a period of unprecedented growth and development, planning attracted a revived consensus of informed opinion.[2]

But the new plans were not as effective as they might have been, and it was not until the publication in 1970 of the *Strategic Plan for the South-East* that the Association could see some consistency with its own objectives. By then, however, as events have shown, it was too late to implement, and the 1970s spelt the beginning of the end for the whole postwar consensus. The logic of the TCPA's case remained, but on the ground the chances of achieving a rational dispersalist policy were receding by the year.

In the face of uncertainties surrounding the future of planning, during the 1970s and 1980s the Association hedged its bets. It retained its general objectives, including the constant espousal of a need for strategic planning, but it also put a greater emphasis than hitherto on the involvement of the consumers of planning. Initiatives in areas like environmental education, planning aid and new communities date from this period. In further widening the aims of the Association in this way (under a general rubric of campaigning for 'people, planning and places'), the 'running effect' of the organization was both weakened and strengthened. It was weakened in the sense that efforts were diffused, and to outsiders it has not always been clear as to what the Association represents. But it was strengthened to the extent that, with more options available, there was a reasonable chance that some would succeed; and, less pragmatically, because there was a belief that in balancing strategic and local issues the Association was returning to the very roots of garden city principles.

By the end of the 1980s there was some evidence to suggest that informed opinion was shifting back once more to an acceptance of planning as an essential part of the machinery of government. In the face of striking evidence of congestion in some areas and neglect and under-development in others, and against a backcloth of public concern for the environment, the idea of strategic planning as a framework for change has returned to the agenda of each of the political parties. Similarly, the populist approach as demonstrated by the Association has found a wider currency, in planning and related fields such as architecture. In this latter context, the commitment of the then Secretary of State for the Environment, Christopher Patten (in his first major policy address on planning), to promote the decentralization of decision-making could, with hindsight, be interpreted as perhaps the beginnings of a turn in the tide.[3]

How far these various shifts in the past twenty years can be said to be due to the work of the TCPA is debatable. The process of influencing politicians and others is a slow and often unrecorded process that defies easy assessment, but it is probably not insignificant. Even if the work of the Association represents but one of a variety of sources of influence, it cannot be discounted. A climate of opinion is created which, when the time comes – through force of circumstances, rather than simply through the force of ideas – provides an environment for change. There is no single message that the Association has communicated, but along with the Royal Town Planning Institute (which has, in recent years, adopted a more promotional role), with environmental pressure groups (like the Council for the Protection of Rural England and Friends of the Earth), and with community organizations (like its six co-publishers of *Network*) various aspects of planning have been kept on the agenda.

As the above paragraphs and preceding chapters indicate, the Association might reasonably claim (as Osborn did in 1949) 'some running effect' on the development of planning, but it has been by no means an unqualified story of success. Not only has the machinery of planning failed to live up to expectations, but the output of planning – as measured by the quality and efficiency of living and working environments – today falls far short of the heady aspirations of the mid-1940s, to which the TCPA and others subscribed.

'Before we build – a plan', proclaimed the first of a series of posters produced in the light of the 1947 Act by the Central Office of Information for the Ministry of Town and Country Planning. In contrast to pictures of congested and smoke-covered towns, and of villages defaced with advertisement hoardings, alternative visions were offered of spacious housing estates, modern factories in a landscaped setting and of protected villages. The new planning machinery offered the key to a better environment, and in another poster the Ministry sought to enlist the support of the public in building a new Britain.

An informed and enthusiastic public behind the planners can make a valuable contribution to ultimate success. It is therefore clearly to our advantage to take a keen and active interest in town and country planning and thereby ensure that our future towns and cities shall become places where all may live, work and play amid pleasant and healthy surroundings.[4]

This was the language and the vision of the 1940s, and it was endorsed in each of the main postwar redevelopment plans and publications of that period.[5] Yet in spite of, and partly because of, the undreamt of improvement in material standards that followed, the reality of town and country some forty years later is a world apart from the earlier vision. Misdirected investment has brought little of lasting benefit. The areas of most intensive urban redevelopment are now problem-ridden inner cities, a failure to match land-use change with transport provision has created congestion on a national scale, and the social and ecological qualities of the countryside have suffered in the face of barely-restrained economic demands. Moreover, the language of the present sounds a far cry from that of the immediate postwar era. Now there is no vision, no pretence that planning will be used to counter market trends in other than a cosmetic sense. It is a recognition of the situation rather than a criticism to observe that modern plans might strike more of a common chord with an accountant or a marketing executive than with the social idealist, let alone the general public.

To the extent that this enormous gap exists between hopes (that were shared, and, in part, shaped) by the TCPA and the reality of an inferior environment, it has to be said that the postwar campaign of the Association must have 'failed'. Certainly, some notable successes have been achieved along the way, and the fact that planning has survived at all has to be seen within a context of constant lobbying and extra-Parliamentary support. But the simple 'dispersalist policy' (so eloquently advocated by Osborn and his successors) of redeveloping towns at lower densities, of relocating the displaced population in planned overspill settlements, and of protecting the intervening countryside has undoubtedly failed in the face of market forces that have proven to be stronger than the instruments of planning.

But why is this? Is the cause for relative failure to be found in the organizational structure of the Association? Is it due to a commitment to aims that are too diffuse? Or is it, quite simply, because no one organization can be expected to resist the pressure of more powerful trends in society.

On the organizational front, any assessment as to whether the Association has been as effective as it might have been has to rest on the consistent fact that it is a small body with limited resources. At any one time, it has had to rely heavily on the abilities of its Director and on a handful of supporting staff. F. J. Osborn, Wyndham Thomas and David Hall have each played a leading role in this respect – with Osborn articulating most clearly the case for a dispersalist policy, with Thomas ably picking up the baton (and carrying it under the watchful eye of his mentor), and with Hall widening the brief to embrace community as well as strategic issues. If energy and enthusiasm for the cause are taken as an index of effectiveness, the record of each of the above is beyond question.

David Hall, Director of the TCPA since 1967.

Moreover, the quality of leadership has been enhanced by the high calibre of supporting officers (including those working on special projects, like Colin Ward and David Lock) and by voluntary committee members from professional, political and academic circles.[6] Over the years, the Association has had little difficulty in attracting an inner circle of active supporters of a high calibre – performing the role of a 'think tank', and located geographically as well as functionally mid-way between the government offices of Whitehall and the still largely gentlemen's clubs of Pall Mall. It is at once a part of an Establishment network of policy-making and influence yet also, in preserving its stance as an active critic of official policies, necessarily outside it.

Within the limits of its own remit, the Association has probably been an effective force. What must be questioned, however, is whether the remit itself has been the right one. The fact is that it has remained a small organization, and has had to work within severe resource and staffing constraints. This, in turn, is commonly attributed to the fact that, with generalist objectives, it has always found it difficult to recruit a large number of members and to stimulate active groups around the country. It has fared notably worse than single interest groups with well-defined goals that have found it easier to build a popular following. Planning itself (apart from the fact that it is tainted by its own poor record) is too abstract a concept, and too orientated towards means rather than ends, to rally the troops.

At various times the cost of this, in terms of a small total of members has been lamented, yet there is no record of a serious attempt to restrict or to change the priorities of the Association to redress the situation.[7] Membership drives have consistently been based on existing goals. On balance, this has probably been the correct strategy, for it would have been wrong to have distorted the principles of the Association for purely functional ends. And the implications of continuing as a small group have at least been recognized through the adoption of practices that rely on the work of an influential elite rather than a mass membership. However, one cannot but note an opportunity cost in terms of lost numbers, resources and a source of democratic vitality – a vision of the Association as it might have been.

All of this, of course, is to beg two related questions. One is that, even if a decision had been made to 'popularize' the aims of the Association, it is by no means apparent how this might have been done. A single-minded commitment, for instance, to new communities would have sent out clear signals as to what it stood for – marking out ground that is taken by no other body – but it is questionable whether it would have had a markedly greater popular appeal than existing aims.

A more pertinent question is to ask whether, no matter how effective a group is in organizational terms, it can ever really have a serious impact on political decisions. This is a fundamental question of agency and structure, of the influence of individuals and groups on the one hand, and of the basic structure and imperatives of society on the other. Can a pressure group like the TCPA hope to exert any real influence, or is it too constrained by the workings of a capitalist society in which political power is unevenly distributed? Empirically, the evidence suggests that it can at times exert some influence and that it can help to shape public opinion, but that for a basically market-orientated system to respond, greater pressure would be required than that which can be exerted by a single group.

Theoretically, the conclusion is much the same; pressure groups occupy an ambivalent role in British society, and any assessment depends very largely on what initial assumptions one is making. If the assumptions are based on a belief that the system is essentially open and democratic, and that the wheels of government and influence are well-oiled, then the potential of a pressure group to influence events is considerable. If, however, it is believed that so-called democratic institutions are a sham and that political power is located elsewhere, then groups such as the TCPA might be knocking at the wrong door. It is in the context of these alternative sets of assumptions that, in the following section, a broader political assessment is made.

A QUESTION OF PRESSURE

> Much of the most important pressure group influence is wielded by groups which do not need to conduct high profile public campaigns. (Jordan and Richardson, 1987, p. 6)

Seeking a measure of consensus in favour of positive planning has called for the exertion of pressure through a variety of means over a long period. What the evidence of this particular process reveals is that the extent to which avowed aims can be achieved is a product not only of the internal organization of such a campaign (or series of campaigns) but also of the changing political context.

These internal and external factors are interconnected and give rise to a number of questions that are generic to pressure group politics in a wider sense. What is the legitimacy of a group to promote a particular case? What constituency is it representing, and what is its professional standing to enable it to do so? What access does it have to sources of decision-making, and when it lobbies what channels does it follow? Finally (recalling R. A. Butler's classic dictum that 'politics is the practice of the art of the possible') how adaptable is such a group and how willing is it to modify its aims to meet new political situations?

On all of these questions, the evidence of the TCPA's campaign has already been presented. The Association claims legitimacy on the basis of being a long-established and generally well-respected organization that has always campaigned on the basis of rational argument. Although it has never enjoyed a mass membership it has attempted throughout its history to represent popular interests. Various means of arousing public opinion and of securing political support have been developed, reflecting political as well as professional skills. And it has proved to be remarkably adaptable to changing circumstances.

Yet all of these observations still beg a further question as to the scope that exists to affect public policy. And this question, in turn, calls for a closer look at the pluralist assumptions that underpin so much of the work of pressure groups and, indeed, of the very idea of consensus.

Various writers have contributed to an understanding of 'pressure groups at work', on the basis of pluralist assumptions of a political system that is open and receptive to this type of intervention. Lowe and Goyder (focusing on environmental pressure groups) have been particularly helpful in this respect.[8] Studies of specific environmental pressure groups within an assumed pluralist framework tend to emphasize organizational characteristics – the extent to which the structure of the group reflects specified aims, relations between the leadership and membership, the degree of professional expertise and the credibility of such groups (sometimes measured by the exclusivity of information available to them), the ability of such groups to communicate information to the media and to target political and administrative personnel, and accessibility to sources of finance.

On the basis of this kind of evidence the ability of groups to influence decisions and to affect policies is most commonly assessed. Successive writers have tended to demonstrate that the most effective groups are those which engage in a continuous process of influence rather than concentrating on sensational or 'one-off' issues. The work of the National Farmers' Union in influencing agricultural policy is a good case in point.[9] Reinforcing the notion that it is sometimes the persistence of quiet work behind the scenes that yields the best results, Eckstein has gone so far as to suggest that 'the influence of groups is enhanced by the lack of any wide public interest in an area of policy.'[10] This line of reasoning is developed by Jordan and Richardson, who assert that the basis of pressure group power is not the threat of non-cooperation; a place exist for groups like the TCPA, although 'it is difficult to see [this body] as one of the commanding institutions of society.'[11] The view is further reinforced by another writer who concludes that 'Whitehall needs the active support of groups such as the Town and Country Planning Association.'[12]

What all of this assumes is that there are corridors of power, some at least of which are open to informed groups. Access is open not simply because it is demanded but because decision-makers themselves find advantage in this process; negotiation and consultation are important features of a pluralist model. Whitehall relies on specialist advice from groups which have professional credibility, which are seen as 'legitimate', which have specific and essentially non-controversial goals, and which, therefore, have *de facto* access in terms of lines of communication. From the pressure group's perspective, it is a process of cultivating contacts and of maintaining dialogue, of 'getting into the In-Tray'.[13] Success in achieving this level of contact and involvement becomes 'a function of limited goals and a bargaining mentality.'[14] There has to exist a measure of professional and mutual respect as a basis for negotiations in what has become an increasingly sectoral and segmented process of decision-making.

In this respect, the TCPA has been able to define a role that is legitimate to government, and it is no coincidence that the offices of the Association are located 'across the Park', just a short distance from Whitehall and the Houses of Parliament.[15] The Association's legitimacy is based, in turn, on professionalism and on effective leadership; it has gained the ear of successive Ministers and senior civil servants in the postwar period, and it continues to be regularly consulted. With few exceptions (an issue like that of the Divis has not been typical) its approach has generally been one of relying on quiet persuasion rather than one of seeking to capture headlines. It has sought to nurture contacts and to engender a sense of cooperation and mutual self-interest; to lodge itself as much as possible within the framework of government.

Such an approach is consistent with a pluralist view of the State. 'The idea of a mutually rewarding relationship between groups and government departments is an important dimension of political science . . . in the United Kingdom . . . in the 20th century.'[16] This view is deeply embedded in studies of the political system, and various writers have strengthened the belief that power is accessible to those who learn to use the system effectively.[17] According to the late political commentator, Robert McKenzie: 'Pressure groups are far more important than the political parties for the transmission of political ideas from the mass of the citizenry to its rulers.'[18] Similarly, influential politicians like Tony Benn have continually stressed the political significance of 'pressure groups as the new centres of democratic initiative outside the party system.'[19] Pressure groups are accorded a key role in sustaining democracy, as illustrated by the view that 'interest groups provide the key to unlock the workings of British politics.'[20]

Pluralist theory has maintained its explanatory power because it has continually shifted to take account of changes in processes of decision-making by government. It is accepted by pluralists that 'democratic processes' are far from ideal and that, for instance, increasing bureaucratization and a growing number of quasi-government agencies may make it more difficult to participate in decision-making. Channels of communication become tortuous, and decision-making is caught up in the log-jam of 'government over-load'.[21] But pluralists hold to the view that ways through can be found, and that the basic problem is one of competition between interests rather than one of outright conflict. Consensus and the idea of a common good remains a beacon of hope, and there is optimism in the view that 'countervailing groups will emerge to reflect and defend common interests.'[22]

Much of what the TCPA has done in the postwar period – working not only to retain a consensus in the idea of planning but to convince successive governments that dispersal policy holds the key to the sensible use of Britain's land – can be located in terms of pluralist theory. During the 1980s, however, a more contentious political context evolved, in which consensus became an unrealistic aim, and in which questions were raised about this way of seeing things. The TCPA itself responded, not by abandoning its long-held commitment to negotiation but by developing a second strand of direct action. This latter approach was more typical of other environmental pressure groups that adopted a confrontational approach; Greenpeace provides one example, Animal Rights activists another. What is at issue (and which can provide a setting for the 1990s) is the very nature of the politics of pressure. Has the ground on which it is based shifted so much that traditional notions of pluralist negotiation no longer hold good? Has a state of conflict usurped a belief in consensus?

Even before the 1980s this debate was being actively explored. In *Politics by Pressure*, for instance, Patrick Rivers argued that whatever sort of parliamentary democracy existed in Britain it was rapidly being replaced by the 'politics of pressure': 'Democracy is in full retreat before the dual forces of informed officialdom and functional representation.'[23] Another environmental author, Frank Fraser-Darling, was less circumspect: 'The uncoordinated growth of each sectional interest produces aimless growth of the aggregate . . . the power to shape society has passed from the old authorities . . . to a new breed of people, centred principally where the money is, in trade, industry, commerce and the bureaucracies with which they coexist.'[24]

Both Rivers and Fraser-Darling lament the growing problems

encountered in seeking to influence decisions and to secure rational politics. Taking this a stage further, for the Marxist this type of situation should evoke no surprise, and a belief that pressure groups have an important role to play is exaggerated. Pluralism, from a Marxist standpoint, is likened to a smoke screen which effectively conceals from the public the realities of power; parliamentary democracy is an illusion. It is argued that pluralists deal only with the perceived 'face' of power, and that they are concerned almost exclusively with action (hence the importance of pressure groups). For the Marxist it is the economic organization of society and its essentially class-based nature which is paramount, and pluralist claims to the contrary serve merely to legitimize inequalities in the distribution of power. Various interests may be seen to be participating, but with 'business entering the pluralist competition on extremely favourable terms in comparison with labour or any other interest.'[25]

From this perspective, then, pressure groups like the TCPA will occupy a very marginal place and will enjoy little in the way of access to the real levers of power. At times when such groups appear to have a more active role there is a danger that this will simply have been allowed in order to legitimize other interests.

Another critical perspective that has informed the pressure group debate is that of corporatism. With this, consensus is shaped not by a multiplicity of interests but through a limited representation; corporatism 'does not outlaw rival interest groups but rather accords certain corporate groups a monopoly over representing given social interests . . .'[26] Pressure groups have a part to play but access to power is very constrained and by no means equitable. Some interest groups (notably, 'insider' groups) enjoy considerably more access than others. Thus, a corporatist explanation might highlight the essentially 'outsider' position of the TCPA, knocking on doors of government offices rather than having a reserved place within. It will be considerably disadvantaged as compared with business interests.

It has to be said, however, that neither the Marxist nor the corporatist models provide totally satisfactory explanations – the former because it has not given sufficient weight to more subtle aspects of persuasion and opinion-forming, and the latter because it has not responded to the realities of a more diffuse decision-making structure (particularly in the light of the impact of the revolution in information technology).[27] Over the last decade a more spirited critique of pluralism has come from the New Right, an ideological stance buttressed by the advantage of having in office a succession of governments of that persuasion.

Of particular relevance to this argument is the New Right's belief that the process of government has become 'clogged up' as a result of an era in which access has been too open. The problem is that of 'overloaded government'. A proliferation of bureaucratic practices during the postwar period has let in too many interests, each demanding a say in policy, and this has led to a breakdown in checks and balances. The demands of organized labour are seen as being particularly threatening, though the critique goes further than that. The public has come to expect too much from the system, and its demands are unrealistic in terms of what can be delivered. Consensus is seen to be both a sign of weak government (encouraging the view that all interests can be met), and also a practical encumbrance in that it invites too many 'cooks into the kitchen'. Its rejection has, not surprisingly, led to a growth in conflict and adversarial politics.

The impact of this approach on many pressure groups has been marked. Some, starved of financial support (as, for instance, with the abolition of the Greater London Council) have simply disappeared altogether. Equally, new groups, responding to a climate of conflict, have been brought into existence. Meanwhile, many existing groups, especially in the environmental field, have reviewed their methods in the light of a less responsive political context. The TCPA's own more strident activities of the 1980s are, perhaps, indicative of a wider trend at a time when rational argument was unlikely to win the day.

The New Right still enjoys a powerful hold on political thinking in Westminster; since the end of the 1970s a generation of civil servants and politicians has worked on these ideas. But the evidence of the postwar period as a whole is that political ideologies are like shifting sands. The message for pressure groups is that there are times when their intervention will be welcome and other times when it will not. There are times when consensus will set the agenda and will determine methods of lobbying, and other times when conflict is prevalent and the methods of pressure groups will themselves be changed.

Even allowing for different critical standpoints, it cannot be concluded that there is any one period when pressure groups will be totally effective or totally ineffective; nor can one conclude that the efficiency of a group can itself provide a full measure of its ability to influence policy. To varying degrees, Marxists, corporatists and proponents of the New Right will each accord a lesser role for pressure groups than pluralists, but the evidence of groups like the TCPA is that the question of influence is really one that is relative rather than absolute. The fact remains that, at the start of the 1990s, the TCPA is still very much in business, although at times over the past decade the walk 'across the Park' must have seemed rather further than earlier campaigners will recall.

UNFINISHED BUSINESS

> The top prize went to the Town and Country Planning Association's Lightmoor project at Telford New Town. In his speech, the Prince delivered yet another of his memorable quotes for the assembled media: he spoke of the need to overcome the 'spaghetti bolognese of red tape' that held up the efforts of ordinary people to create their own environment. As one television programme after another followed the battles of the community-builders with the entrenched bureaucracies, it seems that Howard, Geddes, Turner and the anarchist tradition in planning had achieved ultimate respectability at last. (Hall, 1988, p. 272)

Ebenezer Howard, the heroic simpleton and inventor, had a range of personal beliefs, one of which was reincarnation. He wrote to Cecil Harmsworth in 1911, saying that although 'generally about 600 years elapse between one incarnation and another', special arrangements would be made 'at this extraordinary juncture of affairs' so that 'volunteers who have special work to do on this planet can return to Earth within a few years.'[28]

Whether his remark was serious or playful, it is true that the Association that he inspired has depended all through its history upon a series of volunteers with special work to do. Howard himself, assuming that the opportunity was really available, would certainly feel obliged to seek reincarnation in the light of the work remaining to be done. For he would find to his dismay that in spite of immense efforts by the propaganda he set in motion neither governmental action nor public opinion had finally come to grips with the issues he saw as important ninety years ago.

He would have felt a great sense of loss to learn that, in spite of the efforts of Liberal governments before the First World War and of Labour governments after the Second World War, we have found no political consensus on the crucial issue of retaining the development value of land for the community that creates it. The result is that today in the South of England the price of the site can be 40 per cent of the cost of a house. Consequently, just as affluence brings the demand for more domestic space, actual densities of new housing developments are far higher than they were in Howard's day, in the interwar years or in the first three postwar decades. The assumption that the appropriate use of any piece of land is the one that yields the greatest income on its speculative capital value results in the steady erosion of urban green space, not only in the cities but in small towns and even villages. The moralist in Howard would wonder how his descendants could continue to tolerate the parasitical fortunes won by doing nothing with land except owning it.

He would have been no less dismayed at the superficiality of our response to the situation where London's transport system is, once again, grinding to a halt, with congested streets and an overloaded railway system. We blame everything except our own failure to promote the decentralization of office work. Sensible interim measures like the Location of Offices Bureau had 'enormously facilitated'[29] the outward movement of jobs of this kind, but was abruptly switched into reverse and then abolished by subsequent governments.

He would have been grieved by our tacit abandonment of his own most cherished demonstration project, the garden city. Had he not tried to provide working models to prove his contentions, and had he not had the posthumous satisfaction of seeing something like them inserted into public policy in the new towns? A reincarnated Howard would certainly have agreed with David Hall's contention that there is a greater need for garden cities and new settlements, especially in the South East of England, than at any time since the heyday of the postwar new towns programme.[30] Howard, of course, like his disciple Frederic Osborn, would have had many reservations about new town policy and practice. Above all, he would have thought that one of the immense advantages that he claimed for the garden city – that its assets should accrue to its residents – had been discarded by the sale of these communal assets in the private market.

Disillusionment and grief would be the sentiments felt by the reincarnation of Ebenezer Howard, at the lost opportunities for building his utopia of garden cities and social cities, but the original Howard was far more philosophical. Another of his enthusiasms was the world language Esperanto, and he was able to use that language in addressing an international conference in words which epitomize the experience of the Association:

> One should never be excessively realistic in humane plans.
> There are always too many difficulties and only a small
> percentage of aims may be attained. Our aspirations therefore
> should always be as far-reaching as they can be, so as to make it
> possible to retract from some of them if necessary; for great
> gains are not to be thought of. And the percentage of losses
> depends only on the enthusiasm, energy and perseverance of the
> idealists who undertake it.[31]

A second reason why Howard would not have despaired is precisely because, far from expecting a government to initiate change, Howard valued little local enterprises. 'He had no belief in "the State",' wrote Frederic Osborn,[32] and the geographer Peter Hall perceived that 'one brilliant feature of Howard's plan is that it could be created incrementally, by scores of local initiatives.'[33] This is why Hall sees the TCPA's Lightmoor project not as a diversion from the major tasks of the Association, but as an assertion of an alternative tradition in the planning movement. As 'green' or 'environmental' issues move steadily up the political agenda, Howard's tradition, entirely devoid of sentimental ruralism but concerned with 'the rejection of monolithic state socialism, and the stress on local collective action',[34] grows in stature. He cannot be dismissed as escapist like so many of his Victorian intellectual contemporaries, Hall asserts, since:

> unlike them, he never rejects industry or technology or urbanism in themselves, seeing them rather as the essential means toward his alternative society. But at the same time, by freeing men and women of the burden of inherited land wealth, Howard is able to produce a vision of free, independent and creative spirits. It is the homesteading spirit brought home to industrial England.[35]

The final reason why Howard would not have seen ninety years of effort as wasted is his apolitical stance. Fundamentally, he was interested in social processes, not in the physical details of planning, nor in parliamentary programmes. The Association itself has, like any interest group or cause, been obliged to seek to influence whatever political party chanced to be in office, and as Lewis Mumford observed, 'With his gift of sweet reasonableness Howard hoped to win Tory and Anarchist, single-taxer and socialist, individualist and collectivist, over to his experiment. And his hopes were not altogether discomfited; for in appealing to the English instinct for finding common ground he was utilizing a solid political tradition.'[36] Consensus, indeed, was at the very heart of Howard's plans.

The strengths of his politically empirical approach are illustrated by the planning history of the 1980s, in which governmental rhetoric followed a populist approach of 'lifting the burden'[37] that the inheritance of planning legislation had imposed. But the White Paper which promoted this particular approach also answered the question of the promoting Minister, Lord Young, 'Do we need the present town planning system?' with the answer that '. . . in many ways it has served the country well and the Government has no intention of abolishing it'.[38] Regional and strategic planning was tacitly abandoned, but the green belt was, after several test cases, pronounced to be sacrosanct. In fact:

> Planning is still being practised, there has been no major reform of the Town and Country Planning Acts of 1968 and 1971, and

development plans still have a significant role. Most of the changes in planning have either been revisions of policy within the existing system, or additions to the system, often involving both state intervention and public expenditure. While there has been a sustained attack on planning from the New Right, this has been vigorous in its rhetoric but rather less drastic in its actions.[39]

The New Right itself has re-invested aspects of Howard's proposals in a form rather closer to Howard's conception of the garden city than the actual implementation of a new towns policy by earlier Labour or Conservative governments. The Adam Smith Institute, widely regarded as the 'think tank' of the Thatcher governments of the 1980s, launched a proposal which is closer to Howard than to anything that has actually happened since he set up his two garden cities. *The Economist* reported that

The Adam Smith Institute has just come up with the idea of towns owned by their residents – and selected Scottish new towns as suitable guinea-pigs. Their assets could be taken over by companies in which each resident owns a share. Unlike in par-value cooperatives, which have taken root on some Glasgow housing estates, residents would be able to realise capital gains on their shares when moving on. But rather than allowing shares to be traded freely on the open market, some towns might like to restrict ownership to residents; in Spain's worker-resident towns, newcomers must buy stock and emigrants sell it back to the commune.[40]

This proposal arrived on the scene rather late for adoption by the radical Right; perhaps it will one day be taken up by the radical Left. But it is a reminder that any propagandist group has to operate within the political and social climate of the time. When private philanthropy and limited dividend investment was the accepted mode of innovation, this was the chosen vehicle, inevitably, for Howard's two demonstration garden cities. He had no faith in legislative action except where it could be exploited as an imperfect mode of realizing broader aims. In the abandoned drafts for his book he had written that 'so vast a crowd of constitution members are buzzing around the Parliamentary machine, each waiting to start it to work; so much steam does it require to keep it going . . . that it is, in practice, long after a majority are distinctly agreed on the passing of a measure that it at length emerges in a frequently mangled shape from this complex and cumbrous piece of machinery.'[41]

Fifty years later, in the climate of the Second World War, his

successor Frederic Osborn, endlessly lobbying government committees and commissions and legislators, as well as orchestrating a
propaganda campaign towards the general public and its aspirations
for a better Britain after the war, could well have shared these
sentiments. But since the mood of the time actually demanded large-
scale government action, he sought to exercise the art of the possible.

By the 1970s, with widespread disillusionment with the results of
what was conceived as 'planning', the Association was shifting its
perspective 'towards a more populist stance' through its espousal of
planning aid and environmental education and by flying the kite of
the Third Garden City. In the 1980s it found that a different style
of populism was used to win elections. Language like 'freeing initiative and enterprise from the dead hand of bureaucracy' was used, but
the policies actually adopted by government were designed to ensure
that all strategic decisions were made, with little or no consultation,
by central government. Independent action by local authorities of
whatever political colour was being replaced by centrally funded
token initiatives.

Now, in the 1990s, town and country planning campaigners
approach the new century with the same aims that first obliged a
handful of people to inaugurate the Garden City Association at the
end of the last century, to secure some means by which the betterment value of land accrues to the communities that create those
values, and to transform the cities into the polynuclear social city that
Howard envisaged. These aspirations imply a regionalist, decentralist approach which has been immensely assisted by the transforma-
tions in industry, power sources and communications in the twentieth
century.

One might optimistically conclude that the makings are there for
the emergence of a new consensus. Politicians of different parties
have identified quality of life issues as an item of major concern,
assuring a key role for planning in the 1990s.[42] 'It may be a good time
to consider the possibility of a new consensus', is the view of Peter
Self,[43] a view shared by other commentators.[44] And, spelling out
what might be at the heart of this consensus, Patsy Healey rightly
points to the way in which planning is conducted as well as to what it
addresses. 'The keywords in the redesign of the planning system
should therefore be citizen responsiveness in a democratic society
and environmental consciousness.'[45]

Perhaps, in the last decade of the twentieth century, nothing better
illustrates the potential for achieving this new consensus than the
issue of the environment. Just as 'the housing question' served to
focus campaigning efforts a hundred years ago, now it is the environment that attracts attention. While Howard worked alongside housing reformers, the modern arena for the TCPA is that of green

politics. Pressure groups, in order to remain effective, have not simply to create new political agenda but also to adjust their own priorities in changing circumstances. From garden cities to new towns, from regional and community planning to green politics, the focal point of a continuing campaign has periodically shifted.

After the rearguard actions of the 1980s, when it seemed as if the very future of planning was at stake, the opportunity is now presented to campaign for more effective planning as a means of achieving the higher environmental standards that are widely demanded. A measure of an emerging consensus on this issue can be seen in the form of the policy documents produced in September and October 1990 by each of the three major political parties. The government's own White Paper on the environment, *This Common Inheritance*, sets the scene with its wide-ranging coverage, dealing with issues 'from the street corner to the stratisphere'. Both the Liberal Democrats, in their environmental statement, *What Price Our Planet?*, and the Labour Party, in *An Earthly Chance*, reinforce this type of comprehensive approach. Important differences exist between the three parties, but all are agreed on a need to respond to environmental problems from the local through to the global level.

And all are agreed that an effective planning system is a means to achieve this; the point being well expressed by the Labour Party in the view that 'a revived recognition of the value of planning is long overdue. After a decade in which the value of planning has been consistently undermined by central government, the time is now ripe to recognise that planning is one of the most important instruments we have in seeking to achieve environmental objectives.'[46] Similarly, speaking at the 1990 Town and Country Planning Summer School, the environmentalist Jonathon Porritt argued that a greener future will be inconceivable without an overhaul and extension of the planning system.[47] The environment has emerged as a major political issue, and planning has been relocated from the periphery of political concerns to a central position in this debate.

This is an encouraging context for the TCPA to redirect its continuing campaign. It is not a question of jumping onto a bandwagon, for the issues which are at last attracting mainstream political attention are by no means new. The TCPA's own long-standing work in questioning nuclear power policy is entirely consistent with these new developments, as, indeed (returning to its origins) is the very idea of the garden city, with its enduring aim of creating a healthy environment for all. Understandably, the opportunity will be taken to capitalize on a new foundation of support. Thus, the creation in July 1990 of a working party to examine sustainability, and the annual conference theme in November 1990 of 'planning for sustainable development' is indicative of the organization's response.

For an organization like the TCPA these are challenging times, and there is no shortage of unfinished business. The problem is, however, that which it has been in the past as well – convincing citizens and legislators that it is their unfinished business too, and then of ensuring that planning lives up to its undoubted potential. Opportunities have been lost in the past, but lessons can be taken from this experience to ensure that a new consensus is this time more soundly based.

Tomorrow's consensus must be grounded in a firm understanding of the different and often competing claims on what planning can offer. No policy can afford to neglect the varying needs of different income groups, of those without employment, of ethnic minorities, of the special needs of women, and of the young, old and disabled; nor will the pressing claims of different regions simply disappear.

The return of consensus presents a challenge for planning. New policies will need to appeal to the widest possible constituency, without falling into the old trap of playing down diversity. What will be needed is a version of consensus that is at once pluralistic and responsive, acknowledging the multi-cellular structure of society rather than papering over the joins. Events in the coming years will show whether or not this is possible.

NOTES

'Some running effect'

1. During the 1950s, the aims of the Association were generally listed in the Annual Reports.
2. As a link between the 1950s and 1960s, Peter Self has claimed that his own book, *Cities in Flood*, 'contributed to a consensus about planning goals.' See Peter Self, 'Planning's search for consensus', *The Planner*, Vol. 75, No. 24, 1989, pp. 20–21.
3. The Secretary of State for the Environment, Christopher Patten, promoted this view in his address to the Annual Conference of the TCPA, London, November 1989.
4. Central Office of Information (*c*. 1947) entitled 'How you can help'. An incomplete set of these posters exists in the TCPA archives.
5. For instance, Abercrombie's *Greater London Plan*, 1945, exhorts that 'Courage is needed to seize the moment when it arrives and to make a resolute start' (p. vi).
6. Various interviewees – for instance, Derek Diamond and Mary Riley – have stressed this point, namely, that the TCPA has been well served over the years by the high calibre of its committee members, drawn from a variety of fields.
7. For instance, at the last meeting in 1979 of the Council, John Blake drew attention to the perennial problem of attracting (and retaining) more individual members.

A Question of Pressure

8. Lowe and Goyder (1983).
9. Jordan and Richardson (1987*a*)
10. Eckstein (1960), p. 155.
11. Jordan and Richardson (1987*a*), p. 24.
12. Ashford (1981), p. 51.
13. Jordan and Richardson (1987*a*), p. 40.
14. *Ibid.*, p. 40.
15. David Hall, in discussion, 4th April 1989.
16. Richardson and Jordan (1979), p. 91.
17. For instance, see Dahrendorf (1959), Jordan and Richardson (1987*b*) and Richardson and Jordan (1979).
18. Robert McKenzie, in Hanson and Walles (1980), p. 169.
19. Benn (1981), p. 67.
20. Dearlove and Saunders (1984), p. 56.
21. See, for example, King (1981).
22. Jordan and Richardson, *op. cit.*, p. 62.
23. Rivers (1974), p. 18.
24. Fraser-Darling (1970), p. 48.
25. Miliband (1969), p. 145.
26. Dunleavy and O'Leary (1987), p. 193.
27. See, for instance, Harvey (1989).

Unfinished Business

28. Beevers (1988), p. 181.
29. Hall (1988), p. 13.
30. David Hall, 'The case for new settlements', *TCP*, Vol. 58, No. 4, 1989, pp. 111–114.
31. Waclaw Ostrowski, 'Sir Ebenezer Howard in Poland', *TCP*, Vol. 34, No. 11, 1966, pp. 511–512.
32. Hughes (1971), p. 453.
33. Peter Hall, 'Ebenezer Howard', *New Society*, 11 November 1982, pp. 252–254.
34. *Ibid.*
35. *Ibid.*
36. Mumford, Lewis (1946) 'The garden city idea and modern planning', in Howard (1946 ed.), p. 37.
37. This was the title of a White Paper issued in 1985 by the Minister without Portfolio *et al.* Cmnd 9571. London: HMSO.
38. *Ibid.*, para. 3.1.
39. Brindley *et al.* (1989), p. 1.
40. 'New towns: paradise overdrawn'. *Economist*, 24 September 1988, reported ASI (Research) Ltd (1988) *Livingstone plc I presume*.
41. Beevers (1988), p. 43.
42. For instance, at the 1989 Conservative Party Conference, Christopher Patten, Secretary of State for the Environment, spoke of planning as a 'form of regulation to enhance the quality of life', while John Cunningham, Shadow Environment Secretary, at the Labour Party

Conference, claimed that 'public concern for the quality of life in Britain has never been greater.'

43. Peter Self, 'Planning's search for a political consensus', *The Planner*, Vol. 75, No. 24, 1989, pp. 20–21.
44. For instance, see Peter Hall, 'The TCPA at 90 – some thoughts on past and future', *TCP*, Vol. 58, No. 6, 1989, p. 162.
45. Healey (1989), p. 18.
46. Labour Party (1990), p. 31.
47. Reported in *Planning*, No. 866, 14 September 1990.

CHRONOLOGY OF
IMPORTANT EVENTS 1946–1990

1946 New Towns Act
      Stevenage designated as first new town
1949 TCPA's 50th Anniversary
1951 Festival of Britain: Lansbury as model of urban redevelopment
1952 Town Development Act
1955 National policy for green belts
      Wyndham Thomas appointed Director of TCPA
1959 New Towns Exhibition (to mark TCPA's Diamond Jubilee)
1964 *South East Study* provides context for regional debate
1965 Designation of ten regional councils
1967 David Hall appointed Director of TCPA
1971 Start of Environmental Education Unit
1973 Start of Planning Aid Service
1976 Peter Shore's 'Manchester Speech' heralds end of new towns
      programme
1977 Windscale Inquiry marks start of TCPA's involvement in energy
      policy
1979 Third Garden City: Outline Prospectus
      Opening of Community Technical Aid Centre (Manchester)
1980 Start of Lightmoor project
1981 Start of London Planning Aid Service
1983 Start of Sizewell Inquiry
      Conway neighbourhood survey (start of Laird project)
1984 Start of publication of *Network*
1988 Start of Planning Aid for London
1989 TCPA's 90th Anniversary
1990 *This Common Inheritance* (White Paper) sets planning in context
      of wider environmental debate

BIBLIOGRAPHY

Articles and TCPA policy documents and annual reports are referenced separately in the various chapter notes.

Adams, E. and Ward, C. (1982) *Art and the Built Environment: A teachers' approach*. Harlow: Longman.

Aldous, T. (1975) *Goodbye, Britain?* London: Book Club Associates.

Aldridge, M. (1979) *The British New Towns: A programme without a policy*. London: Routledge and Kegan Paul.

Ambrose, P. (1986) *Whatever Happened to Planning?* London: Methuen.

Ardill, J. (1975) *New Citizen's Guide to Town and Country Planning*. London: Charles Knight.

Armstrong, J. (1985) *The Sizewell Report: A new approach for major public inquiries*. London: TCPA.

Ashford, D. E. (1981) *Policy and Politics in Britain: The limits of consensus*. Philadelphia: Temple University Press.

Bailey, J. (1975) *Social Theory for Planning*. London: Routledge and Kegan Paul.

Ball, A. R. and Millard, F. (1986) *Pressure Politics in Industrial Societies: A comparative introduction*. London: Macmillan.

Banham, M. and Hiller, B. (eds.) (1976) *A Tonic to the Nation: The Festival of Britain*. London: Thames and Hudson.

Barker, T. (ed.) (1978) *The Long March of Everyman 1750–1960*. Harmondsworth: Penguin.

Bauer, C. (1952) *Social Questions in Housing and Town Planning*. London: University of London Press.

Beevers, R. (1988) *The Garden City Utopia: A critical biography of Ebenezer Howard*. London: Macmillan.

Benn. T. (1981) *Arguments for Democracy*. London: Jonathan Cape.

Bentley, A. F. (1908) *The Process of Government*. Cambridge, Mass.: Bellknap Press.

Best, R. (1964) *Land for New Towns*. London: TCPA.

Beveridge, W. (1951) *New Towns and the Case for Them*. London: University of London Press.

Blowers, A. (1984) *Something in the Air: Corporate power and the environment*. London: Harper and Row.

Bogdanor, V. and Skidelsky, R. (eds.) (1970) *The Age of Affluence 1951–1964*. London: Macmillan.

Brindley, T., Rydin, E. and Stoker, G. (1989) *Remaking Planning: The*

politics of urban change in the Thatcher years. London: Unwin Hyman.
Buckman, P. (1970) *The Limits of Protest.* London: Panther.
Cherry, G. E. (1975) *Environmental Planning, 1939–1969.* Vol. 2: *National parks and recreation in the countryside.* London: HMSO.
Cherry, G. E. (1979) *The Evolution of British Town Planning: A history of town planning in the United Kingdom during the 20th century and of the Royal Town Planning Institute 1914–74.* Leighton Buzzard: Leonard Hill.
Cherry, G. E. (ed.) (1981) *Pioneers in British Planning.* London: Architectural Press.
Cherry, G. E. (1981) 'George Pepler 1882–1959' in Cherry (ed.) (1981).
Cherry, G. E. (1982) *The Politics of Town Planning.* London: Longman.
Cherry, G. E. (1988) *Cities and Plans: The shaping of urban Britain in the nineteenth and twentieth centuries.* London: Edward Arnold.
Coleman, A. (1986): *Utopia on Trial.* London: Hilary Shipman.
Cooke, P. (1990) *Back to the Future: Modernity, postmodernity and locality.* London: Unwin Hyman.
Coxall, W. N. (1985) *Political Realities: Parties and pressure groups.* London: Longman.
Craig, F. W. S. (ed.) (1975) *British General Election Manifestoes, 1900–1974.* London: Macmillan.
Crossman, Richard (1975) *The Diaries of a Cabinet Minister.* Vol. 1: *Minister of Housing 1964–66.* London: Hamish Hamilton.
Cullingworth, J. B. (1975) *Environmental Planning 1939 – 1969.* Vol. I *Reconstruction and Land Use Planning, 1939–1947.* London: HMSO.
Cullingworth, J. B. (1979) *Environmental Planning 1939–1969.* Vol. III: *New Towns Policy.* London: HMSO.
Culpin, E. G. (1913) *The Garden City Movement Up-to-date.* London: GCTPA.
Dahl, R. (1967) *Pluralist Democracy in the United States.* Chicago: Rand McNally.
Dahrendorf, R. (1959) *Class and Class Conflict in Industrial Society.* Stanford: Stanford University Press.
Davies, J. G. (1972) *The Evangelistic Bureaucrat: A study of a planning exercise in Newcastle-upon-Tyne.* London: Tavistock.
Dearlove, J. and Saunders, P. (1984) *Introduction to British Politics.* London: Polity Press.
Dennis, N. (1970) *People and Plannning: The sociology of housing in Sunderland.* London: Faber and Faber.
Dix, G. (1981) Patrick Abercrombie 1879 – 1957, in Cherry (ed.) (1981).
Donnison, D. and Soto, P. (1980) *The Good City: A study of urban development and policy in Britain.* London: Heinemann.
Dunleavy, P. and O'Leary, B. (1987) *Theories of the State: The politics of liberal democracy.* London: Macmillan.
Dunnett, Mc G. (ed.) (1951) *Guide to the Exhibition of Architecture, Town-Planning and Building Research.* London: HMSO.
Eckstein, H. (1960) *Pressure Group Politics: The case of the BMA.* Stanford: Stanford University Press.
Environmental Board (1978) *Final Report of the Environmental Board's*

Working Party on Environmental Education. London: Department of the Environment.

Eserin, A. and Hughes, M. (eds.) (1990) *The Sir Frederic Osborn Archive: A descriptive catalogue.* Hertford: Hertfordshire County Council.

Eversley, D. (1973) *The Planner in Society: The changing role of a profession.* London: Faber and Faber.

Fishman, R. (1977) *Urban Utopias in the Twentieth Century.* New York: Basic Books.

Foot, Paul (1968) *The Politics of Harold Wilson.* Harmondsworth: Penguin.

Fraser-Darling, F. (1970) *Wilderness and Plenty.* London: BBC.

Fyson, A. (1976) *Change the Street.* Oxford: Oxford University Press.

Fyson, A. (ed.) (1987) *Planning in Post-War Britain: The J. R. James Memorial Lectures.* London: Royal Town Planning Institute.

Gamble, A. (1988) *The Free Economy and the Strong State: The politics of Thatcherism.* Basingstoke: Macmillan Education.

Garside, P. and Hebbert, M. (eds.) (1989) *British Regionalism 1990–2000.* London: Mansell.

Gibson, T. (1984) *Counterweight: The neighbourhood option.* London: TCPA.

Goodey, B. (1974) *Urban Trails: A preliminary list of trails and sources.* Birmingham: Centre for Urban and Regional Studies.

Goodman, R. (1972) *After the Planners.* Harmondsworth: Penguin.

Green, P. (1973) Facsimile edition of Patrick Geddes (1904) *City Development: A study of parks, gardens and culture institutes.* A Report to the Dunfermline Trust. Shannon: Irish University Press.

Greentown Group (1979) *The Garden City in Milton Keynes.* Milton Keynes.

Hall, P. *et al.* (1973) *The Containment of Urban England*, Vols. 1 and 2. London: Allen and Unwin.

Hall, P. (1988) *Cities of Tomorrow: An intellectual history of urban planning and design in the twentieth century.* Oxford: Basil Blackwell.

Hall, P. (1989) *London 2001.* London: Unwin Hyman.

Hanson, A. H. and Walles, M. (1980) *Governing Britain. A guidebook to political institutions.* London: Fontana.

Hardy, D. (1991) *From Garden Cities to New Towns: Campaigning for town and country planning, 1899–1946.* London: Spon.

Harvey, D. (1989) *The Condition of Postmodernity: An enquiry into the origins of social change.* Oxford: Basil Blackwell.

Healey, P., McDonald, G. and Thomas, M. J., (eds.) (1983): *Planning Theory: Prospects for the 1980s.* Oxford: Pergamon.

Healey, P. (1989) *Planning for the 1990s*, Working Paper Series, No. 7, Department of Town and Country Planning, University of Newcastle-upon-Tyne.

Hebbert, M. (1981) Frederic Osborn 1885–1978, in Cherry (ed.) (1981).

Heseltine, M. (1987) *Where there's a Will.* London: Hutchinson.

Howard, E. (1946 ed.) *Garden Cities of Tomorrow.* London: Faber and Faber.

Hughes, M. (ed.) (1971) *The Letters of Lewis Mumford and Frederic J. Osborn: A transatlantic dialogue, 1938–70.* Bath: Adams and Dart.

Jenkins, P. (1989) *Mrs Thatcher's Revolution: The ending of the socialist era.* London: Pan.

Jordan, A. G. and Richardson, J. J. (1987*a*) *Government and Pressure Groups in Britain.* Oxford: Clarendon Press.

Jordan, A. G. and Richardson, J. J. (1987*b*) *British Politics and the Policy Process.* London: Allen and Unwin.

Keable, G. (1963) *To-morrow Slowly Comes.* London: TCPA.

Keeble, L. (1961) *Town Planning at the Crossroads.* London: Estates Gazette.

Kimber, R. and Richardson, J. J. (1974) *Pressure Groups in Britain.* London: Dent.

King, A. (1981) The Problem of Overloaded Government, in Potter, D. *et al.* (1981).

Kingdon, J. W. (1984) *Agendas, Alternatives and Public Policies,* Boston: Little Brown.

Labour Party (1990) *An Earthly Chance.* London.

Liberal Democrats (1990) *What Price our Planet?* London.

Lock, D. (1989) *Riding the Tiger: Planning the South of England.* London: TCPA.

Lowe, P. and Goyder, J. (1983) *Environmental Groups in Politics.* London: Allen and Unwin.

Lynch, K. (1960) *The Image of the City.* Cambridge, Mass.: MIT Press.

McKay, D. H. and Cox, A. W. (1979) *The Politics of Urban Change.* London: Croom Helm.

McKie, D. and Cook, C. (1972) *The Decade of Disillusion: British Politics in the Sixties.* London: Macmillan.

Marwick, A. (1982) *British History since 1945.* Harmondsworth: Penguin.

Midwinter, E. (1972) *Projections: An Education Priority Area at Work.* London: Ward Lock.

Miliband, R. (1969) *The State in Capitalist Society.* London: Weidenfield and Nicholson.

Ministry of Housing and Local Government (1964) *The South-East Study, 1961–81.* London: HMSO.

Ministry of Local Government and Planning (1951, reprinted 1953) *Town and Country Planning 1943–1951.* Progress report by the Minister of Local Government and Planning on the work of the Ministry of Town and Country Planning. Cmd. 8204. London: HMSO.

Mitchell, E. B. (1967) *The Plan that Pleased.* London: TCPA.

Montgomery, J. and Thornley, A. (1990) *Radical Planning Initiatives: New directions for urban planning in the 1990s.* London: Gower.

Mullan, R. (1980) *Stevenage Ltd.: Aspects of the planning and politics of Stevenage New Town, 1945–78.* London: Routledge and Kegan Paul.

Orlans, H. (1952) *Stevenage: A sociological study of a new town.* London: Routledge and Kegan Paul.

Osborn, F. J. (1918) *New Towns after the War.* London: Dent.

Osborn, F. J. (1970) *Genesis of Welwyn Garden City: Some Jubilee memories.* London: TCPA.

Osborn, F. J. and Whittick, A. (1977) *The New Towns: Their origins, achievements and progress.* London: Leonard Hill.

Owen, G. (ed.) (1987) *The Thatcher Years: The policies and the prospects.* London: Financial Times.

Paris, C. (ed.) (1982) *Critical Readings in Planning Theory.* Oxford: Pergamon.

Partridge, P. H. (1971) *Consent and Consensus.* London: Macmillan.

Plaskow, M. (ed.) (1985) *The Life and Death of the Schools Council.* Brighton: Falmer Press.

Potter, D. *et al.* (1981) *Social Science: A Foundation Course* esp. Block 4 'Politics, Legitimacy and the State', Milton Keynes: Open University Press.

Ravetz, A. (1980) *Remaking Cities: Contradictions of the recent urban environment.* London: Croom Helm.

Ravetz, A. (1986) *The Government of Space: Town planning in modern society.* London: Faber and Faber.

Reade, E. (1987) *British Town and Country Planning.* Milton Keynes: Open University Press.

Richardson, J. J. and Jordan, A. G. (1979) *Governing under Pressure.* Oxford: Martin Robertson.

Riley, D. W. (1966) *The Citizen's Guide to Town and Country Planning.* London: TCPA.

Rivers, P. (1974) *Politics by Pressure.* London: Methuen.

Royle, E. (1987) *Modern Britain: A social history 1750–1985.* London: Edward Arnold.

RTPI/TCPA (1989) *Garden Cities of Tomorrow.* London: RTPI/TCPA.

Sandbach, F. (1980) *Environment, Ideology and Policy.* Oxford: Basil Blackwell.

Secretary of State for the Environment *et al.* (1990) *This Common Inheritance: Britain's Environmental Strategy.* White Paper Cm. 1200. London: HMSO.

Self, P. (1953) *The Planning of Industrial Location.* London: University of London Press.

Self, P. (1957) *Cities in Flood: The problems of urban growth.* London: Faber and Faber.

Self, P. (1982) *Planning the urban Region: A comparative study of policies and organisations.* London: Allen and Unwin.

Senior, D. (ed.) (1966) *The Regional City.* London: Longmans Green.

Simmie, J. (1974) *Citizens in Conflict: The sociology of town planning.* London: Hutchinson.

Simpson, M. (1985) *Thomas Adams and the Modern Planning Movement: Britain, Canada and the United States, 1900–1940.* London: Mansell.

Sissons, M. and French, P. (eds) (1964) *Age of Austerity, 1945–1951.* Harmondsworth: Penguin.

Sked, A. and Cook, C. (1979) *Post-War Britain: A political history.* Harmondsworth: Penguin.

Skeffington Report (1969) *People and Planning: Report of the Committee on Public Participation in Planning.* London: HMSO.

South-East Economic Planning Council (1967) *A Strategy for the South-East.* London: HMSO.

South-East Joint Planning Team (1970) *Strategic Plan for the South-East:*

Report by the South-East Joint Planning Team. London: HMSO.

Stansfield, K. (1981) Thomas Sharp 1901–1978, in Cherry (ed.) (1981).

Stott, M. and Taylor, P. (1980) *The Nuclear Controversy: A guide to the issue of the Windscale Inquiry*. London: TCPA.

TCPA (1946) *Building our New Towns*. London: TCPA.

TCPA (1947) *Greater London Plans in Action*. London: TCPA.

TCPA (1955) *Green Belts: Their establishment and safeguarding*. London: TCPA.

TCPA (1959) *New Towns*. London: Royal Academy Galleries.

TCPA (1961) *The Growth of London and the Future Development of South-East England*. London: TCPA.

TCPA (1962) *The Paper Metropolis: A study of London's office growth*. London: TCPA.

TCPA (1964) *The Intelligent Voter's Guide to Town and Country Planning*. London: TCPA.

TCPA (1966, 1974) *Citizen's Guide to Town and Country Planning*. London: TCPA.

TCPA (1968) *Papers on Regional Planning*. London: TCPA.

TCPA (1971) *London under Stress: A study of the planning policies proposed for London and its region*. London: TCPA.

TCPA (1971) *New Towns: The British experience*. London: Charles Knight.

TCPA (1972) *Region in Crisis: An independent view of the Greater London Plan*. London: Charles Knight.

TCPA (1978) *Inner Cities of Tomorrow*. London: TCPA.

TCPA (1978) *Planning and Plutonium*. London: TCPA.

TCPA (1979) *A Third Garden City: Outline Prospectus*. London: TCPA.

TCPA (1984) *Lightmoor: A new kind of neighbourhood*. London: TCPA.

TCPA (1987) *North-South Divide: A new deal for the regions*. London: TCPA.

TCPA (1989) *Bridging the North-South Divide*. London: TCPA.

TCPA (1989) *The Future Planning of the Countryside*. London: TCPA.

Thornley, A. (1991) *Urban Planning under Thatcherism: The challenge of the market*. London: Routledge.

Truman, D. B. (1951) *The Governmental Process*. New York: Knopf.

Ward, C. and Fyson, A. (1973) *Streetwork: The exploding school*. London: Routledge and Kegan Paul.

Ward, C. (ed.) (1987) *A Decade of Anarchy, 1961–1970*. London: Freedom Press.

Whittick, A. (1987) *F.J.O. – Practical Idealist: A biography of Sir Frederic Osborn*. London: TCPA.

Williams, R. (1976) *Keywords: A vocabulary of culture and society*. London: Fontana.

Wood, A. (1988) *Greentown: A case study of a proposed alternative community*. Energy and Environment Research Unit, Occasional Paper 57. Milton Keynes: Open University.

Young, H. (1989) *One of Us: A biography of Margaret Thatcher*. London: Macmillan.

PLANNING PERSPECTIVES

An International Journal of
Planning, History and the Environment.

EDITORS: **Professor G. Cherry**   **Professor A. Sutcliffe**
University of Birmingham, UK   University of Leicester, UK

Planning Perspectives reflects the interest of those concerned with the planning of the environment as well as those who seek to provide explanations for the origins and consequences of planning ideas, methods and activities.

The Journal's scope is international, linking the past with the present and the future on a worldwide basis and thus tracing the development and transfer of different planning practices.

Planning Perspectives brings together a variety of disciplines which combine to produce a fuller understanding of the complex factors which influence planning. These include academic disciplines such as historical sociology and geography, and economic, social and political history, as well as the more applied fields of public health, housing, construction, architecture and town planning.

An important feature of **Planning Perspectives** is its substantial book review section. This allows a wide-ranging and critical appraisal of the broad area of current international planning research.

For further information, a free sample copy of **Planning Perspectives** or subscription enquiries, write to

     Journals Promotion Dept.
     E & FN Spon
     2–6 Boundary Row
     London, SE1 8HN, UK

OR

     Journals Promotion Dept.
     E & FN Spon
     29 West 35th Street
     New York, NY 10001-2291, USA

E & FN SPON
An Imprint of Chapman & Hall

INDEX